Ten Cities That Led the World

Paul Strathern is the author of numerous books about science, history, philosophy and literature, including two series, *Philosophers in 90 Minutes* and *The Big Idea: Scientists Who Changed the World,* and the *Sunday Times bestseller The Medici: Godfathers of the Renaissance*.

He also won a Somerset Maugham award for his novel *A Season in Abyssinia*. He formerly lectured in philosophy and mathematics at Kingston University. He lives in London.

Ten Cities That Led the World

From Ancient Metropolis to Modern Megacity

HODDER

First published in Great Britain in 2022 by Hodder & Stoughton
An Hachette UK company

This paperback edition published in 2023

5

Copyright © Paul Strathern 2022

The right of Paul Strathern to be identified as the Author of the Work has been
asserted by him in accordance with the Copyright, Designs and Patents Act 1988.

[Add disclaimer for fiction if applicable]

A CIP catalogue record for this title is available from the British Library

Paperback ISBN 9781529356441
eBook ISBN 9781529356458

Typeset in Plantin by Manipal Technologies Limited

Printed and bound in Great Britain by Clays Ltd, Elcograf S.p.A.

Hodder & Stoughton policy is to use papers that are natural, renewable
and recyclable products and made from wood grown in sustainable forests.
The logging and manufacturing processes are expected to conform
to the environmental regulations of the country of origin.

Hodder & Stoughton Ltd
Carmelite House
50 Victoria Embankment
London EC4Y 0DZ

www.hodder.co.uk

To Matthias

wer die Zukunft erforschte
while I thought about the past

Vienna Lockdown 2020

Contents

Prologue

What Survives

Cities come and go, some destroyed by humanity, others by nature, others simply abandoned. Several decades ago, I happened upon an example of the last kind, in India. The red-stone city was deserted, its wide, empty, paved streets extending into the distance towards the fortified walls. The branches of trees burst from the sides of some of its buildings. The interiors of its domed temples, pillared palaces and long colonnades were dark and silent. The only visible signs of life were the monkeys, which scampered away as you approached, running up the steps of a temple, along the tops of the ornate walls. The city of Fatehpur Sikri, which had once been capital of the Mogul Empire, was now an abandoned, gradually crumbling ruin.

According to legend, more than four centuries previously the Moghul Emperor Akhbar, whose rule extended across the north Indian subcontinent from Bengal to Afghanistan and Central Asia, was travelling through the countryside with his entourage. Here he encountered a holy man sitting beneath the shade of a tree. The holy man asked him, 'What is it you desire, oh mighty emperor?' The emperor replied: 'It is a great sadness to me that my wife and I have no children. Above all things on earth I would wish my wife to give birth to a son, who can one day succeed me as emperor.' The holy man answered him: 'Your wish will be granted. You will have a son.'

The following year the emperor's wife gave birth to a son. Emperor Akhbar was so overjoyed that he returned to the very spot where he had encountered the holy man, declaring: 'Here I will build my new capital city.' Some time later, the Emperor Akhbar, his wife and son, as well as his court and all his administration, took up residence amid the splendours of his newly built city, to which he attached the name 'Sikri', meaning 'thanks'.

Just over a decade later Fatehpur Sikri had drained all available water from the surrounding countryside, and Akhbar was forced to abandon his imperial city, leaving it deserted, much as I saw it over four centuries later when I first walked through the large, intricately carved, monumental gateway.

The greatest cities of all time have changed the world. At their peak they literally make history. However, after such superhuman effort, their influence wanes. Some fall back upon themselves. Others may continue to thrive, but in a supporting role, rather than as the leading actor in the unfolding drama of events.

In this book we shall see how Athens produced a template for the future western world; how Rome established the power and organisation to carry forth these ideas; and how, centuries later, Paris would produce the ideas of the Enlightenment, which would in time inform both the constitution of the United States and the practice of communism. From the past to the future, we shall see how the modern megacities of Mumbai and Beijing embody not only the future of our cities, but of our whole world. They *are* our future, in two different versions. The freely evolving wonders and chaos of democratic Mumbai, and the 'directed' economic supergrowth of communist Beijing, which views democracy as an obstacle. These cities of the future are stuffed with humanity, bursting at the seams. Yet the future may also have room for emptiness. Water diverted to the ill-advised cotton plantations of the Soviet era resulted in the emptying of the entire Aral Sea, once the fourth-largest lake in the world. Climate change will doubtless bequeath us with similar voids: vanished seas, vanished cities…

Empty cities are not an ancient phenomenon, like Fatehpur Sikri. Indeed, nowadays we are experiencing the entirely new phenomenon of empty cities that have never had any inhabitants at all. Some years ago, I visited the city of Cartagena, on the Caribbean coast of Colombia. I was surprised to find that across the bay, beyond the hillside shanty towns, and far from the four-hundred-year-old picturesque streets of the old town, was a spectacular skyline consisting of mile upon mile of white skyscrapers receding like a mirage beneath the blue Caribbean sky. A few were luxury hotels, but most of these ultra-modern buildings appeared to be empty.

A few days later I arrived at Panama City, to be greeted by the sight of a similar functioning old city, far-off shanty towns, and an almost identical skyline of spectacular white skyscrapers stretching into the distance along the shore. Apparently, until recently the ground now occupied by these pristine buildings had been empty sand dunes. In 2005 the United States tax authorities had begun pressurising Swiss banks to reveal the identities behind certain numbered bank accounts. Not long afterwards, Cartagena and Panama City experienced a building boom. The skyscraper district in Panama City was confidently expected 'to house nine out of ten of Latin America's tallest buildings', according to Andrew Beatty of *Business News*. These immaculate architectural edifices were nothing less than monuments to laundered cash, hiding in plain sight, owned by Russian dolls of offshore shell companies far beyond the reach of any tax, or judicial, jurisdiction.

Other ghost cities have sprung up in the modern world too. As China rose to global power status during the early decades of this century, megacities began mushrooming all over the country. New cities, capable of housing populations of up to a million or more, were built to drive the new economic powerhouse. These were part of the miraculous transformation of the world's most populous nation, a commercial enterprise on a scale hitherto unknown in human history. Today many of these megacities, their names all but unknown in the West, are producing a flood of low-priced goods and technology that China ships to every corner of the globe.

However, not all of these new cities have proven to be a success. A few, with rows of high-rise blocks and industrial parks, many designed piecemeal by Australian architects, have populations of around a hundred thousand living amid the dwarfing structures intended to house up to a million inhabitants. Others of similar size are completely devoid of inhabitants. These cities were intended to be magnets, attracting a population keen to better themselves with new jobs and modern accommodation. But the young workers and peasants couldn't afford the rent for these lines of new flats rising thirty storeys above the ground. And so there was no one to work in the factories, which remained empty. No customers for the large shopping malls, no people to fill the empty restaurants. Yet the government found itself unable to slash the rents in order to attract new workers. The building of these cities had played a considerable part in raising China's Gross Domestic Product, a GDP that had helped drive the entire world economy to new heights. Slash the rents, and the value of the nation's assets would also be slashed. Worse still, economic wisdom dictated that a collapse in house prices inevitably led to a recession. Better to leave these cities empty – ghostly monuments to a future that might never come. Some are simply left unfinished, others are in full working order, right down to the eerily changing traffic lights on the deserted streets. These remain devoid of inhabitants, apart from the occasional lone uniformed security guard.

The deceptive existence of such ghost cities, as well as their smoke-and-mirrors-legacy, remains enigmatic. Perhaps they are best viewed as monuments to that almost abstract practice – the spirituality of our time, if you like – namely, financial manipulation.

A Chinese ghost city, complete with working traffic lights.

For the most part, modern cities have long been very much the opposite of such vacuity. Some time after I visited Fatehpur Sikri in India, I travelled on to Calcutta (modern Kolkata). This was the 1960s and many were preoccupied with the world's fast-growing population, with increasing numbers flooding from the countryside into already overcrowded cities. Concerned discussions regarding the future 'failure of the city' were beginning to take place.

Waking on my first morning in Kolkata, I opened my shutters to the glare of sunlight. Below was a cacophony of blaring lorry and car horns, rickshaws, handcarts, calling vendors, pedestrians, careering cyclists, their flow all parting around a seemingly indifferent cow seated in the middle of the road.

Along the broken pavements on either side of the road, spilling into the traffic, the homeless were waking up and going about their morning business. Men in shabby dhotis stood brushing their teeth with twigs and spitting, squatting women fanned the choking smoke of small fires with palm leaves, naked infants ran amok, other men and women squatted to defecate into the gutters. The sheer volume of variegated cries and noise, the stench of smoke, excrement, cooking and petrol fumes, was all but impossible to absorb.

Later, in the cool of the night, I was driven back to my hotel across the long, high, cage-like skeleton of the Howrah Bridge. Below, a white mist was drifting off the silent waters of the Hooghly River. Along the extended pavements on either side of the empty road across the bridge stretched row upon row of shrouded figures, the homeless restively sleeping, huddled against the chill of the night. Next morning, the back page of the leading newspaper listed the number of homeless people on the Howrah Bridge who had died during the previous night. This was usually in double digits.

The 'failure of the city' was not some future concept, I realised. It had already taken place, some time ago, here in Kolkata. The city may have failed, but its inhabitants were continuing as best they could, unaware of this new concept that was becoming such a talking point among the sociologists, architects and intellectuals of the world.

As the philosophers have long reminded us, the way of the living runs through the cities of the dead. Even as we move forward, we can never escape our past. So the twentieth-century poet of Alexandria, Constantine Cavafy, put it:

> I'll go to another city, go to another shore,
> find another city, better than this one.

But as he replied to himself:

> You cannot find another city, you cannot find another shore.
>
> As you have made your life here, in this small corner,
>
> So you will make the same of it wherever you go.
>
> You will walk the same streets, the same quarters,
>
> You will always end up in this city. This city will always be with you.

Much the same can be said even of a mythological city. Writing in the fourth century BC, Plato described the lost city of Atlantis. He claimed that the Greeks first heard the story of Atlantis in Ancient Egypt, and he places the island of Atlantis west of the Pillars of Hercules (what we know as the Straits of Gibraltar). The large island supposedly contained a city with concentric canals, and appears to have been host to a quasi-utopian civilisation that was unfamiliar to the Greeks. But tragedy struck and one day Atlantis was said to have experienced a tumultuous earthquake, causing it to disappear beneath the waves and sink for ever to the bottom of the sea.

Atlantis was long supposed to have been a legend. Even Plato appears to have used it primarily to illustrate a philosophical point concerning the superiority of Greek values and just government. However, some scholars now believe that the sinking of Atlantis beneath the waves was an actual event marking the end of Minoan civilisation, one of the earliest in the Mediterranean region. At around the time of mythical Atlantis's mysterious and sudden ending in roughly 1,600 BC, a massive volcanic eruption all but destroyed the island of Thera (Santorini). The eruption is known to have been one of the most powerful in the earth's history, blasting millions of tons of rock and earth and ash twenty-five miles into the atmosphere. Ensuing tsunamis, some of them hundreds of feet high, swept out across the Aegean, obliterating Minoan coastal settlements through the region. Fortunately, the capital of Minoan civilisation, Knossos, was mostly (but not completely) spared from destruction as it lay several miles inland on Crete.

In the early years of the twentieth century the British archaeologist Sir Arthur Evans excavated the palace of King Minos at Knossos, uncovering the secrets of this colourful, all but legendary Bronze Age civilisation. The bull appears to have played a central role in Minoan culture. We are familiar with the legend of the Minotaur, the half bull, half man who lived in a mysterious labyrinth beneath the palace of King Minos, devouring all who entered. This labyrinth had been skilfully designed by the polymathic artist Daedalus, who would go on to design the wax wings that enabled his son Icarus to embark on his ill-fated flight.

But bulls also appear in the lighter aspect of Minoan culture. A vivid fresco on the palace wall depicts a scantily clad youth vaulting acrobatically between the horns of a bull. This seemingly impossible feat, gracefully and athletically performed by both young men and girls, is thought to have taken place as part of a ritual, whose significance we can only grasp as fleetingly as the passage of those slender young bodies somersaulting between the lethal horns of the bull.

Parts of the city of Knossos were deeply damaged by the Thera tsunami, the clockwork of its civilisation irreparably broken. The site gradually fell into disrepair, and there it lay for all of 3,500 years, an undiscovered mystery. Even so, the bull-worshipping of the Minoans would survive at the other end of the Mediterranean. The practice of bull-fighting in Spain is a direct consequence of Minoan influence. Many years ago, on a visit to Spain, I decided to discover for myself the attraction of this gruesome 'sport'. The small, slightly tacky bullring in northern Spain was packed out, the more expensive seats in the shade, while I found myself among the vociferous section beneath the glare of the late afternoon sun. The proceedings began with the customary blare of brass playing the fanfare, whereupon an open-top pastel-coloured Cadillac bearing a bevy of young women clad in traditional dress and black mantillas drove slowly into the ring across the sand. From that moment on, through the ensuing antics of the toreadors and the choreographed slaughter of the bulls, I sat both repelled and entranced. I couldn't escape the feeling that something deep was unfolding before me, something savage and chthonic that was both human and animal. This was the travestied performance of a primitive ritual that I didn't understand, but could only feel stirring within me. Whatever Minoan culture was, whatever had once taken place in the city of Knossos, was still capable of speaking to the blood many millennia after its disappearance.

A similar fate to that which befell Knossos would also mark the end of human life in Pompei. On this occasion the volcanic eruption was less violent, though much closer to the city. When Vesuvius erupted in AD 79 it expelled a vast cloud of superheated ash and volcanic debris. This rained down on the city below, to a depth of almost ten feet, both burying its inhabitants and preserving the city as if in a time capsule. Excavations have now managed to reveal the precise bodily position of fallen, fleeing citizens. Also preserved were the lavish villas of the rich, some with murals depicting idyllic pastoral scenes, early evidence of the rural nostalgia that continues to afflict urban dwellers to this day. Similarly preserved were the minutiae of daily life: taverns, rows of open circular-seated public wooden lavatories, graffiti outlining the prices and positions offered by prostitutes.

Thus the vagaries of nature failed to obliterate the legacy of ancient cities. But human destruction can, if anything, be even more violent. By the early third century BC the Phoenician city of Carthage, situated in modern-day Tunisia, ruled over an empire that extended through much of the western and central Mediterranean. Its trade routes reached out as far as the tin mines of Cornwall in western Britain, the Crimea in the northern Black Sea and the ancient Phoenician ports of Tyre and Sidon on the coast of modern Lebanon. This sea-faring expansion brought Carthage into conflict with a younger embryonic empire that was developing on the Italian peninsula in Rome. The two cities clashed three times between 264 BC and 146 BC in what has become known as the Punic Wars.[1]

During the second of these three wars, the Carthaginian general Hannibal, largely regarded as one of the finest military strategists of all time, would march his army across the Alps, complete with dozens of elephants. For fifteen years Hannibal's army rampaged through the Italian peninsula, the Roman battle squares unable to withstand the force of Hannibal's charging elephants. But when the Romans withdrew into their walled cities, Hannibal was unable to dislodge them, having lost his siege equipment while crossing the Alps. He only returned to Carthage when he was forced to defend the city against a surprise attack led by the Roman general Scipio.[2] In 202 BC Hannibal lost to Scipio in the Battle of Zama, and the Carthaginians sued for peace.

At the outset of the Third Punic War in 149 BC, the Romans crossed the Mediterranean, using their new tactics to defeat the Carthaginians in battle. The Romans then laid siege to Carthage for three years. The Carthaginians defended themselves with increasingly ingenious weapons, even going so far as to use ropes woven out of their women's hair to make catapults. But in 146 BC the Romans breached the city walls. Formerly, Carthage had boasted some five hundred thousand inhabitants; now just fifty thousand survived to be marched off into slavery. The city was set ablaze, its fire burning for fifteen days; the smoking ruins were

---

1   Punic was the Roman name for these wars, derived from the Latin *Punicus* (or *Poenicus*) meaning 'Carthaginian'.
2   Later named Scipio Africanus in honour of his military exploits in Africa, Scipio was the only Roman general to prove a match for Hannibal.

then razed until not one stone stood upon another. According to legend, the site of the city was afterwards ploughed, its furrows sewn with salt so that nothing would ever grow there again. '*Carthago delenda est*' (Carthage must be destroyed), as Cato the Elder, Roman soldier turned politician, had insisted. He repeated these words at the end of every speech he gave in the Senate, no matter what the subject under discussion.

The orgy of destruction that wiped the city of Carthage from the face of the earth was even more thorough than the forces of nature. Indeed, it has been claimed that the only things to have been bequeathed to us by Carthage are remnants of the world's first alphabet and a rare purple dye. This is the only cultural legacy of a city that at its height dominated the entire western Mediterranean. However, over twenty-one centuries later, genetic tests have revealed a wider legacy. Research completed in 2008 by IBM and the *National Geographic* has revealed that as many as one in seventeen men living in the Mediterranean basin possess a Y-chromosome derived from a Phoenician ancestor. According to David Platt of IBM: 'One boy in each school class from Cyprus to Tunis may be a direct male-line descendant of the Phoenician traders.'

But suppose the Punic Wars had gone the other way? What if Carthage had conquered Rome? Western Europe might have been a Phoenician empire. Imagine all the Roman elements in our culture, from law to architecture, technology to philosophy, replaced by a more nautically flavoured eastern Mediterranean influence.

Just a hundred miles or so south of the original Phoenician heartland cities of Tyre and Sidon lies the city of Jerusalem. Here the Romans aimed to obliterate the gentle message preached by Jesus of Nazareth, inflicting on him a similar brutality, public dishonour and finality to that which they had shown in the destruction of Carthage. Yet the idea sown by this one small voice would eventually spread throughout the Roman Empire, even outlasting it, so that Christ's ideas remain central to our entire western culture and spiritual outlook, whether one believes in his god or not. It was the idea that survived, as ineradicable as the genes of the Phoenicians.

So what constitutes a city? What makes a city great? Cities come in all manner of shapes and sizes, from Freeport City, Kansas (population 5) to Chongqing, China, whose multi-hub population of 30,484,300 occupies an area the size of Austria. How can we characterise the city?

After glimpsing various facets of our subject by means of anecdote and example, we now home in on a brief but sweeping analysis of the difficulties involved. The Danish poet Søren Ulrik Thomsen, who learned the essence of a city by walking its streets day and night, concluded that a good, functioning city needs three qualities: it should be complex, chaotic and colossal. This insight is worth pondering. To the outside eye, or from the distant view of posterity, a city may appear hopelessly complicated and disorganised, containing a teeming mass of inhabitants whose cultural habits either remain unknown to us, appear utterly alien, or revolt us in their barbarity. But modern rationality means that we still cling to the belief that every working part of a city fulfils a purpose. And not always in an expected or wholesome fashion. Instances abound: the Ancient Romans simply left unwanted babies on street corners to die and be collected as refuse. Instances of our failures to understand also abound, as shown by the claims of the early twentieth-century English historian W.J. Colville in his *Ancient Mysteries and Modern Revelations*: 'the whole scientific world of today is coming very near to an acceptance of that esoteric teaching which alone accounts intelligently for the behaviour of all forms of existence observed under the microscope'.

Esoteric mysticism does not explain the behaviour of microbes beneath a microscope, any more than modern sociology can fully explain the behaviour (and madness) of crowds. Analogy may illuminate, but does not fully comprehend. We can only partially account for the riots between supporters of the 'blue' chariot race teams and the supporters of the 'green' chariot teams, which brought sixth-century Constantinople to a halt for days on end, resulting in over a thousand deaths. These were both more, and less, than clashes between modern football hooligans, or the periodic quasi-spontaneous flash riots that spread through modern cities. These are usually triggered by single specific events, often a particular perceived injustice. But these are just one among many similar events. Why is it the one specific event in one place on one particular day that inflames an entire population? Such events remain an unpredictable aspect of city life. And afterwards the scatter-fire of explanations – tipping points, festering social grievance, the latent anarchy of the human heart – can never fully explain the particular unforeseen event. As with the present, so with the past. L.P. Hartley observed: 'The past is a foreign country, they do things differently there.' We all, to a greater or lesser extent, inhabit this foreign country, trying as best we can to step forward out of the shifting sands of our past history.

All leading cities in history have thrived on a crushed underclass, often composed largely of slaves. Yet, without the fear of this 'mob', there would be no one for the emperor to appease, no one to whom the ambitious populist could appeal, no one for the revolutionary leader to inspire, no one to drive the ambition and dread of those who wish to avoid or escape such shameful destitution. The dynamics of a great city are seldom in equilibrium. Functioning institutions and established mores will always chafe the libertarian, the visionary and the creator.

To stress once more: the greatest cities of all remain those that have, at some point in their existence, changed the world. They are the centres of progress, which have made history by leading us forward from our past: their moment of glory, before passing on the baton to their successor. The ten cities I describe in this book have been chosen using this qualification in the widest sense: greatness comes in many forms. Central to the success of these cities appears to be some nexus of power and ideas. The message of Christ would not have spread if it had not penetrated the central city of Roman power. It may at first have existed as the religion of slaves, whispered among the city of catacombs beneath the city itself; but it would later emerge into the light of day and have sufficient power to capture the imagination of the powerful.

The epoch-making city must also be possessed of originality, some indefinable yet immediately recognisable new quality that is utterly its own: the Ancient Greek culture of Athens; New York, as a beacon for the 'land of the free'; Moscow's seemingly similar appeal to the downtrodden workers of the world. Such are the cities that made our history, and continue to do so.

1

Babylon: The Building Blocks

Babylon had flourished in the Green Crescent of Mesopotamia for almost one and a half thousand years by the time it reached its peak during the Neo-Babylonian Empire under Nebuchadnezzar II in the sixth century BC. (Think present-day Rome since the Fall of the Roman Empire.)

According to several ancient sources, Nebuchadnezzar II was responsible for building one of the landmarks that would contribute to the city's legendary status throughout the Middle East and beyond: the Hanging Gardens of Babylon. The Ancient Greeks would later name it as one of the Seven Wonders of the Ancient World, along with the likes of the Great Pyramid of Giza and the 300-foot-high Lighthouse of Alexandria.

Several second-hand descriptions of the Hanging Gardens have come down to us, though the precise location of the gardens, and even their very existence, remain debated. The Romano-Jewish historian Josephus, who lived some four centuries after Nebuchadnezzar II, wrote about the gardens:

> In this palace he erected very high walls, supported by stone pillars; and by planting what was called a pensile [hanging down] paradise, and replenishing it with all sorts of trees, he rendered the prospect an exact resemblance of a mountainous country. This he did to gratify his queen, because she had been brought up in Media, and was fond of a mountainous situation.

Other sources describe the gardens as a construction reaching over 50 cubits (anywhere up to 100 feet) high, having tiered sections with sufficient depth of earth to contain roots of the largest trees. To replenish these gardens, water was drawn from the nearby Euphrates by means of Archimedes screws.[1]

The Hanging Gardens of Babylon remain the only one of the Seven Wonders that was never described by a reliable eyewitness; and, as yet, no evidence for these gardens has been found on the site of ancient Babylon. However, the contemporary British archaeologist Stephanie Dalley recently published a book claiming evidence for an edifice, similar to that described by Josephus and others, which existed in Nineveh, some four hundred miles north of Babylon. According to Dalley these gardens were watered by a network of canals and aqueducts that carried water from mountain streams around fifty miles away.

On the other hand, some historians have suggested that the reason the site of the Hanging Gardens of Babylon has never been discovered is that they now lie beneath the waters of the Euphrates. Over the centuries the river has changed course, and currently flows several hundred yards west of its course during the time of Nebuchadnezzar II, thus obliterating much of the west bank of the old city.

The other legendary structure of Babylon is the Tower of Babel, which according to the Book of Genesis in the Bible was built some time after the Flood. The aim was that it would be built so high that it would reach heaven. The Bible explains that God was so angered by this human presumption that he confounded the speech of its builders so that they could not understand

---

1 This device operates by raising water from a pool or river to a higher level by turning a screw-shaped surface closely fitted inside a pipe. The screw carries the water up the pipe, spilling it out into a higher irrigational ditch. Although the device is named after Archimedes, it had been in use in Mesopotamia and Ancient Egypt some five hundred years before Archimedes was born.

one another – giving birth to all the different languages of the world. The reality on which the Tower is based was probably the 300-foot-high ziggurat of Etemenanki, whose name means 'platform between heaven and earth'. According to an inscribed contemporary stele discovered in 1917, this too was built by Nebuchadnezzar II: 'The house, the foundation of heaven and earth, I made it, the wonder of the people of the world, I raised its top to heaven, made doors for the gates, and I covered it with bitumen and bricks.'

Curiously, this origin-of-language myth is even more prevalent among ancient civilisations than the Flood myth. The same story appears in pre-Columbian myths of Central America, where flat-topped pyramids appeared to be reaching for the heavens. Similar myths also appear as far afield as Myanmar, Nepal and Africa – in tribal cultures from Botswana to the Kongo people – yet no one here built pyramids.

Other Babylonian constructions included its famed outer wall, which is known to have stretched over six miles to enclose the population of more than two hundred thousand, making it the largest and most populous city in the world at that time. Because there was no stone available, these walls were built of clay bricks, which were either baked in ovens or left to dry in the sun. The identically sized bricks were then bound together by bitumen to construct the walls, which were so wide that they could accommodate chariot races. These walls were said to have had no less than 100 gates.

By the time of Nebuchadnezzar II there were also long, tall, bitumen-covered embankments lining either side of the Euphrates to contain the river's regular flooding. The flooding had long ago been recognised as a seasonal occurrence, but the greater inundations remained unpredictable, requiring the services of the priests on the ziggurats to predict or ward off such events. Indeed, these ziggurats seem initially to have been built in order to provide refuge from the floods for the ruler, the priests and the upper echelons of Babylonian society.

Other ominous natural phenomenon, particularly eclipses, had also been studied by priests from the top of their sacred ziggurats, who learned to plot their recurring patterns. This led the Babylonians to gain an astronomical and mathematical expertise that led the world, with its influence still visible to this day, and some of its astronomical predictions concerning eclipses even now proving correct.

What we know as Babylonian mathematics actually originated before the city of Babylon in the earliest civilisation, the Sumer, which flourished in Mesopotamia from 3,500 to 3,000 BC. Here, when two groups wished to trade, they soon realised that they had to adopt a common number system. The number system first adopted was sexagesimal; that means with a base of 60 (our present number system for example has a base of 10). Why 60? This appears to have been chosen because five (fingers) multiplied by twelve (months of the year) is equal to sixty. This links the human body with the passing of time. Sixty is also an extremely versatile number, which not only enabled trade, but also enabled mathematics itself to advance. This is because sixty is a highly composite number, being divisible by many factors.[2] This greatly facilitated the use of fractions, which are vital when it comes to dividing quantities in trade.

The legacy of the Babylonian sexagesimal number system remains with us to this day, in both our temporal measurement and geometry. We still have sixty seconds to a minute, and sixty minutes to an hour. And a circle is still said to contain 6×60 degrees i.e. $360°$, a fact that remains reflected in our map-making, navigation and geography. In geometry, all angles are measured in such degrees; a triangle contains $3 \times 60°$, which equals $180°$.

---

2 These factors are 1, 2, 3, 4, 5, 6, 10, 12, 15, 20, 30 and 60.

Babylonian mathematics, much like ours, also had a place value system: that is, digits in the left column represent larger values. For instance, 126 in our decimal system represents 1 hundred, 2 tens and 6 singles. Unfortunately, the Babylonian system had no zero, so a zero was simply left blank, which meant you had to remember it. If you didn't, your 106 apples were liable to become 16 apples. Thus, financial manipulation in its infancy.

Despite this drawback, the sexagesimal number system enabled the Babylonians to calculate π as 25/8 which = 3.125. That is just 0.5 per cent below the true value. More remarkable still, these anonymous mathematicians, members of a priestly caste who lived apart from the main population, were able to calculate $\sqrt{2}$ to a value of 1.41421296... The modern value has the last three numbers as 356. All this was recorded in cuneiform script, made by pressing reed stalks into the damp surface of clay tablets, which could then be baked in the hot sun to render their markings permanent.

A baked-clay Babylonian tablet with cuneiform script indicating sophisticated mathematical knowledge.

But the most extraordinary Babylonian mathematician of all, we actually know by name – even if practically nothing else is known of him. This was a man called Kidinnu, who lived during the reign of Nebuchadnezzar II. His astronomical feats are truly extraordinary, even if many of them were built upon a foundation of earlier observations of eclipses and the movements of the stars in the heavens. Kidinnu traced the different movements of the sun and the moon, noted the rotating pattern of the stars in the heavens, and how the speed at which they travelled differed from day to day. His precise measurements are now known to have involved the use of geometric techniques, such as angular measurements on the celestial sphere, which until recently were thought to have been invented in Europe almost two millennia later.

Using these methods, Kidinnu was able to calculate that the average time between new moons was around 29.35 days. This is known as the synodic, or lunar, month. Such precise information is key in the calculation of lunar and solar eclipses, which can only take place when the sun, moon and earth are all aligned. By means of such observations Kidinnu was able to produce a lunisolar calendar predicting eclipses. Solar eclipses, he calculated, took place every 233 synodic months – a period known as a 'saros'. Thus the saros is approximately equal to 6,585.3211 days. In other words, a saros is equivalent to 14 common years, 4 leap years and 11.32 days; or 18 years, 11 days and 8 hours. After a solar eclipse occurs, we have to wait another saros for the next eclipse to occur. These eclipses will be of varying degree – some are total eclipses, others to a lesser extent (and yet others may be invisible from different parts of the planet). But they will occur at precisely these intervals. Kidinnu's predictions, well over two and a half millennia ago in Babylon, still hold true to this day. Indeed, the modern mathematical historian Aaboe Asger has gone so far as to claim that 'all Western efforts in the exact sciences are descendants in direct line from the work of the late Babylonian astronomers'.

In Babylonian times eclipses were considered to be omens of ill fate, such as the imminent death of a ruler, so the ability to predict an eclipse was of major importance to Babylonian kings. According to modern archaeologist Ruth Schuster, this meant the kings 'could abdicate briefly, handing the reins to some unfortunate, who would then, fitly, be killed'. This tradition persisted well into the Hellenic era. According to Schuster, 'Alexander the Great is believed to have sacrificed just such a substitute king named for an eclipse to save his own skin'. Such was the continuing power of eclipses that in the century following Kidinnu's predictions, the eclipse on 28 May 585 BC even caused the Medes and the Lydians to abandon their war in Anatolia (modern Turkey) because they thought this to be a sign of the gods' annoyance. Babylonians mathematics was infected by a similar superstitiousness. Having been awed by the seemingly miraculous powers to be found in the manipulation of numbers, many mathematicians were tempted to seek a deeper meaning within the very numbers themselves. This they found in such pursuits as numerology. As with the eclipse, this too assigned a magical occurrence to numerical prediction.

Similarly, astronomers were liable to fall into astrology. Here the constellations depicting particular groups of bright stars, and the position of these constellations, were of particular relevance in the prediction of future events.[3] The stars also divined the character of the leader and his fate. This was of great importance, as the fate of the king and the fate of his nation were initially deemed as inseparable. Only in a later development would these positions of the stars be seen as predicting the personality and fate of lesser individuals and normal citizens. With some small justification, this development has been seen as the first stirrings of the psychological impulse to 'know thyself'. However, even at the time

---

3 These constellations had not yet evolved into what are now called the signs of the zodiac, which would be a Greek development.

there was some disparagement of this pseudoscience and several sources speak of the Babylonian astronomers' distaste for the practices of the astrologers, to the point where they refused to share accommodation with them.

Nebuchadnezzar II's name would originally have been written as Nabu-kudurri-usur, meaning 'Nabu protect my eldest son'.[4] This indicates the emphasis placed on continuity of rule. The overthrow of a dynasty usually marked the end of an empire, and great upheaval. Nabu was the name of one of the most ancient Mesopotamian gods, dating from the era of Akkadian rule and the world's first empire during the eighth century BC. In a similar blurring to that between astronomy and astrology, Nabu was seen as the god of wisdom, writing and rationality, while his Akkadian name in fact meant 'he who gives prophecies of the future'. The cult of Nabu would spread over the entire Mesopotamian region and beyond. He was even worshipped in Ancient Egypt as the god Thoth; he is mentioned in the Old Testament as Nabo; and in the Greek pantheon he appears in the form of Apollo.

Nebuchadnezzar's father, Nebopalassar, was a high-ranking official who had led a revolt that brought about the end of the Neo-Assyrian Empire. He led an army that attacked the Assyrian capital Nineveh in 635 BC, finally overcoming and sacking the city. Nebopalassar would establish his capital at Babylon, thus founding the Neo-Babylonian Empire in 626 BC. He abdicated, probably incapacitated by ill-health, in 605 BC, and died a few months later. His heir apparent was his twenty-nine-year-old son Nebuchadnezzar, who had already distinguished himself in battle. Nebuchadnezzar would reign for forty-three years, during which Babylon achieved its ascendancy. He led armies into Syria and attacked the combined forces of the Assyrians and the Egyptian pharaoh

---

4 The name we use, Nebuchadnezzar, is the Hebrew version, as it appears in the Bible.

at the Battle of Carcamesh. According to a large cuneiform clay tablet known as the Nebuchadnezzar Chronicle, now displayed in the British Museum: '[Nebuchadnezzar] crossed the river to go against the Egyptian army which lay in Karchemiš. They fought with each other and the Egyptian army withdrew before him... the Babylonian troops overtook and defeated them so that not a single man escaped to his own country.' We know that the above report is not entirely truthful, as the defeated pharaoh Necho II managed to flee the field. He would later achieve renown as the ruler who commissioned the Phoenicians to sail out from the Red Sea, south and then west around the tip of Africa, and back up to the Nile delta.

Despite Nebuchadnezzar's repeated attempts he would never succeed in his aim of conquering Egypt. During the course of his campaigns he would lay siege to Jerusalem in 597 and 587 BC. It was after the successful second siege that he destroyed the Temple of Solomon before marching the Israelites into captivity in Babylon. This is described in several books of the Old Testament. In the Book of Daniel, the noble young author describes how Nebuchadnezzar converted to the Jewish god Yahweh after His divine intervention saved three of Daniel's companions, when they were sentenced to burn in a fiery furnace. Daniel also describes how Nebuchadnezzar succumbed to madness, as he had prophesied. For seven years the king was apparently 'driven from men, and did eat grass as oxen, and his body was wet with the dew of heaven, till his hairs were grown like eagles' feathers, and his nails like birds' claws'. In the light of historical evidence, Daniel's colourful tales appear to have been pure fantasy. The experience of the Israelites in Babylon was in fact closer to the heart-rending sadness described in Psalm 137:

> By the rivers of Babylon, there we sat down, yea, we wept, when we remembered Zion.
> We hanged our harps upon the willows in the midst thereof.

For there they that carried us away captive required of us a song; and they that wasted us required of us mirth, saying, Sing us one of the songs of Zion.
How shall we sing the Lord's song in a strange land?
If I forget thee, O Jerusalem, let my right hand forget her cunning.

This sounds more like the true suffering endured by the slaves of Babylon.

However, Professor Jonathan Tenney of Cornell University, who has made a comprehensive study involving the translation of over five hundred cuneiform tablets from this period, presents yet another picture. According to Tenney, the life of slaves in Babylonian society was not as harsh as one might expect. Details of the daily life led by weavers, musicians, water sprinklers and others in government service (i.e. slavery) included such items as food for babies. He believes that the majority of these slave households contained nuclear families, who were 'free to develop their own individual culture and identity... instead of slaves living together or in groups'. At least eight thousand of these government workers were classed as temple employees.

In fact, the foundation of the legal status of all citizens of Babylon had been laid down over a millennium previously by King Hammurabi during the First Babylonian Empire. Some time around 1754 BC, Hammurabi established what many consider to be the first complete legal code in world history. This was carved into a black diorite stele in the shape of an admonishing forefinger. It records 282 laws, with a scaled list of punishments for breaking each one. Most famously, Law 196 records:

If a man destroy the eye of another man, they shall destroy his eye. If one break a man's bone, they shall break his bone. If one destroy the eye of a freeman or break the bone of a freeman he shall pay one gold mina. If one destroy the eye of a man's slave or break a bone of a man's slave he shall pay one-half his price.

This basically establishes the legal principle of 'an eye for an eye, a tooth for a tooth'. Yet it should be noted that there is a graduation of punishments, dependent upon the status and gender of those involved. A man will always be regarded as superior to a woman, a free man to a slave, and so forth. But the essential point here is that the law applied to all levels of society. However, although the law did apply to slaves, they were clearly at the bottom of the scale, able to inflict lesser punishments, and receive greater ones. For instance, if a physician's treatment led to the death of a wealthy patient, he would have his hands cut off; yet if he killed a slave he needed only to pay a fine. Slaves were also regarded as property, as in Law 15: 'If any one take a male or female slave of the court, or a male or female slave of a freed man, outside the city gates, he shall be put to death.' Respect for property was central, as seen in Law 22: 'If any one is committing a robbery and is caught, then he shall be put to death.' Perjury in a murder trial was also punishable by death.

Like slaves, wives were also regarded as property, but this could be tempered by natural affection. If a woman committed adultery with another man 'they shall bind them and throw them in the waters'. But if 'the owner of the wife' wished to save her, he could do so. On the other hand, if a woman could prove that a husband had rejected her, or abused her, 'then no guilt attaches to the woman, she shall take her dowry and return to her father's house'.

Quite apart from the law, the sheer organisation of a city the size of Babylon had evolved over the centuries. Hammurabi's Code may provide us with an insight into the mores of Babylonians, but the actual life of the city is another matter. Scenes from the bustling streets to the serenity of the pleasure gardens of the palaces, from the clamour of the market places that sold goods from as far afield as Oman (spices), Turkey (honey) and Afghanistan (lapis lazuli), to the daunting Halls of Justice, can only be imagined.

Some have compared the workings of a city to the performance of an orchestra, with every instrument playing its part in the overall performance. Without the abject prisoner awaiting death in his cell, there can be no judge to interpret the legal code. Without the mathematical knowledge gained by an astronomer-priest scanning the night heavens on his ziggurat, there can be no precisely measured mud plot after the annual flooding for the farmer to till, pay his taxes and provide a son to the military. But what is the overall symphony that this orchestra is playing? To every age its own interpretation: To the greater glory of God, of the leader, of the nation... All such analogies disintegrate in the face of our modern analysis: social, anthropological, economic, financial. Once again, we could do worse than fall back on our modern spirituality: namely, money. For this is one of the sites where money originated.

Babylon was the city whose unit of exchange began as the shekel (derived from the ancient Akkadian word *šiqlu*, which meant 'weighing'). The shekel began as a standard unit of weight on a scales, used for measuring transactions ranging from millet to dates. As trade expanded into foreign lands, travelling merchants began to carry with them their own metal weights, stamped with their own markings, indicating their authority and their weight. This enabled Babylonian traders to operate as far afield as the ports of the Red Sea, the Persian Gulf and the Mediterranean. The Phoenicians traded tin from Cornwall, Indian Ocean voyagers provided cloves from Zanzibar and copal (resin) from Madagascar, while camel trains from India and Persia produced gold, frankincense and myrrh.[5]

---

5 The Three Wise Men (or Magi) of the Bible, who brought these gifts to the infant Christ, have been identified in some sources as Zoroasters (fire worshippers) from Persia. Magi is the origin of our word 'magic'. The black-faced Balthazar is traditionally identified as a Babylonian merchant.

Yet such exoticisms don't bring us any closer to imagining the actual life as it was lived on the streets of Babylon. Must all attempts to recapture that full awareness of place, as captured by all five senses, necessarily represent a failure of the imagination? Perhaps these streets and alleyways were somewhat like the streets of Kolkata? But Babylon wasn't a city that failed. Defeated maybe, but not collapsing of its own accord. During twenty-three years following the long and glorious reign of Nebuchadnezzar II in 539 BC, the city would fall into decline, largely through inept administration.

In 539 BC Babylon was overrun by the expanding Persian Empire of King Cyrus the Great, and a new era was ushered in. The Persians had identified a weakness in the city's monumental defences. While the Babylonians were celebrating one of their national feasts, the Persians made a secret plan to divert the waters of the Euphrates, enabling their soldiers to slip beyond the outer city along the mudbanks of the lowered river. Unaware of the approaching Persian forces, the citizens of Babylon continued celebrating – the great city fell into enemy hands without anyone realising.

The new Persian Babylonians took over quickly and established their culture and government. According the contemporary Ancient Greek Herodotus, widely regarded as the father of history, the Persians wore turbans and splashed their bodies with perfume. They buried their dead in honey and peopled their temples with ritual prostitutes. And the three Persian tribes who occupied the city are said to have eaten only fish. Under their king, Cyrus the Great, astronomy was given a new lease of life, enabling the Babylonian mathematicians to complete their maps of the constellations. Cyrus also issued a decree allowing the Israelites to return to their homeland.

The prophet Jeremiah, who had correctly prophesied the fall of Jerusalem to the Babylonians in 587 BC, had also prophesied that one day the Israelites would return to Jerusalem. He had also prophesied the downfall of Babylon: 'Therefore the desert creatures will dwell with the howling animals. And in her the ostriches will dwell. She will never again be inhabited. Nor will she be a place of residence throughout all generations.' Not until many centuries later, when Mesopotamia descended into chaos, would Babylon be abandoned. It would remain a vast ghost city of crumbling ruins, the grit in desert wind gradually sandpapering the walls of the buildings, silting up the streets and the doorways. The entrance to the city's archive chambers was buried in sand and grit, sealing inside thousands upon thousands of baked-clay tablets marked with a cuneiform script that had now passed beyond human understanding.

Sequence

But many of the secrets contained in the language of those inscrutable cuneiform tablets had already passed on into other languages, spreading through the eastern Mediterranean region, where they eventually reached an entirely different type of people, who lived in small city states around the Aegean Sea: the Ancient Greeks.

In Babylonian times, the scientific knowledge contained in these tablets had been within the purview of the priests, its direction guided by the dictates of the powerful gods of the religion to which they adhered. Even the practitioners of this science had been members of the religious caste. The gods of Mesopotamia and Ancient Egypt were serious, mysterious, all-seeing figures, whose powers required appeasement. On the other hand, the Greek gods were human, only more so, and took advantage of their god-like powers in much the same fashion as any human would have done if granted such powers. They could be jealous and angry, but also subtle and deceitful. When Zeus, the most powerful of the gods, lusted after the beautiful Leda, who was married to the king of Sparta, he transformed himself into a swan, so that he could rape her.

Clearly such gods had little to do with spirituality, moral behaviour or the quest for knowledge. This liberated Greek thought to develop in an utterly original fashion, engendering the beginnings of philosophy. In Ancient Greece this pursuit, which literally means 'love of knowledge', covered all human knowledge, including moral, speculative and scientific knowledge.

The first philosopher is generally accepted as being Thales of Miletus, Miletus being a Greek city state on the Ionian coast of Anatolia. In 585 BC Thales predicted the eclipse that took place on 28 March of that year. This was the very eclipse that had persuaded the Medes and the Lydians to abandon their war in the heartland of Anatolia. Thales almost certainly gained foreknowledge of this eclipse from Babylonian sources.

As a philosopher, Thales observed and pondered the world around him. When he climbed the hillside above Miletus, he saw seashell fossils set in the cliffs. Looking out over the sunlit blue Aegean Sea, he observed vapour rising to form clouds. When these drifted inland on the wind, they deposited rain on the green valley. This water drained into the winding River Meander, which carried it back out to sea.[6] From the evidence of the seashells, the rain, the clouds and so forth, he deduced that the world was fundamentally made out of just one substance, namely water. Such reasoning, and deduction from appearances, without any appeal to the gods or some metaphysical agency, is the very nature of philosophy.

Thales was mocked by his fellow citizens, however. If he was as clever as he claimed, how come he was not rich? Thales eventually decided that it was time to put an end to such criticism. On hearing that a bumper olive harvest was due, he laid down options to hire every olive press in Miletus. When the bumper olive crop duly

---

6 The origin of our word 'meander'.

arrived, he set his own high price for hiring out the olive presses, making a small fortune in the process. This is widely regarded as the earliest example of derivative trading, which involves options and futures. Once again, an important advance in human abstract human thought appears to have coincided with a new sophisticated form of financial manipulation.

A follower of Thales, who also lived in Miletus, was Anaximenes, whose observations and contemplation led him to the conclusion that the fundamental substance was in fact air. Mist, liquids and solids were all more or less concentrated accretions of air. In 546 BC when Anaximenes was forty, Miletus was overrun by Cyrus the Great, as the Persian Empire spread westwards; but Anaximenes appears to have been allowed to continue teaching philosophy.

However, in 499 BC Miletus led the Ionian Revolt against the Persians. This was savagely put down: Miletus was sacked, its men all slaughtered, its women and children sold into slavery and its youths all castrated, thus ensuring that there would be no further citizens of Miletus.

Some fifty miles up the coast, and also under Persian rule, was the city of Ephesus, which produced the Greek philosopher Heraclitus. Developing on Anaximenes' thought, Heraclitus came to the conclusion that the ultimate substance was not material at all. It was the flickering, ever-changing form of fire. From this he concluded 'all is flux', leading him to declare: 'No man steps into the same river twice.'

Some years later, the northern Greek philosopher Democritus would use rational thought to arrive at the ultimate idea of the *a-tomos*, literally meaning 'that which cannot be cut'. Thus, the ultimate constituent of matter was deemed to consist of atoms. By this point philosophical thinking had reached Athens, the epicentre of Greek culture.

Athens: The Template

Athens was the largest and most powerful city state in Ancient Greece, only rivalled in power by Sparta in the nearby Peloponnese. Ancient Greece was not a country; it consisted of almost a thousand squabbling, semi-independent city states, some with trading colonies as far afield as the northern Black Sea and Spain.

Many question whether these 'Greeks' even shared a common racial or genetic inheritance. But they did share a common language, and a common cultural ethos. Evidence of this ethos can be seen in their shared belief in the same gods, who were said to inhabit Mount Olympus, the tallest mountain in Greece. Similarly, the many oracles, such as the celebrated one at Delphi, were consulted by all Greeks. However, although religion was important, the spheres of religion and knowledge were – as we have seen – kept separate, which gave birth to philosophy as a foundation stone of Ancient Greek culture.

The Greeks also shared a sophisticated literary heritage, reaching back to the blind poet Homer, who may in fact have been a conglomeration of oral sources dating from around the twelfth century BC. Then there were the regular pan-Hellenic athletic competitions that were held annually in Olympia, known to us as the Olympic Games. During the games a pan-Hellenic truce was declared to enable athletes from all cities to travel and take part.

Even amid this exceptional cultural efflorescence, Athens excelled. During the course of this era, the city gave birth to all kinds of ornaments to western civilisation – ranging from tragic drama to democracy, from the perfection of sculpture to the art of rhetoric, from the invention of logic to the creation of the world's first analog computers.[7] Perhaps most important of all was Athens' reputation for philosophical thinking – Athenians stood out for their mastery of the subject and transformed it into what we recognise as 'philosophy' today.

Athenian inventions and institutions would foster an exceptional collective spirit. Take the Agora, for instance – the marketplace that played a central role in the city's social life. This was more than a mere collection of stalls selling produce: it was the economic heart of the city and became a gathering place for all free citizens to exchange news and gossip, form opinions and debate matters of the day. This was where many of the philosophers practised their trade – the Stoics even gained their name from the stoa (pillars) where they gave lessons in the shade at the edge of the market.

Tragedy, too, was a collective social experience: dramas were performed before the entire (male, free) population, gathered in the amphitheatre of Dionysius, which was capable of seating 17,000 spectators. Appreciation, criticism and freely expressed opinions of these communal events provided a crucial collective experience. All this fostered the individuality, creativity and unique

---

7 Evidence of this was found in the form of the so-called Antikythera Mechanism, which dated from around the second century BC, but was only discovered on an ancient wreck off Antikythera by sponge divers in 1901. The complex clockwork mechanisms of this instrument were so rusted and clogged with marine accretions that it would take decades of painstaking cleaning and restoration before the technical virtuosity and purpose of this intriguing lump of corroded metal became evident. Its mechanism could be used to calculate the positions of the stars and eclipses many decades in advance. Here was a technology that could perform similar tasks to the Babylonian minds who created the astronomical cuneiform tablets, no less.

ethos that nurtured a cultural supremacy that would surpass that of any other that had preceded it, even the fabled wonders of Babylon that had flourished over three centuries previously.

Evidence of the sheer width and breadth of this Greek cultural phenomenon can be seen in our language to this very day. It is no accident that we continue to use such Greek words as philosophy, psychology (from the Greek *psyche* meaning 'soul', and *logos* meaning 'word' or 'learning'), democracy (from *demos* 'the people' and *kratos* 'rule'), epistemology (*episteme* 'knowledge') and so on and so forth. From tragedy to autocracy, from geometry to geography – we still speak Greek.

As with Babylon, the foundations of Athenian society during its ascendancy were laid down by a law-maker. This was Solon, who was born in Athens in 630 BC, possibly a descendant of Codrus, the last semi-mythical king of Athens, who had ruled around 1070 BC before the city became a magistracy. Although Solon was of aristocratic lineage his family were impecunious, for he initially embarked upon a career in commerce, which was considered unworthy of high-born citizens. Despite this, he evidently rose to prominence. In a war against the nearby city state of Megara, he was chosen to lead the Athenian army, whose spirits he rallied by reading a patriotic poem he had written. At the age of thirty-six he was chosen as an archon, one of the nine magistrates who ruled the city during this pre-democratic era. Below the magistrates was the assembly known as the Ekklesia, whose members were largely noble or wealthy citizens, with ordinary citizens and the poorer classes excluded.

By this time, the city of Athens had declined into a parlous state of political, moral and economic decline. Solon was tasked with drawing up a series of reforms designed to overcome this malaise. He initiated these by extending membership of the Ekklesia to all freeborn male citizens, regardless of class or wealth. This is generally recognised as an early Athenian move towards democracy, which would only come to full fruition some eighty years later, under the law-maker Cleisthenes.

Economically, the rich had a stranglehold over the poor. This often led to poorer members of society falling into debt to their masters, who were allowed to seize their debtors, or their children, and make them their slaves. At the same time, there was considerable strife between the rural citizens of the city state, and their urban counterparts, with this being further complicated by family and tribal rivalries. In order to raise the rural economy above subsistence level, as well as ameliorate such conflicts, Solon introduced a scheme whereby fathers were obliged to find their sons a trade. Only then would their sons be obliged to look after them in their old age. Also, in a move to free up the economy, all debts were suspended.

In an attempt to bring about a more open moral climate, as well as bring practice in line with the law, Solon is also said to have introduced public brothels and to have regulated the widespread practice of pederasty (relationships between adult men and younger teenage boys) by introducing the notion of consent. Some sources have viewed such scurrilous tales as no more than later satirical comment on Solon's reforms, but there is widespread evidence that they were serious, and did in fact take place.

Paradoxically, considering the high regard in which they were later held, Solon's reforms were not an immediate success. He also appears to have become embroiled in a scandal regarding his proposed suspension of debts – it seems many of his friends, who had prior warning of the suspension, quickly ran up large debts. Consequently, Solon would spend the next ten years travelling abroad to evade prosecution. Thus, democracy appears to be yet another advance that was accompanied by financial chicanery.

Despite the initial failure of Solon's reforms, they are now seen as laying the foundations for Athens' golden age. This would come to fruition under the leadership of the statesman and general Pericles, whose thirty-two-year period of rule during the fifth century is regarded as the peak of Athenian ascendancy.

Yet before this could take place Athens was forced to defend itself against the might of the expanding Persian Empire. The city's survival was due to a series of all but miraculous victories. During 490 BC, in response to Athens' support for Miletus during the Ionian Revolt, the Persian army crossed the Aegean. Despite being heavily outnumbered, the Athenians chose the battle site with care, at Marathon, where marshy ground rendered the Persian cavalry unusable. On the fateful day, ten thousand Athenians and their allies faced some three hundred thousand Persians in the narrow pass between the mountains and the sea. The Greek army formed a phalanx, its leading soldiers creating a wall of linked shields advancing in lockstep towards the Persian lines. After bitter fighting, the Greeks finally drove the Persians back towards the marshy ground, where they broke ranks and began fleeing for their beached triremes in a panic.[8]

Following the battle, the runner, Philippedes, was despatched back to Athens to relay news of this famous victory, which he did, dramatically dying of exhaustion after conveying his message. The modern marathon running race commemorates this event, taking place over some 26 miles and 385 yards, the distance from Marathon to Athens.

This victory demonstrated that the Greeks were capable of resisting the might of the Persian army, who would not return for another ten years. When the Persians did return, however, they proved all but unstoppable. Despite another famous victory by the Greeks, this time at the sea battle of Salamis in 480 BC, the following year the Persians would overrun Athens and sack the city. Eventually,

---

8 The Ancient Greek historian Herodotus, the 'father of history', records how the Greek god Pan instilled fear among the Persians, causing them to 'panic' – the origin of our present word.

an alliance of Greek city states, the Delian League, would drive the Persians from Greece altogether during the 470s BC.

By now the battle-hardened Pericles was a rising young figure in Athens. He was elected to power in 461 BC, aged just twenty-seven. His success as a general during the ensuing First Peloponnesian War against Sparta consolidated his popularity. It was during these years that he ordered the building of a new Parthenon on the Acropolis, which still stands today. In Pericles' day the Parthenon served as both a temple to the goddess Athena, the patron of Athens, and as the treasury for the Delian League, whose members would become the Athenian Empire. The reign of Pericles would also see the construction of other superb examples of Greek architecture, making Athens the envy of all Greece. Athens produced some of the finest achievements in Greek art, especially in sculpture, which saw the perfection of marble depictions of the human form. The most notable examples of these are the *Venus de Milo* and the *Winged Victory of Samothrace*.[9] Similar sculptural masterpieces include the so-called Elgin Marbles, which formed the frieze of the Parthenon.

Our appreciation of the classic proportions and sheer beauty of these pure white marble works was somewhat undermined by the recent discovery that the Greeks originally coloured their sculptures with bright blue, red and green paint. Furthermore, the *Venus de Milo*'s missing arms were probably decorated with metal jewellery, as were her head and ears. Even the Parthenon itself, it seems, was originally decorated in garish reds and greens, such as to make it the envy of any modern-day oligarch.

All we can usefully say of this is that taste changes, often radically so – and we must accept the fact that there is no accounting for

---

9 Widely believed to have been created to celebrate the Athenian naval victory, against all the odds, over the Persians at the Battle of Salamis. The result of this battle was considered to be such a forgone conclusion that the Persian King Xerxes had a golden throne set up on the mountainside overlooking Salamis so that he could witness his famous victory.

it, regardless of the guise in which it is presented. Can we seriously claim that our taste is superior to that of the geniuses who created such timeless, once colourful masterpieces? Which prompts some seriously undermining questions. What is the basis of our historical perception? What are *our* misconceptions? Why do we assume that our view of the past is correct, that only we understand? How will such lapses in epistemology, in taste, in vision even, be judged by an aghast, uncomprehending posterity?

Which leads us to the most spectacular of all classical Greek cultural achievements: the invention of dramatic theatre. This began as a ritualised religious performance at the bi-annual celebrations of the god Dionysius. It involved the *exarchon*, or leading priest-figure, who was accompanied by a choir, or masked chorus, who performed dithyrambic hymns involving singing and ritual dancing. These celebrations took place on a platform facing out towards the bowl of stepped semi-circular rows of seats of the *theatron* (literally 'watching place') where the citizens would gather to witness the rites. The platform was known as the *orchestra* (literally 'dancing place') and behind this was the rectangular building known as the *skene*, which formed the backdrop and also served as a dressing room. Above the orchestra was an arch known as the *proscenion*, which served to enclose the open-air stage. All these elements have their recognisable counterparts in theatres to this day.

The chanted interaction between the *archon* and the leader of the chorus, *coryphaeus*, gradually evolved into a dialogue. But it was a man called Thespis who was the first *archon* to appear on stage and not speak in his own voice. Some time around 535 BC he is said to have startled his audience by leaping onto a wooden cart onstage and delivering a speech impersonating another character, thus becoming the first *hypokrites* ('actor'). His dialogue with the leader of the chorus soon meant that there were two actors on the stage, backed by the chorus, whose interjections and running commentaries pointed out the significance of what was being said by the two characters. This situation quickly developed into an active narration of important, often tragic historical events, giving rise to further actors and action mimicking the events themselves.

One of the earliest of these dramatic narrations was called *The Fall of Miletus*. The contents of this drama are now lost, but, most importantly, there was something that could be lost – in other words a written text, which was learned by the actors. Not long after this, in 472 BC, the Athenian Aeschylus produced a tragedy called *The Persians*, based on his own experiences at the Battle of Salamis. It soon became clear that Aeschylus was using his dramas to demonstrate the effect of tragic circumstances to explain the psychological and theological implications of the human condition. In the process, this evoked terror and empathy in his audiences, which had a cathartic effect. Such tragedies both united and inspired the citizens of Athens in a unique, quasi-spiritual experience. In just sixty years, little more than a lifetime in that era, an archaic religious ritual had been transformed into an utterly new and profoundly engaging art form that is capable to this day of holding up a mirror to our lives.

In a final twist, Ancient Greek drama would also develop an antithesis to tragedy, in the form of comedy. Comedies, with their political satire, scatological innuendo and general buffoonery, provided a different kind of release for the assembled citizens in the form of laughter. Such satire, or mockery, would become an integral part of Athenian cultural life, an essential ingredient to the ethos of democracy. No citizen was precluded from the ridicule of his fellow citizens.

All this leads us back to the finest flowering of Greek culture, its three great philosophers: Socrates, Plato and Aristotle. Socrates was born around 470 BC and was widely regarded among the people of Athens as something of a public buffoon. Indeed, he even appears as such in one of the plays by the city's first great comic playwright,

Aristophanes. Socrates encouraged this aspect of his character by revelling in the self-applied nickname 'the gadfly of Athens'.

Socrates wrote nothing down, so we have to rely heavily upon his description in the dialogues written by his pupil Plato, who was devoted to his master and took his philosophy very seriously indeed. Yet even in Plato's loving description it is not difficult to discern an impish contrarian element to Socrates' character, which did in fact colour his entire philosophy.

When the Delphic Oracle was asked: 'Who is the wisest man in Greece?' it replied, 'Socrates of Athens'. After this news reached Athens, Socrates professed astonishment. How could he be the wisest man in Greece when he knew that he knew nothing? And if he knew nothing, then what did the wise men of Athens know? Socrates set about visiting each of these wise men in turn to find out what they knew. Using his dialectical method of question and answer, he probed the roots of their so-called knowledge, exposing the false assumptions upon which it was built. Having demonstrated the erroneous nature of their beliefs, he would then reply: 'I, too, know nothing.'

Socrates also made the apparently contradictory claim: 'There is only one good, knowledge, and one evil, ignorance.' This contradiction is resolved in his assertion: 'The unexamined life is not worth living.' Previously, philosophers had questioned the world around them. Socrates sought to reverse this speculation about nature, urging his pupils to examine human nature. He urged them to follow the advice of the Delphic Oracle: 'Know thyself'. Only by building upon such secure foundations could we hope to attain genuine knowledge.

Socrates' introspection led him to a profound ethical understanding of the human condition. A question such as 'How can one live the good life?' was liable to lead to ever more profound and far-reaching questions, such as 'What is the nature of good?', leading to 'What is a good and just society?'

Despite Socrates' rejection of the more scientific attitude taken by previous philosophers, his method of probing questions and doubting assumptions have continued to inform science to this day. Even though science nowadays tries to know the answer to everything, and philosophy appears to have the answer to nothing, philosophy will always remain more profound. Its questions go deeper. One example will suffice. Physics, arguably the most successful branch of science, rests on quantum theory. And according to one of the finest physicists of our age, Richard Feynman, 'Nobody understands quantum mechanics.' We only use it because it appears to work, though we still have not understood quite why this is so.

Socrates is said to have given his lessons amid the clang and bustle of a blacksmith's shop just outside the agora, where he attracted quite a following among the young. In contrast, other Athenian philosophers would occupy the less crowded edges of the agora, which young men were not permitted to enter. Socrates abhorred pretension and advised his enthusiastic young followers to question the false knowledge of their elders. Such subversive teaching eventually led to him falling foul of the authorities. He was charged with 'corrupting the young' and stood trial before the democratically assembled citizens of Athens. Here his behaviour was characteristically provocative. He refused to defend himself, instead insisting that rather than being charged he should be provided with free board and lodging for his valuable service to the community. Despite such apparent impudence, this is a valuable point. Today, all reputable democracies have a paid leader of the opposition, whose job it is to question the decisions taken by their leaders. But Socrates was far ahead of his time, and the jury condemned him to self-administered death by drinking hemlock.

Plato was outraged at the way democracy had treated his beloved mentor, and consequently his philosophy would condemn this form of government in favour of government by a philosophically educated class of leaders like himself. However, contrary to Socrates' stance on knowledge, tradition has it that the Academy Plato founded had above its entrance a sign reading: 'Let no one ignorant of geometry enter here.'

The core of Plato's philosophy lay in his belief that the world we see around us consists of mere shadowy appearances. The *real* world, which made up these appearances, consisted of ideas (or ideals). For example, an orange consisted of nothing more than a conglomeration that partook of the ideal (or essence) of the colour orange, of roundness, of solidity and so forth. This outlook was certainly coloured by Plato's belief in the fundamentally idealistic nature of mathematics. Here all straight lines are no more than an approximation of an ideal straight line, all numbers are mere appearances of ideal numbers. As he said: 'God forever geometrises'.Behind the world of appearances was a god who dealt in ideals. God did not move in mysterious ways, but in mathematical ways.

However, this is merely Plato's view of epistemology. In his dialogues he discusses the whole range of philosophical problems, from the nature of justice to the motives for human action, from good and evil to truth and falsehood, from aesthetics to ethics. Indeed, it is little exaggeration to claim – as many do – that all philosophy since has been mere footnotes to Plato. For example, modern mathematicians continue to debate whether numbers, theorems and indeed all of mathematics are created by mathematicians, or already exist in some ideal platonic world and are merely discovered by mathematicians. Likewise, is there an ideal of justice: a universal Justice to which all should agree? Or are there simply different forms of justice, each of which has evolved among different peoples in accord with the development of their own differing societies?

Aristotle was the most able pupil at Plato's Academy, but he quit in a huff when Plato died and he was not chosen as his successor.

Later, Aristotle would be employed by King Philip II of Macedonia to tutor his son, the young man who would grow up to become Alexander the Great. Aristotle instilled in Alexander a belief in the superiority of Greek culture, which may well have inspired his insatiable quest to conquer the world and turn it into a Greek empire.

Where Plato's thoughts ranged over the whole of philosophy, Aristotle's ranged over the whole of human knowledge. Where Plato saw the world as devolving from a higher world of ideas, Aristotle saw it as precisely the opposite. To him, the world was real and the ideas it generated were merely universal likenesses created by the human mind. Form and matter co-existed in the particular object, rather than creating it. In other words, the form and matter of an orange exists within each particular orange; the orange does not partake of some ideal world of absolute ideas, it is what it is, and it is our investigations that discover any universal characteristics it may possess. This is a scientific, rather than a metaphysical or mystical, view of the world: we investigate the inherent properties of objects, rather than dismissing them as mere appearances.

In this way, Aristotle's scientific worldview enabled him to investigate everything from plants to the passage of projectiles through the air, from animals to theories of politics. He was interested in physics, rather than metaphysics.[10] It was the mystical other-worldly aspect of metaphysics that he tended to dismiss; though he did investigate metaphysical subjects, such as the first causes and ultimate principles of things. He was particularly interested in teleology, from the Greek *telos*, meaning 'end or purpose', and *logos*, 'knowledge'. That is, he believed the best way to understand any aspect of nature – from a bird's wings to the leaves of a tree – is to discover the purpose

---

10 Ironically, the very word 'metaphysics' appears to stem from his writings. When later commentators were assembling his works, they listed them in order, and all those that came after his work on physics were labelled 'meta-physics', i.e. 'beyond physics'.

it fulfils. This can be done by examining the object in question, and then applying rational thought to discover what it is for.

It was in this notion of rational thought that Aristotle made his supreme contribution to human knowledge: namely, logic. Put simply, he invented the syllogism: a number of proven truths, from which a further truth can be deduced. For example:

All men are mortal.

Socrates is a man.

Therefore Socrates is mortal.

Aristotle would extend this logical way of thinking, the syllogism, into a method of extreme subtlety, which would hardly be bettered for two millennia. For instance, it could be generalised:

All objects of class A are members of class B.

C is a member of class A.

Therefore C is also a member of class B.

However, logic is a process requiring the utmost rigour, and is thus prone to pitfalls, or false generalisations. Its arguments have to be watertight, include no unproven assumptions and be utterly undeniable. Aristotle's one serious logical mistake would influence human thought for centuries to come, and when this came to be allied with theology it would be further strengthened – almost to the point of becoming incontrovertible. Aristotle's notion of teleology gave him profound insight into the ways of nature, but his mistake was to generalise this principle to the world and all human life, deducing that these were directed towards a final end.

This would appear to be an inspired piece of logical deduction, whose fatal flaw was not revealed for over two millennia, when Darwin discovered the principle of evolution, which is not purposeful but blind. Evolution moves forward by the survival of the fittest, not towards some ultimate end. The same could be said of history. Though, as elsewhere, the element of unforeseeable chance often plays a major role.

Somewhat ironically though, after making Athens a leading centre of philosophy, it was Aristotle's own pupil, Alexander the Great, who would grow up to conquer the whole of Greece and later bring about its downfall.

Sequence

If Alexander the Great had chanced to launch his campaign of conquest west into Europe, rather than east as far as the border of India, the embryonic Roman Empire would have been overrun and western Europe might have been part of a Greek rather than a Roman Empire.

According to one of Rome's founding legends, alluded to by the poet Virgil in the *Aeneid*, Rome was in fact founded by Greeks. When Troy was destroyed at the end of the Trojan War, the Trojan prince Aeneas set sail to found a new Troy. After a long sea voyage, Aeneas and his companions made landfall on the banks of the River Tiber. By this time, the women in the group had grown tired of their continual voyaging and wanted to remain on land. A woman named Roma, along with some female companions, decided to burn the ships so that they could not leave. At first the men were furious, but they finally decided that they had found an ideal spot to establish a settlement, which they named after Roma. According to Virgil's version, Romulus and Remus, the twins who are often credited with the founding of Rome, were merely distant descendants of Aeneas. However, most sources agree that Romulus killed his brother Remus, giving Rome a violent and bloody baptism.

3

Imperial Rome

It would take eight and a half centuries before Rome achieved its peak under the Emperor Trajan, who ruled from AD 98 to 117. By this stage, the Roman Empire had reached its furthest extent, from the cold, misty clime of Hadrian's Wall in Britannica, through western Europe and North Africa, to the baking heat of Babylonia and the shores of the Sinus Persicus (Persian Gulf).

Despite Virgil's *Aeneid*, his mythic poem describing the founding of Rome, the city was by no stretch of the imagination Greek in origin. Though initially adopting certain Greek traits, it had unmistakably evolved its own mores. Take its idea of public entertainment: instead of an amphitheatre seating the small population of a Greek city state, Rome had built the Colosseum, a venue said to have been capable of accommodating over eighty thousand spectators. And instead of enacting cathartic tragedies and farcical comedies that fostered a shared ethos, Rome had its own brand of entertainments. Armies of gladiators fought battles to the death, the victors the last men standing in a field of carnage. The grand arena could be flooded with water from the nearby aqueduct in order to stage battles between galley ships manned by slaves and desperate, condemned men. And in the intervals between these mass spectacles, public executions took place. Rapists, murderers, Christians and the like were driven, often naked, into the arena to suffer *damnatio ad bestias* – where they would be savagely attacked, clawed to the ground and torn limb from limb by starved lions, tigers, leopards, or even crocodiles. Instead of communal catharsis the spectators experienced blood-lust, jeering in mockery, yet simultaneously experiencing an inner abject terror. This was how Rome celebrated its victories over its enemies, its subversives, its slaves: all damned to excruciating horrors. Watching citizens beware!

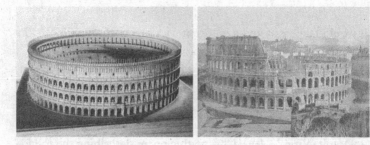

The Colosseum as it would have appeared in Ancient Roman times, and its ruin today.

Where the Greeks were inclined to pose abstract questions, the Romans favoured concrete answers. Philosophy was downgraded in favour of technology. Where the Athenians built the timeless proportions of the Parthenon, the Romans built engineering miracles such as the Colosseum and the Pantheon.[11] The latter, started during the reign of Trajan, certainly had had

---

11 The name given to this temple suggests that it was probably dedicated to the worship of all the gods, though this remains disputed. The Romans had adopted a number of the Greek gods (many of which had even earlier pre-Greek origins). For instance, the Greek god Poseidon, the sea god, became Neptune for the Romans; while the Greek goddess of love, Aphrodite, became the Roman Venus. By and large these adopted gods retained their original function. However, the elephant in the room was the fact that, by now, some emperors had begun declaring themselves to be gods. For the most part, this elevation was only formally observed, though any heretical derision of such status was, of necessity, covert.

a large Greek-style porticoed entrance, its eight pillars matching those of the Parthenon, but its inner marble-floored circular temple was utterly Roman. It was topped by a vast dome, the like of which the Greeks had not even contemplated. Their architects had remained ignorant of how to secure an arch with a keystone, let alone translate such a two-dimensional edifice into a three-dimensional dome. This Roman feat required anti-intuitive engineering and ingenuity of the highest order, whereby the weight of the stones (the force of gravity) was used to hold the structure together, reinforcing its strength, rather than bringing it crashing down. The 142-foot diameter of the dome on the Pantheon remains to this day the largest unreinforced concrete dome in existence – a fact that speaks for itself concerning the achievements of Roman architectural engineering.

The same keystone principle was used to build the Colosseum: row upon row of supporting arches, rising to a pillared fourth level reaching a height of over a hundred and sixty feet.[12] And instead of the semi-circle of a Greek amphitheatre, the Colosseum encloses a vast oval arena: a shape that ensured maximum visibility for all spectators. Other indicative differences can be seen in the seating arrangements. The citizens of the Athenian city state certainly sat in different rows according to their class, with the *hoi polloi* ('common people') seated in the upper rows at the back of the arena; but the seats were the same for all. The Colosseum, on the other hand, had four separate tiers of seating, one above the other, and even these were subdivided by metal barriers. There were over forty different numbered entrances to the Colosseum, and these were used to separate people from different classes and different districts of the city.

---

12 By comparison, the Amphitheatre of Dionysius in Athens is sixty feet high, with the Parthenon just forty-five feet.

The focus of the Colosseum was the podium, where the purple-robed emperor sat on his dais, accompanied by his entourage and protected by the Praetorian Guard, the only soldiers permitted to bear arms within the precinct of central Rome. Nearby, in the closest seats to the arena sat the senatorial class, clad in white togas.[13] The highest levels of the thirteen stories of seats were occupied by the plebeians, the rabble of common people. And beneath the arena (now exposed among the ruins) was a network of tunnels where the gladiators and animals were caged prior to their entrance into the arena.

One unavoidable element of having such a large amount of people in one space was the fact that they could voice their collective opinion. Here perhaps was the last remnant of republican Rome, with its measure of democracy, which ended in 46 BC when Julius Caesar overthrew the Republic, ushering in the imperial age. In the Colosseum the emperor came face to face with the people, and always did his best to gain their cheers, with scattered free gifts and mock-ingratiating gestures, obsequiously returned by the vast roar of the spectators. However, such attempts to win over the crowd were not always successful, and on occasion groups of unruly spectators could be rounded up and thrown into the arena to fend for themselves.

Another locus of public activity was the Forum, which performed a similar function to the agora in Athens, only on a much larger scale. The Forum was a paved open space almost three hundred yards long and two hundred wide in the flat valley between the Capitoline and the Palatine, two of the seven hills on which Rome

---

13 Togas, and their material, were a sign of rank, usually worn on social occasions. Senators wore white togas of finest cloth; those who also acted as magistrates wore a white toga with a broad purple stripe. Togas rubbed with chalk, to emphasise their whiteness, were worn by candidates for public office – this 'whiter than white' was intended to indicate the purity of their moral character.

was said to have been built.[14] Originally a marketplace, the Forum became the central focus of the city, where crowds gathered and all manner of social, political and religious activity took place. It was surrounded by many of Rome's oldest and finest buildings, including the pillared temples, the Senate House and the triumphal arch of Septimus Severus, who would become emperor in AD 193.

Then there were the baths – public baths were scattered throughout the city, evidence of the Roman obsession with bodily cleanliness. Each bath house had a *tepidarium* (a hot plunge pool), a *caladarium* (a steam room with underfloor heating, where attendants massaged the bather's body with perfumed oil before scraping their skin), and a *frigidarium* (a large cold-water bath used for swimming). Such baths were separated by gender and used on a daily basis by the more affluent classes, while even the poor tended to visit on a weekly basis. Like the Forum, the baths served as a useful social venue where members of different classes could mix and exchange news and gossip.

Roman baths were frequently attached to a gymnasium, an institution that originated with the Ancient Greeks as a place of exercise and training for such sports as wrestling, boxing and ball games.[15] The close alliance of cleanliness and fitness is implied in the Roman saying '*Mens sana in corpora sano*' (Healthy mind, heathy body). This aspect of the gymnasium is reflected in modern usage – in the German-speaking world a gymnasium is a school, whereas in the English-speaking world it is of course a place for fitness and training.

---

14 One version of Rome's founding has it that Romulus and Remus founded the city on the latter hill on 21 April 753 BC.

15 In Greece, competitors in such sports, and indeed in all the Olympic Games, were invariably naked. This was claimed to promote 'aesthetic appreciation of the male form'. Such practice is reflected in the Greek word *gymnós*, meaning 'naked'. The Romans preferred to play their games in suitable clothing. They also had no word for homosexuality and were seemingly less prone to 'aesthetic appreciation of the male form'.

Landmarks like the Forum, the Colosseum, public baths and triumphal arches became features of Roman cities throughout the empire, and their ruins serve as a visible reminder of a civilisation that had a formative influence on the western world. The Arc de Triomphe in Paris, Marble Arch in London and the Washington Square Arch in New York are all direct copies of their Roman predecessors. So too, pillared buildings with a Corinthian facade such as London's British Museum and Le Panthéon in Paris would be immediately recognisable to any Ancient Roman, as would much of the public architecture of Washington, DC, state capitols throughout the US, and other monumental government buildings from Buenos Aires to Berlin and St Petersburg. What also spread out from Rome throughout the length and breadth of the empire was, of course, the Latin language, which derives its name from Latium, the original name for the region in which the city of Rome was founded. Classical Latin was spoken by administrators, its inscriptions carved into monuments and buildings; it was also the language of communications and decrees and was spoken by all citizens with pretentions to social status. The plebeians (the common people) and the common soldiers of the Roman Legions communicated in Vulgar Latin. This was seldom written down and has mainly come down to us through phrases that crop up in Roman plays, as well as the graffiti found on ruins such as those in Pompei. In fact, we rely on this ancient graffiti to extrapolate much of everyday Roman life as it was lived by the people. The crowded tenements inhabited by the Roman plebs were not built for posterity.

After nearly a millennium of glorious and vicious rule, the Roman Empire began to disintegrate from the third to the fifth centuries. As things fell apart, the Latin language began to split into distinct regional dialects, many of which are known to have incorporated elements of the Vulgar Latin used by the Roman soldiers and common people in these former Roman provinces.

Today, the separate languages spoken in Portugal, Spain, France, Italy and Romania are all Latin based, as is much of the English language. To this day, government institutions, schools, families and the like often adopt Latin mottos, from Canada's national motto '*A Mari usque ad mare*' (From sea to sea), to the '*Semper fidelis*' (Always faithful) of the US Marine Corps.

Perhaps though, of all the many aspects of Rome's legacy, Ancient Roman law is the most enduring. In the fifth century BC, it was decided that laws needed to be written down so that they could be applied equally across the increasingly large and diverse empire. As a starting point, the Romans looked to Athens and the laws that were set down there some two hundred years previously. After much ensuing debate, twelve laws were drawn up, known as the Law of the Twelve Tables. At least, this is how these disputed events are recorded by the influential Roman historian Livy in his '*Ad Urbe Condita*' (From the Founding of the City). In his work, Livy recounts at length the history of Rome from the time of Romulus to the final years of the first century BC during his lifetime. However, much as parts of Livy's extensive history remain lost, so too do we only have fragments of the Law of the Twelve Tables. From what remains, it seems the Twelve Tables were far from being a comprehensive set of laws as in the Hammurabi code in Babylon. Instead, they were more a series of steps intended to formalise many of the prevailing customary laws, as well as including a gesture towards making plebeians more equal to their fellow citizens before the law.

Despite the gaps in our understanding of the origins of Roman law, its later application reveals a philosophy of law that is certainly recognisable as the foundations of modern democratic government. It is in Roman law that we first encounter the principle of checks and balances. Prior to Julius Caesar's takeover in 49 BC, Rome was ruled by two elected consuls, either of whom could veto the other.

This ensured that no one man held power. These checks and balances also ensured that the consuls had to work in some measure of harmony with the Senate, as well as the People's Assembly, a legislative body that elected magistrates and enacted laws. At one time there had been a specific Plebeian Assembly. Later, there was a Tribal Assembly, where the three tribes of Rome, into which the population was traditionally divided, were represented by tribunes.

Other important legal concepts established by Roman law include the separation of powers, the right of veto, limited terms of office, and regular elections in which Roman citizens could vote. Over the years, there were various definitions of Roman citizenship, which was a privileged position throughout the empire. For the most part, all freeborn Italian males qualified for Roman citizenship, which could be passed on to their sons. Full Roman citizens had the right to vote, to sue others in court, and were granted certain tax exemptions. Those who had served their full time in the Roman legions could also acquire a form of Roman citizenship, though usually this did not allow them to vote or hold public office. Women also held a limited form of Roman citizenship with similar restrictions. Generals and emperors could grant Roman citizenship, and many citizens of allied nations were granted it. We can see this in the case of St Paul, who was born Jewish but inherited Roman citizenship. This meant that when his activities as a Christian proselytiser led to him being charged with treason, he was able to invoke his right to be tried in Rome and 'appeal unto Caesar'. It also meant that when he was finally sentenced to death, he would be decapitated rather than suffer the horrific indignity of being crucified. But by this time his work was irrepressible: he had spread Christianity beyond the confines of Judea. Christianity was no longer just a Jewish religion.

Rome was the capital, the seat of power and the beating heart of an essentially military society. All roads literally led to Rome, and its legions ruled an empire spanning three continents. Legionaries were recruited from conquered territories, but to ensure no divided loyalties they would be posted to regions of the empire far distant from their homeland. Evidence of this can be seen in objects unearthed at Hadrian's Wall, the northernmost posting in the empire. Legionaries serving here at various times brought with them items such as red clay dishes from as far afield as Africa, statuettes from India, and blue glass bottles from Egypt.

The central command of Rome over its vassal states and its enemies seldom faltered. When it did, and such a lapse was overcome, Roman revenge was capable of extreme brutality. We have already seen what happened to Carthage in 146 BC. Insurrections even closer to home could be put down with yet greater barbarity. When the gladiator Spartacus led a revolt in 73 BC, he and his followers were crushed in 71 BC by the Roman-born general Crassus (though credit for this feat was claimed by Pompey). Spartacus himself probably died in battle, though his body was never identified. However, the 6,000 survivors of this final stand would be crucified on crosses lining the Appian Way from Rome to Capua, a distance of 100 miles.

This atrocity was the work of Crassus, a fully rounded monster. Crassus had previously motivated his reluctant army, many of whom covertly sympathised with Spartacus, by reviving the Ancient Roman military practice of 'decimation', when one in ten soldiers were randomly selected to be killed. According to the first-century writer Plutarch, Crassus had the selected men tortured and killed in front of the remaining army, ensuring the process involved 'many things horrible and dreadful to see'. Not surprisingly, Crassus' army soon realised that their general was capable of far worse things than their enemy, and were accordingly motivated to pursue the enemy with sufficient enthusiasm.

Crassus is best remembered as the 'richest man in Rome', who eventually accumulated a fortune in the region of £20 billion in

modern terms. This was achieved by ingenious and persistent chicanery. Crassus had been born of an old plebian family made good,
whose fortune had been seized by 'proscription'. This process
involved a consul putting a 'public enemy' (i.e. one of *his* enemies)
on the proscribed list: the enemy was subsequently put to death, or
sometimes exiled, and all his property seized.

Naturally, when Crassus' skill as a general enabled him to
achieve consular office, he made full use of this method. He con-
nived to have many rich men's names added to the proscribed
list, then quickly took over their property at a token price – thus,
according to Plutarch, 'making public calamities his great source
of wealth'.

He also introduced Rome's first fire brigade, staffing it with 500
of his own slaves. This was a long-overdue measure, as serious fires
broke out among Rome's crowded housing on an almost daily basis.
Crassus made a habit of turning up with his fire brigade and engaging with the distraught owner of the burning building. Crassus
would offer to buy the building at a highly reduced price. If the owner agreed, the fire was at once put out. If not, nothing but smoking
ruins remained. Most owners quickly agreed to Crassus' terms, as
did the owners of surrounding houses blighted by the fire. Crassus made sure that he bought slaves with architectural and building
experience. These people would then be set to work restoring any
damaged building, which was frequently leased back to its owner at
an inflated price. So successful was this business model that, according to Plutarch, Crassus 'bought the largest part of Rome'.

Crassus' barbarity was but an excessive case of normal practice
during this time. Rome was also capable of equal barbarity towards
its own generals or politicians on the occasions when they revolted
and attempted to seize power. Such events brought about a sequence
of civil wars, which were both chaotic and bloody. The most significant of these was prompted by Julius Caesar's seizure of power in

49 BC. Caesar was opposed by his former friend Pompey, who in 48 BC fled for Egypt after his defeat by Caesar and was hacked to death as his boat landed on the beach. Caesar himself was then stabbed to death by a group of senators in 44 BC in a plot led by his former political ally Brutus. In Shakespeare's *Julius Caesar*, Mark Antony, formerly Caesar's closest friend, delivers his duplicitous eulogy:

> Friends, Romans, countrymen, lend me your ears;
> I come to bury Caesar, not to praise him.
> The evil that men do lives after them;
> The good is oft interred with their bones...

Mark Anthony may not have delivered these actual words, but they are as slippery as the man himself, who was a close companion of both Caesar and Brutus. Mark Antony would later lead an army to chase down Brutus, defeating him in battle in Greece, after which Brutus opened his veins. Antony then joined forces with the general-statesman Lepidus, and Julius Caesar's adopted son Octavian, to form a ruling Triumvirate, which presided over the final years of the Republic. The Triumvirate fell apart when the three men turned on each other. Lepidus was expelled from the Triumvirate in 36 BC, after allegedly planning an uprising. Octavian then declared war on Mark Antony, who was living in Egypt with Caesar's former lover Cleopatra. After his defeat in 30 BC, Mark Antony sliced open his own stomach and Cleopatra famously clasped to her bosom an asp (a venomous Egyptian cobra). The way was now open for Octavian, who declared himself Augustus Caesar in 27 BC, becoming the first Roman emperor in all but name.[16]

This violent sequence of events is actually a highly simplified version of the tale of woe that comprised these complex machinations.

---

16 Augustus Caesar and his successor were in fact referred to as Principate (First Citizen), but are now generally regarded as the first Roman emperors.

Over some twenty years of chaos Rome was transformed from a Republic (in name only, it was by then an oligarchy) into an autocratic empire. During the course of these civil wars, armies loyal to their various generals fought in Spain, Italy, Greece, Egypt and Africa, with the blood-letting of their generals echoed throughout the ranks.

Fortunately for Rome, Augustus proved to be a capable ruler. This would be the beginning of the '*Pax Romana*' (Roman Peace), a period of two hundred or so years during which relative stability prevailed throughout the Roman Empire, largely enforced by the presence of the Roman army.

As emperor, Augustus instituted a much-needed reform to the tax system, established a civil police and recruited a reputable Roman fire brigade. He also set about rebuilding parts of the city that had fallen into decay. In a move to prevent further military disorders within the city he established the Praetorian Guard and stationed a loyal standing army outside the city.

By now the city of Rome had a population of over one million and would remain the largest city in the world for some three centuries. Uniquely, Rome was simply a centre of government; it had no established manufacturing base, nor did it actually produce anything. In order to buy the favour of the people, emperors were forced to institute a policy of '*panem et circenses*' (bread and circuses). This involved supplying free grain for bread, and regular entertainments (in the form of spectacles at the Colosseum and the like). Vast amounts of grain were shipped in via the port of Ostia from provinces such as Egypt and north Africa.

Augustus Caesar proved such a popular and able ruler that after his death the Senate voted that he be deified, thus instigating a notorious system that would be exploited by later emperors claiming god-like status. Unfortunately, he was succeeded by his stepson Tiberius, who was described by the Pliny the Elder as 'the gloomiest of men'. In the event, Tiberius was a degenerate recluse who retired to indulge in his perverse pleasures on the island of Capri and left the government in the hands of his administrators. Emperors good, bad and ugly would succeed him, while Rome's golden era faded and the city gradually declined.

Despite Rome's history of recurrent turbulence, the city produced a lively cultural and artistic legacy. Initially over-influenced by Ancient Greek culture, the city soon developed its own original characteristics in a succession of writers, artists and thinkers. The playwright Terence, born as early as 185 BC, is best remembered today for his saying: 'Nothing human is alien to me.' In other words, we should seek to understand, and realise, that all of us are capable of the most depraved, as well as the most saintly, acts. Such thought certainly inspired the playwright Seneca, who developed the notion of Greek tragedy to new heights – and depths. His work would later inspire Shakespeare's tragedies.

Seneca was also a skilled stoic, a philosophy that encouraged calm acceptance of indomitable fate. Such thought would prove particularly consoling among the upper classes, who found themselves powerless in the face of wilful or vindictive emperors. Seneca practised what he preached, and when he fell foul of the Emperor Nero in AD 65 he opened his veins, encouraging his surrounding friends to adhere to their stoic philosophy, even as he slowly bled to death.

A contemporary of Seneca, the poet Lucretius, was also heavily influenced by Greek thought. His long poem *De Rerum Natura* ('About the Natural World') is in part a scientific treatise in verse form, which among other things remains the only source we have for Democritus' idea that the world ultimately consists of atoms.[17]

---

17 Lucretius' poem includes an astonishingly perceptive description of what we now call Brownian motion: the random motion of tiny particles floating on the surface of water. It was from this, and Democritus' logical notion of the *atomos* ('uncuttable') that Lucretius derived his idea of the atom. Almost two millennia later, in 1905, Einstein would use Brownian motion in his first scientific proof of the existence of atoms.

Like Seneca, Lucretius was a philosopher, though his ideas were very much opposed to those of the Stoics. Lucretius taught Epicureanism, which insisted that we should try to enjoy life. But this was no call to thoughtless hedonism, as it is sometimes characterised. Lucretius proposed that Epicureanism should be practised in a civilised, discriminating fashion, avoiding over-indulgence, tending towards the pleasures of the mind rather than the body.

The most significant and influential Roman scientist was in fact a Greek called Galen, who was born at Pergamum in Asia Minor in the second century AD, but later moved to Rome where he would achieve fame and fortune as a physician. The science of medicine had been founded in the sixth century BC by the Greek Hippocrates. His practise was based on the theory of the four humours, and would later be echoed by Aristotle when he adopted the prevalent theory that the world was made up of four elements: earth, air, fire and water. According to Hippocrates, the four humours were Black Bile (related to earth, whose properties were cold and dry), Yellow Bile (the choleric that produced anger), Blood (which caused heat and prompted optimism) and Phlegm (which caused lethargy and melancholia).[18] These four humours governed our behaviour, our emotions, our disposition and our health. We became ill, in mind or body, when these four elements no longer balanced.

Galen would then go on to develop the four humours into a sophisticated, all-embracing medical ideology, using medicines and elixirs intended to counter-balance any over-emphasis of a particular humour. The dissection of cadavers was forbidden on religious grounds, but Galen managed to gain deep insight into human anatomy by working as resident physician at a school for gladiators. Their gruesome slashes and penetrating wounds

---

18 Although we no longer believe in the four humours, the words 'bilious', 'choleric', 'melancholic' and 'phlegmatic' all still hold meaning for us.

revealed to him much of the inner workings of the human body. He gained further insight by carrying out dissections on animals such as pigs and sheep. While Galen was practising in Rome, soldiers returning from the Middle East brought a plague to the city. From his various case notes we can guess this plague may have been smallpox. Galen found that he was able to diagnose whether or not a patient was likely to survive, but was unable to discover a cure.

The Emperor Trajan is generally listed among the five 'good' emperors. Others include Hadrian and the remarkable Marcus Aurelius, who ruled from AD 161 to 180. During his reign he instituted a number of social 'reforms', some of which were undeniably retrograde. For instance, he reintroduced the concept of class into criminal law: with the *honestiores* (the 'upper classes') receiving lighter sentences than the *humiliores* (the 'plebs' and such, who could be tortured to obtain evidence). However, his aim was social stability, which also accounted for his ambivalent attitude towards the increasing number of Christians in Rome. The religion was officially illegal, but the law was largely ignored, except when it suited the emperor. Despite Marcus Aurelius' deep involvement in administrative affairs, as well as leading a military campaign at Vindobona (modern Vienna), he still found time to pen his *Meditations*, the philosophical thoughts that ensure he is remembered to this day. These are stoic in character, but the fact that they were written in Greek has cast controversy over their intent. Were they merely the private *aide-mémoires* of an emperor? Yet how could his stoic thinking be in accord with his social position? On top of this, his governance was hardly stoic. Despite such inevitable and undermining speculations, there is no doubt that his thinking reflected that of many in this period. The meaning of his *Meditations* is thus judged according to our personal prejudices, while their worth and originality is subject to similar ambiguities. Three examples will have to suffice: 'You have power over your mind – not outside events. Realise this and you will find strength'; 'The soul becomes dyed by the colour of its thoughts'; and 'The art of living is more like wrestling than dancing.' Written by a philosopher, these certainly add to our self-knowledge; written by an all-powerful emperor, they have more than a whiff of hypocrisy.

Marcus Aurelius was to be the last of the 'good emperors'. After his death in AD 180 he was succeeded by a series of inept, often corrupt rulers, and over the following two centuries the empire would decline and gradually fall apart. Like Babylon, and then Athens, its legacy now passed on.

Sequence

Civil wars, corruption, administrative incompetence, breakdowns in Rome's grain supply and a series of plagues all contributed to the fall of Rome. As did the invasion of western Europe by barbarian tribes from Scandinavia (Goths) and the Germanic lands (Visigoths and Huns). A population explosion in Central Asia drove further waves of barbarian tribes (Huns) west into Europe. Marauding tribal groups of twenty thousand or more cut swathes through the former imperial territory. In AD 410 Rome itself fell to the Goths.

By this time the capital of the Roman Empire had moved out of Rome. In 313 the Emperor Constantine had been persuaded by his mother to convert to Christianity and issued the Edict of Milan, declaring Christianity to be the official religion of the empire. Despite making this seismic change, Constantine himself never fully grasped the concept of Christianity, and when he moved the capital of the Roman Empire east to the millennium-old city of Byzantium on the shore of the Bosporus, he would rename it Constantinople in his own honour. Hardly an act of Christian modesty.

Gold coins dating from the reign of Marcus Aurelius discovered in China attest to Roman trade along the Silk Route with the Han Dynasty. The Han ruled over an empire comparable in size to that of the Roman Empire, and their technological achievements include such inventions as the magnetic compass, the seismograph, paper and the spinning loom. However, despite the ornate palaces and fine sculptures of its three successive capital cities, these did not match the size, sophistication or lasting influence of Rome at its height. Similarly, Indian statuettes found at Hadrian's Wall and in Pompei suggest Roman trading links with the Satahavana Empire of India. The cities of this empire, too, achieved significant advances in astronomy, medicine and science, though none matched the sheer scale of achievements attributable to Rome. Meanwhile, isolated from the rest of humanity in Mesoamerica, the Mayas also evolved a sophisticated civilisation. Its many cities produced fine artefacts and a calendar that remains in use to this day among indigenous people in Guatemala and southern Mexico.

Yet such cities as these can hardly be compared to Rome, even in its decline. Which leaves only the second great capital of the Roman Empire as a serious contender for the leading city of the ensuing era.

Constantinople/Istanbul:
Capital of Two Empires

The divided legacy of this city is echoed in its divided name. Constantinople was the capital of the Eastern Roman Empire, better known as the Byzantine Empire, for over a thousand years (twice as long as Rome was imperial capital of its Western equivalent). Then, in 1453, the Christian city of Constantinople was conquered by the Muslim forces of the Ottoman Turks, after which it eventually became known as Istanbul. This city would then become capital of the Ottoman Caliphate, which at its height was even more extensive than the Roman Empire under Trajan.

No other city in world history has been capital to two such vast and disparate empires as the Byzantine and the Ottoman. The two regimes were different in religion, culture, appearance and population demographics, despite the fact that they occupied much of the same eastern Mediterranean, North African and Levantine territories.

A major role in Constantinople's history was played by its geographical location. Not only did it command the southern entrance to the Bosporus, and all trade between the Mediterranean and the Black Sea, but it also overlooked the nearby inlet known as the Golden Horn, a large harbour that was guarded by a large chain strung across its comparatively narrow entrance.

As early as AD 330 the Emperor Constantine had a wall constructed around the entire headland, as well as across from the shore of the Golden Horn to that of the Sea of Marmara, protecting the isthmus. The city was impregnable to any attack by sea or land.

Less than a century later, just three years after the fall of Rome, the fifth-century Emperor Theodosius II would begin the building of a second outer defensive wall across the isthmus between the Golden Horn and the Sea of Marmara, a task that would take over a quarter of a century to complete. The dominating remains of this wall still stand, just a hundred yards or so west of the earlier Constantine's wall, providing an impressive gateway to the modern city. At the time of construction, this outer wall was nothing less than astonishing. The wall was four miles long from coast to coast; it was forty feet high and twenty feet thick, incorporating no less than ninety watchtowers along its length. In front of the walls was a moat sixty feet wide and twenty feet deep. The wall was rightly deemed impenetrable. There was just one snag: Constantinople lay close to the boundary between two of the earth's tectonic plates; whenever these shifted, the city was prone to earthquakes.

In AD 477, Atilla the Hun was preparing to march his vast army towards Constantinople when an earthquake caused serious damage to the area, including several breaches in the city's defences.[19] At this time, the city was already suffering with an outbreak of plague. However, such was the organisation, will and energy of the citizens that the walls were all rebuilt within sixty days. In some aspects at least, the Eastern Roman Empire was certainly a match for the Western Empire at its greatest. On hearing that the walls had been rebuilt, Atilla called off his march on Constantinople and turned west.

---

19 Reports vary as to the size of this army, with a reliable upper estimate of over two hundred thousand warriors.

Over the years, Constantinople's formidable defences would be further supplemented by artillery and naval vessels employing a revolutionary new weapon known as 'Greek Fire'. This secret weapon was the invention of a Greek called Kallinikos of Heliopolis, who was born in AD 650. The weapon consisted of a highly flammable liquid that could be squirted, through siphons, projecting it onto nearby ships, or infantry, thus coating them in an adhesive burning substance that was impossible to extinguish. It was also inserted into clay balls, which could be hurled into the ranks of advancing troops (followed by a flaming arrow to ignite the liquid). In this respect, Greek Fire was a forerunner of the modern hand-grenade. It also preceded the modern flame-thrower, and its adhesive qualities can be likened to napalm.

A further advantage of Greek Fire was that it was lighter than water, so it could be poured onto the surface of the sea, set alight, and be carried by wind or current towards a fleet of oncoming enemy ships, engulfing them in unquenchable flames. According to contemporary descriptions, the burning flames of Greek Fire were accompanied by thunder and smoke; it was also described as sticky fire, adhering to clothing, objects and surfaces. In the centuries to come, this weapon would prove the salvation of Constantinople during two serious sieges.

The actual substance of Greek Fire remained a tightly guarded secret, which is now lost. Speculations concerning its ingredients suggest it might have contained saltpetre, and was thus a form of gunpowder (which had been discovered in China a century or so previously, but was not thought to have reached the West until some five centuries later). Others claim it contained quicklime, accounting for the increase in its flammable qualities when it came into contact with water. Modern researchers point to the availability of crude oil in wells around the Black Sea, suggesting that alchemists had learned how to distil this substance and obtain petroleum, which was then mixed with resin to increase its adhesive qualities.

Had the secret of Greek Fire not been lost, the course of history would certainly have been changed. Imagine the consequences if medieval western European armies and navies had got their hands on it. In all, it appears that Greek Fire was one of the great 'might have beens' of early warfare, which never achieved its potential to change world history. As we shall see, this would prove to be a characteristic of the Byzantine Empire.

A Byzantine manuscript illustrating the use of Greek Fire.

With such artillery power and defensive walls, Constantinople was undoubtedly the world leader in military hardware during the post-Roman era. Its geographic position also made it the major trading power of the eastern Mediterranean. The westward extent of the Silk Road trading routes terminated at Levantine ports such as Tyre and Antioch, both of which remained part of the Eastern Roman Empire. Other branches of the Silk Road terminated at ports from Alexandria to the Black Sea and the Crimea. All these came under Byzantine control, except the Crimea, whose sea routes south beyond the Black Sea were controlled by the Bosporus. The Silk Road brought such lucrative goods as oriental silk and spices to Europe, where demand continued to grow once the barbarian invasions ceased and the continent embarked upon a more settled era.[20]

By the sixth century, the Visigoths and other invading tribes had occupied most of Iberia (the Kingdom of the Visigoths) and France (the Frankish Kingdom). Yet the Byzantines, who had continued to occupy the Balkans, Asia Minor and the Levant, soon expanded to occupy all of northern Africa, much of Italy and part of southern Spain. This meant the entire Mediterranean was under Byzantine control, much as it had been under the old Roman Empire.

As well as dominating the Mediterranean, Constantinople also established another new important trade route with the Vikings, who had sailed down the river systems of a country inhabited by people they called Rus'. Moving south from Novgorod, down the Dnieper, past Kiev, the Vikings emerged into the Black Sea and were soon trading with Constantinople. In return for silk and spices, Constantinople gained amber and slaves from the Vikings. Sitting at the centre of this vast trading web, at its peak Constantinople had the most advanced economy in the world.

However, unlike the previous Roman Empire, the Eastern Roman (or Byzantine) Empire exhibited certain fundamental differences. Where the old Roman Empire had been essentially militaristic in tenor, the Byzantine Empire was at its core religious. Constantine's

---

20 The Silk Road in fact consisted of a network of linked trading routes between China and Europe, crossing the deserts, steppes and mountains of central Asia. It first began transporting luxuries, e.g. silk and spices, to Europe during the Roman era. Trade fell into abeyance with the arrival of the marauding Huns and the collapse of the Western Roman Empire.

conversion to Christianity cemented a new unity of church and state power. Previously Roman emperors' claims to be gods, or the representatives of god on earth, had been of little profound religious significance. Constantine's conversion took on a more meaningful aspect, backed as it was by a well-developed theology.

Constantinople regarded itself as the last outpost of true Christianity. In western Europe the bishops of Rome (that is, the popes) were forced to make accommodations with the pagan invaders. In the West, the light of Christian faith and learning was kept alive in – often isolated – religious communities.

Over time, a schism emerged between the Western (later Catholic) Christianity and the indicatively named Orthodox Christianity in Constantinople. This division gradually widened, as both developed after their own fashion. This was inevitably exacerbated by their increasing geographical and racial separation. However, there were other causes, the main one being linguistic differences. The Roman Catholic language was Latin, while the Orthodox language increasingly became Greek. This often caused problems with the interpretation of even basic texts. Most important of all were doctrinal differences. These may appear to us, from the view of posterity, as minor theological quibbles, but they were seen at the time as matters of profound importance. The Nicene Creed (and its successors) was the fundamental credo of Christian faith. It opens with a declaration that can be paraphrased as: 'I believe in God the Father, God the Son and God the Holy Ghost…' Within a self-proclaimed monotheistic religion this Holy Trinity was always going to present difficulties. Could this trio be regarded as one and the same thing? Did the Holy Ghost emanate from both God the Father and God the Son? Or, on the other hand, was Jesus Christ the Son of God, and the Holy Ghost the Spirit of God? Such matters were debated heatedly and at great length. Not for nothing has the word 'byzantine' entered our language as a byword for excessive complication or deviousness. Such abstruse controversies would last for centuries, until finally in 1054 they resulted in a permanent formal schism between these two wings of the same religion.

Initially, Constantine's dual role as emperor and head of the Church (the unification of the sacred and the secular in one role) had certain beneficial effects. In 532, the Emperor Justinian I embarked upon the building of a vast cathedral. In keeping with the growing Greek influence, this would become known at Hagia Sophia (Greek for 'Holy Wisdom'). This would take just under six years to build, with more than ten thousand construction workers, and no expense spared in materials. Gold, a particular favourite of Byzantine artists, decorators and architects, would become a major feature. It is estimated that the finished building contained over 160 tons of worked gold, at a modern cost approaching $200 billion.

Hagia Sophia would prove to be the architectural wonder of the Christian world, the supreme masterpiece of Byzantine art, a building that would remain unmatched in beauty, proportion and achievement for almost a millennium, until the Renaissance. Its geometric proportions mirror the finest Ancient Greek mathematics of Alexandria; its decor incorporates symmetries and patterns of great aesthetic beauty. Indeed, the entire structure is riddled with mathematical ingenuity – most intriguing of all being the avoidance in its proportions of irrational numbers.

However, the crowning glory of this building was, and remains to this day, its dome. This is 102 feet in diameter, and soars 184 feet above the marble floor of the nave. Although it is in fact smaller than the dome of the Pantheon in Rome, it far exceeds its Roman counterpart in its striking setting of supporting domes and the transcendent quality of light produced by the forty windows set into the dome's base. In the words of the sixth-century historian Procopius: 'It seems not to be founded on solid masonry, but to be suspended from heaven.'

The other main benefit from the Church's combination of religious and secular political power would be its expansion of the Christian religion, brought about by missionaries who travelled along the Viking trade routes into the land inhabited by the Rus' people. In 869 the man we know as St Cyril produced a script for these eastern Slavic people, so that they could write down their language (and also so that missionaries could use biblical texts in the local language for their missionary work). The letters of this script were based on the Greek alphabet, and would be known as Glagolitic script. This would later be adapted into a form that spread through Eastern Europe, Russia, the Caucasus and Central Asia, where it remains in use to this day. This is now known as Cyrillic script, after its pioneer, the Byzantine monk St Cyril. Such developments played a major part in the conversion of these eastern Slavic people to Christianity. This commenced on a larger scale when the people of Kievian Rus' converted to Christianity in 867. Consequently, the Russian people would adopt Orthodox Christianity; and echoing the practice of Constantinople, the ruler of the Russian people, the tsar, would be regarded as God's representative on earth. There would be no separation of church and state power.

Yet this cultural exchange worked both ways. In the opposite direction along trade routes came the Vikings, who made their presence felt in Constantinople. Viking warriors and Kievian Rus' troops were recruited as members of the elite Varangian Guard, who provided personal protection for the emperor. Among these immigrant Vikings was one Harald Sigurdsson, who saw service throughout the Mediterranean from Sicily to the Holy Land, and would later become King of Norway.

The Varangian Guard took on increasing importance as the emperor's personal protectors, especially when the Byzantine army began hiring less reliable mercenary troops to control the far-flung regions of the empire. Graffiti carved by Viking mercenaries – in the form of runes and names – can still be seen carved into an upper marble parapet in Hagia Sophia.

Meanwhile, following the initial mutual encouragement, the identity of secular and religious power in Constantinople was beginning to have a detrimental effect on Byzantine cultural life. Imagination gradually gave way to time-honoured ritual and superstition. With hindsight, hints of this are in the superstitious avoidance of any irrational numbers in the construction of Hagia Sophia, as well as the over-emphasis of gold as an artistic medium. Gold was the substance that inspired alchemists' art, and there followed a revival in sorcery and alchemy among the common citizens. Astrology, too, took on a new lease of life, despite being banned in the early days of Christianity. By the reign of Manuel I Komnenus in the mid-1100s, the emperor himself was employing astrologers to guide him in his personal as well as his political affairs.

But the decline in Byzantine culture is most vividly apparent in its art. The colourful, flowing naturalistic sculptures of Ancient Greece and Rome gave way to stylised golden icons depicting saints and biblical figures. What had once appeared free and imaginative now became severely limited in both subject and form. Just as Ancient Greek thought blossomed once it became free from the constraints of religion, now the reverse became true in Byzantine Constantinople. The pure speculation of philosophy was stifled by the constraints of orthodoxy.

Ironically, as capital of the united Roman Empire, Constantinople had initially accumulated many classical works of philosophy and science. While libraries were destroyed by barbarian invaders in the West, Constantinople accumulated much learning that might otherwise have been lost. Works by Plato, Aristotle, Archimedes and the like survived in the vaults of Constantinople long after other copies had disappeared or been lost in the fire at the Great Library of Alexandria. Many of the books stored in these vaults remained unused, dismissed as pagan learning that had no place in a Christian world. Others were vandalised using a method that had been developed in ancient Rome to overcome shortages of material; ancient texts on scrolls of vellum or parchment were scraped clean of their previous script so that a new text could be inscribed to form a palimpsest. This term derives from the Greek *palimpsestos*, which can be translated as 'scraped clean and ready to be used again'. In a telling metaphor, religious texts were now written over the ghostly, remnant lettering of ancient philosophy, poetry and mathematics.

As Byzantine culture in Constantinople decayed, stifled by religious orthodoxy and lack of creative thought, a new religion was arising some two thousand miles away on the western edges of the Arabian Desert. Unlike Orthodox Christianity, this new religion firmly united both theology, political and speculative thought.

In 610 the religion revealed to the Prophet Muhammad began to galvanise the spiritual, intellectual and physical energies of the Arab people. At the outset, this was a warrior religion. In 629 Muhammad conquered Mecca; within a dozen years his followers had overrun the entire Arabian peninsula; thirty years later his followers had conquered territory from Libya to Afghanistan. Inevitably, his warriors soon began making inroads into the Byzantine Empire, sweeping through the Levant and invading Asia Minor. By 674 the city of Constantinople found itself under siege. After four long years, Emperor Constantine IV eventually managed to liberate his city and destroyed the Arab fleet with the empire's secret weapon, Greek Fire.

Although Constantinople may have been saved temporarily, Muslim forces increasingly took possession of Asia Minor, stripping the Byzantine Empire of its remaining north African possessions. Contrary to the Byzantine example, the new Arab religion did not stifle creative, scientific or philosophical thought. To know the world was to know the mind of God. Texts by Ancient Greek authors, especially Aristotle, were translated into Arabic, further encouraging intellectual speculation.

In the early 1300s Osman I became the leader of a small, predominantly Sunni Muslim Turkish tribe living on the southern shore of the Sea of Marmara, just sixty miles across the water from Constantinople. In a lightning conquest, like that of the Arabs, the followers of Osman, the Osmanlis (known to us as the Ottomans) struck east across Anatolia, and then north and west into the Balkans. As Constantinople became increasingly encircled, Orthodox monks fled to western Europe bearing with them such cultural treasures as they could carry. Most importantly, these contained many hundreds of scrolls, some containing works by the likes of Plato, Aristotle and Archimedes, many of which remained unknown in the West. When translated, these works would spark a Renaissance of classical learning in Italy, particularly in Florence, that would inspire the beginning of the modern age.

By 1453, the twenty-one-year-old Mehmet II, a direct descendant of Osman I, had 200,000 troops camped outside the formidable double walls of Constantinople. Mehmet had recently conquered Hungary, and had learned of a master iron-founder called Orban, who boasted he could build a cannon capable of blasting 'the walls of Babylon'. As good as his word, Orban proceeded to cast a 27-foot-long brass cannon weighing almost 17 tons (the weight of more than three of Hannibal's elephants). This weapon could fire granite cannon balls weighing half a ton (four small elephants) over a distance of half a mile, i.e. well beyond the range of any Greek Fire or the Genoese crossbowmen employed by the Byzantines. Mehmet II selected what he considered to be the weakest point in the walls, the Gate of San Romano, and on 11 April he ordered his mammoth cannon to begin firing night and day at its target, only pausing when its barrel became dangerously overheated. Almost fifty days later, a large scalable breach had begun to appear in the city's outer defensive wall.

In a meticulously pre-planned operation, overnight more than a thousand Ottoman soldiers began filling in the moat. Next morning Mehmet II's troops stormed across the earth-filled moat, poured in through the breach, and began fighting their way towards the inner wall. The Turkish soldiers met with considerable resistance, until the gate in the inner wall swung open, and the Byzantine soldiers began fleeing through this back into the safety of the city. In a characteristic Byzantine mishap, the last troops fled so quickly that they were unable to lock the gate behind them, and the Ottoman troops soon swarmed into the city. Here they inflicted massacre and mayhem on the terrified population, finally reaching the Imperial Palace where the Emperor Constantine XI died fighting alongside the soldiers of his Varangian Guard. On 29 May 1453 Constantinople finally fell, marking one of the major events in world history.

The city we now call Istanbul became the capital of the Ottoman Empire, with Mehmet the Conqueror (as he became known) as its sultan. Hagia Sophia was turned into a mosque, and many of the surviving populace were sold into slavery. Afterwards, according to the Venetian physician Nicolò Barbaro, who survived these events, bodies of Turks and Christians alike clogged the surrounding sea 'like melons along a canal'.

Mehmet II's declared intention of conquest was simple: 'If you embrace Islam, we will leave you alone, if you agree to pay the poll tax, we will protect you if you need our protection. Otherwise it is war.' Territory thus conquered was known as '*dar al-islam*' (Realm of Peace); all territory beyond this was known as '*dar el-harb*' (Realm of War), which had to be conquered in order to establish a caliphate of universal peace. However, elements of such absolutism would soon become tempered in the Ottoman Empire, just as they had been during the previous Arab caliphates that had ruled over the Middle East during the medieval era. Over time, the Ottoman Constantinople developed into a culturally rich and diverse city. Believers in other religions were in some cases permitted to retain their faith, and even hold positions of authority, but they were required to pay a more or less punitive extra tax for the privilege of doing so.

Having taken Constantinople, the Ottomans continued their campaign of conquest, marching rapidly north up the Dalmatian coast. Then, one night in 1476, the lookout posted atop the campanile in Venice noticed fires burning on the distant hills to the east. These fires were the advanced scouts of the Ottoman army. Venice immediately despatched a delegation to Constantinople to sue for peace, and the city was spared.

But this did not stop Ottoman designs on other regions of Italy. In 1479 Ottoman troops suddenly invaded Otranto on the heel of Italy, giving them control of the southern entrance to the Adriatic. How much further this invasion of Italy was intended to progress will never be known – two years later Mehmet the Conqueror died, and the Turkish troops withdrew as suddenly and unexpectedly as they had arrived.

Under Mehmet the Conqueror's grandson, Selim I, the empire now expanded east, defeating the Mamluk Caliphate in Egypt, before pushing on to the Holy Cities of Mecca and Medina. Following such conquests Selim I decided to take on the title of Caliph, a post always previously always occupied by a descendant of the Prophet Muhammad. The Ottoman Empire had come of age and was now the Sunni Caliphate of the Muslim world (disputed only by the Shi'ite Muslims of Persia, whose own Caliph claimed descent from a different branch of Muhammad's family).

Selim I proved to be a man of deep contradictions. Despite acquiring the title Selim the Grim, he was an accomplished poet in both Persian and Arabic, encouraging a cultural revival in his court at Constantinople. At the same time, he issued a decree forbidding on pain of death the importation of the newly invented printing press. His courtiers knew well enough to take him at his word; Selim was known for his explosive temper, which resulted in the summary execution of seven of his grand viziers during his eight-year reign.

Ottoman ambivalence towards western developments, especially during the ensuing centuries of rapid European progress, would be a prevalent trait throughout the Ottoman era. Despite the sultan's position as head of the caliphate, in which the Muslim religion forbade any representation of the human form, there are surviving portraits of almost all Ottoman sultans, some painted by Venetian artists of the calibre of Bellini and Titian.

Such was the prelude to the glorious forty-five-year reign of Selim I's son, who would become known as Suleiman the Magnificent. His reign would establish Muslim Constantinople as once again a city that led the world. By 1550 the city had a population of 660,000 (almost double the size of Europe's largest city, Paris, with 350,000) and Suleiman ruled over an empire of 25 million, while the population of the whole of Europe was just 70 million. More importantly, Constantinople held the guardianship of Mecca, the pilgrimage centre of the Muslim religion, which stretched from west Africa to the Philippines, with particularly numerous populations in the Indian subcontinent and Central Asia.

Suleiman the Magnificent was a man of many parts. He personally led the Ottoman army to the gates of Vienna. He also oversaw a widespread reform of the empire, assisted by his able grand vizier Makbul Ibrahim Pasha (Ibrahim the Favourite). Together they scrutinised the decrees of Suleiman's predecessors, annulling all contradictions and anomalies, and created a new set of laws for the entire empire. Pasha travelled to Egypt to reassure the muftis of Cairo, regarded as the leading theologians of Islam, that these civil reforms remained within the bounds of the sacred (Shariah) law. This new code, which became known as Ottoman Law, would be implemented equally throughout the empire for the following three centuries. Pasha also proved an able diplomat, negotiating important Ottoman agreements with Venice and France.

Unfortunately, Pasha then fell out with his master, for reasons that remain unclear. Consequently, Suleiman had him strangled to death by mute executioners during the course of a dinner party, whereupon he was no longer referred to as Makbul Ibrahim Pasha (the Favourite), but as Maktul Ibrahim Pasha (the Executed).

The most lasting of all Suleiman the Magnificent's projects was the building programme he instigated, which would transform the face of Constantinople and remains the glory of Istanbul to this day. Suleiman hired the highly gifted architect Mimar Sinan, and together they embarked upon building a series of beautiful and important mosques. This would result in a series of Sinan's exquisitely proportioned white marble mosques, with their rising multiple domes offset by rows of finely proportioned minarets. In the view of many, Sinan's mosques are a match for the French chateaux of the Loire and even the Taj Mahal, which were also being constructed around this period.

Islamic Constantinople had some of the world's finest buildings, strong foundations of law, and ruled over an empire extending into three continents. Yet despite all this, how precisely did this city lead the world, in any sense comparable to Babylon, Athens or Rome? One answer lies in its sheer existence, which acted as a catalyst for events that would change the world forever. Had Constantinople not fallen into Muslim hands, those precious manuscripts carried by monks fleeing the Ottoman army might not otherwise have reached Europe, and inspired the Renaissance. Similarly, when Mehmet the Conqueror took control of the city, the entire balance of world trade shifted radically. The riches of the Silk Route trade from China and the Orient could no longer pass through Christian Constantinople to Europe. This caused the European powers to seek out other routes to the East. The Portuguese rounded the Cape of Good Hope just thirty-five years after the Fall of Constantinople. And in the following decade Columbus, intent on reaching China by a westward route around the globe, accidentally happened upon the New World. Others such as the English, the Dutch and the French would soon follow in their wake.

A new era had begun. The European Renaissance, the European Age of Discovery and the European colonisation of the globe – all these were to a large extent jolted into motion by the Ottoman conquest of Constantinople in 1453. Islamic Constantinople may not itself have achieved these advances in world history, but it can certainly be argued as their ulterior cause or catalyst. Through the coming centuries, Ottoman Constantinople would be recognised as the leading city in the Mediterranean world and throughout the Middle East. Its power, its mosques and its wealth would be legendary throughout Europe.

Sequence

Before our next leading city we must return to western Europe during the early centuries of the Common Era, during which the Western Roman Empire disintegrated. This plunged Europe into the so-called Dark Ages, as the continent was overrun by waves of tribal migrations – by Goths, Visigoths and the like – sweeping westward from Central Asia.

As the tribes settled, sovereign territories gradually emerged and the migrations of the Dark Ages evolved into the more stable medieval era. The role of Christianity in preserving the culture and learning associated with civilisation meant that it assumed a major role during the medieval era. Yet over the centuries this religious dominance in the intellectual sphere tended towards a state of cultural stasis. However, this was far from being as stultifying as the religious dominance of Byzantine thought. The building of great gothic cathedrals involved the development of architectural innovations such as the flying buttress that enabled the construction of high vaulted ceilings and resonant interiors.

Choral singing involving plainsong and counterpoint attained new sophistication in order to exploit the acoustics of these vast, echoing interior spaces.

Towards the end of the medieval era there were a number of significant developments. With hindsight, we can view these as presaging the age to come. Gutenberg's printing press was but one: books that could be printed in bulk, rather than being laboriously copied by monks, enabled the rapid spread of learning among the literate class. Likewise, the invention of reading spectacles towards the end of the thirteenth century meant that ageing scholars could continue to add to their learning. The invention of the mechanical clock enabled a greater focus on social co-ordination and the more fruitful use of time. The emergence of bills of exchange (a forerunner of paper money) used by banks facilitated a boom in foreign trade. The increased use of the rotation of crops improved agricultural production, prompting improvements in water mills and the spread of windmills.

The introduction of gunpowder from China was initially a novelty, revolutionising the spectacle of public entertainments with fireworks. Its use in cannons was initially spectacular, as in the Fall of Constantinople. Only gradually did the military mind grasp its full implication. The age of fortified castles and sieges was coming to an end. There was no defence against intelligently deployed artillery fire.

Such incremental advances helped introduce a dominant progressive element in modern history, which has continued to increase exponentially to this day. The end of medieval stasis and the beginning of modern progress inspired an entirely different attitude towards the world. This would prove one of the transformative moments of human evolution. Our feeble life in this world was more than a period of suffering before death and our entry into eternal life, where our soul would be judged according to how we had behaved on earth. Instead, what mattered was how we, as individuals, made use of our life. The focus of existence gradually switched from a spiritual afterlife to the exercise of our human powers in this life. And thus the new philosophy of Humanism was born.

Hand in hand with the Renaissance inspired by a rebirth of classical learning (which also focused on life, rather than the hereafter), this Humanism would result in a metamorphosis of western civilisation. This was both vast and varied, affecting all elements of human culture. Here it is only possible to summarise briefly, alluding to major achievements. This transformation would inspire great artists (Leonardo, Michelangelo, Raphael), great architecture (St Peter's in Rome, the chateaux of the Loire), great literature (from Dante and Cervantes to the 'sound and fury' of Shakespeare), and perhaps most sensationally of all, the rebirth of science. Copernicus would show that the earth was not the centre of the universe, and Galileo would lead the way to a new empirical view of the world and how it worked: 'Mathematics is the language in which God has written the universe.' For contradicting the works of Aristotle, and thus the teachings of the Church, Galileo would be lucky to avoid being burned at the stake.

Ironically, much of the earlier Italian Renaissance was funded by the riches of the Catholic Church, which collected dues from Greenland to Vienna. Yet enough was not enough. More funds were required to finance the Church, which had once kept alight the flame of Christianity in a dark world but was now leading the West in both culture and corruption. Further revenue was accrued by the sale of Indulgences, whose purchase could shorten the period a soul would spend in Purgatory prior to its ascent to Paradise.

The German priest Martin Luther caught the imagination of many when he rebelled against such practices, and the Western Church split in what became known as the Reformation, dividing Christendom into Roman Catholics and Protestants. For the latter, there was no need for priests to intercede with God on someone's behalf. People could pray to God directly. Here, too, was a deeper emphasis on individuality.

Meanwhile, along with the expansion in learning and culture, Europe expanded in a more physical sense. The discovery of America, and the passage around Africa to India and China, led to a more widespread western self-realisation. What had once been secretly suspected by a learned few, now become common knowledge. Not only was the earth not the centre of the universe, but Europe was not unique in possessing its own advanced and complex culture. In the Americas, Inca and Aztec civilisations had evolved their own entirely different systems of social cohesion. Meanwhile, in India, the advanced Moghul Empire held sway over the subcontinent and beyond, its influence permeating far into South-East Asia. It was this civilisation that was responsible for the spread of Islam to the Philippines and beyond, even into China. And it soon became clear to the 'civilised' Europeans that China was very much more than a source of silk, spices and other exotic novelties from porcelain to gunpowder. Marco Polo's tales of an ancient, vast and highly sophisticated civilisation, which had evolved after its own fashion with no European input, were more than the over-elaborated fantasies of a Venetian trader, as had previously been believed. What had once been mere traveller's tales became a tangible adjunct to the new expanding European knowledge. What had once been viewed as imagination was now becoming reality in all fields of human endeavour. And after their own fashion, China, India and the Americas also had to take into account the arrival in their domain of a new militaristic, white-skinned people driven by their demonic motives that could neither be fathomed nor trusted.

Such developments resulted in an increase in all manner of novel cultural exchanges. This is perhaps best illustrated by the least subtle and least intended of these social interactions. Diseases imported by Europeans devastated the indigenous peoples of America. In exchange, Europe became infected with the scourge of syphilis. At the other end of the scale, Europe discovered the joys of tomatoes and tobacco. Words, and the objects they designated, crossed frontiers with the ease of migrating birds. *Sag* in India became *sabanik* in the Levant, *espinacas* in Spain, *épinard* in France, and finally arrived in England as the novelty vegetable known as spinach.

Yet it should not be forgotten that the European exploration of the globe had been financed for commercial purposes. After initial trading, and some rebuffs, European traders soon found it more convenient to occupy the lands they traded with, thus establishing colonies around the globe.

But the European self-realisation and self-understanding encouraged by Humanism did not apply to the less advanced cultures encountered by the European traders. In a tradition that preceded Babylon, co-existed with the philosophical achievements of Ancient Athens, aided the social fabric of Rome and provided for the societies of both Constantinople and Istanbul, slavery once more took on a major role in human civilisation. This time it would be western European commerce that benefited, as never before.

Enslavement had long been practised among the tribes of Africa; now a more lucrative European buyer entered the market. It was quickly understood that the mass importation of black slaves to the new humanist Europe would probably not have been acceptable to contemporary sensibilities. So the scheming European traders devised an innovative method to make use of this new resource. Mirrors, gaudy colourful trinkets and the like were readily available in Europe. Such novelties – along with gold buttons and doubloons of doubtful provenance – proved irresistibly appealing to the slave masters of western Africa. Slaves were exchanged for these and shipped in chains across the Atlantic in conditions worse than those previously endured by animals. On arrival in Latin America, the West Indies and the American South, these people were sold for gold, which would eventually be divided among the ship's captain and his backers in Bristol, Liverpool, Bordeaux, Nantes, Lisbon or Cadiz.

In the American plantations new settlers who were producing crops such as tobacco, sugar and cotton were finding them difficult to harvest. White servants and European convicts were unable to withstand the heat and toil of such tasks. Instead, these were now replaced by African slaves.

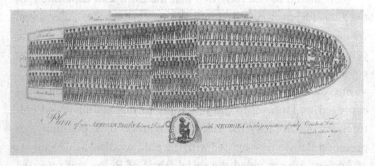

A Plan of an African slave ship.

It is worth bearing in mind that most of the ensuing western cities with any claim to have led the world, all to a more or less extent owed their riches to the African slave trade. From the financing of the English Industrial Revolution, and most of its technological successors, to the colonisation of the globe and the armaments that sustained this enterprise, to say nothing of the politics that encouraged such ambitions – all remain tainted, just as Leonardo, Michelangelo and Raphael owed their wages to a corrupt papacy intent upon extracting the maximum penance from those in their pastoral care. Here it is perhaps worth placing my previous allusion to Shakespeare in its wider context:

> It is a tale
> Told by an idiot, full of sound and fury,
> Signifying nothing.

Paris: City of Enlightenment

Faced with such a world of contradictions, it comes as no surprise that the French rationalist philosopher René Descartes adopted such a drastic approach in his search for ultimate truth. He chose to doubt everything, even his own experiences and thoughts. As though life is a dream or a mirage or a hallucination, he imagined the possibility that a malicious demon of 'utmost power and cunning has employed all his energies in order to deceive me'. Yet Descartes realised that there was just one thing he could not doubt: the fact that he was thinking. This led him to his famous conclusion: '*Cogito ergo sum*' (I think therefore I am).

Upon this single indubitable foundation, the ultimate certainty, Descartes realised that he could rebuild an entire world of rational thought and knowledge. The similarity to Socrates' dialectic questioning ('I, too, know nothing') is striking, and would produce a similar effect. Following in Descartes' footsteps would come the new Platos and Aristotles of the modern age.

Descartes embarked upon his philosophical investigations in Paris. However, he did most of his serious thought lying in bed until late in the morning, and visitors would keep interrupting him. So he chose a profession in which he would not be subject to such importunate disturbance, and became an army officer in the Netherlands. Naturally, this absented him from Paris, if not from his bed.

Descartes, along with other leading intellectuals of the period, was able to rely upon a unique agent, who made it his business to circulate ideas in the form of letters, fielding replies and passing on objections where appropriate. This was Father Marin Mersenne, a priest and highly talented polymath who resided in a monastery in Paris. The list of his friends and correspondents is like a who's who of the European intellectual world on the eve of the Enlightenment, the period that evolved in the wake of Renaissance Humanism. Besides Engineer Officer Descartes, Mersenne maintained contact with the mathematician Fermat (a judge in Toulouse), the philosopher-scientist Pascal (who made sophisticated calculating machines to assist his tax-collector father in Rouen), Galileo (whose ideas had led to him remaining under house arrest outside Florence), the pioneer English political philosopher Hobbes, the Dutch scientist Huygens who proposed the wave theory of light, the Copernican astronomer Gassendi, and many, many more. Indeed, it is now generally recognised that the Royal Society of London and the Academie des Sciences of Paris, founded in the decades following Mersenne's death in 1648, were institutions inspired by his invaluable activities.

Like Babylon, Paris had thrived for more than one and a half thousand years before it attained its prime in the Enlightenment of the eighteenth century. The city was probably founded as a defensive settlement by Julius Caesar in 52 BC on a strategic island in the Seine (the Île de la Cité, site of Notre Dame). By the height of the medieval era the city had a population of around two hundred and fifty thousand, making it the largest city in Europe; it was also the greatest centre of learning during this period. Its university, the Sorbonne, was situated on the Left Bank of the Seine in the area known as the Latin Quarter (because scholars spoke Latin). It attracted students from as far afield as Scandinavia and Bohemia, who would walk many hundreds of miles to reach Paris, in order to hear lectures by the finest philosophers and theologians of the era such as Thomas Aquinas and the Scottish priest Duns Scotus.

By the beginning of the Enlightenment, around the turn of the eighteenth century, France was the major political and military power in Europe. Its aim to establish a hegemony over the continent was only thwarted by shifting alliances between the Holy Roman Empire, the many minor states of Germany, Austria, Spain and England. The country was ruled by the 'Sun King' Louis XIV from his vast ornate palace at Versailles, some ten miles south-west of the city centre, overlooking a park and gardens covering an area larger than one and half thousand football fields. The palace itself was so large that it could accommodate nearly ten thousand people, including all the senior aristocracy of the country and the requisite servants and lackeys. Proximity to the king enabled nobles to win favours, but it also kept them in order. Unfortunately, the architects had not taken into account the possibility of the palace accommodating quite so many occupants, which meant that apart from in the royal apartments, plumbing and bathing facilities were few and far between. Chamber-pots in the form of elegant chairs were placed at strategic intervals along the corridors and near apartments, but these emitted a stomach-churning pong, and were not always regularly emptied by the servants, which meant that they often overflowed, leading to carpets and wall-hangings becoming fouled. The pervasive stench rendered essential the use of nosegays.

On the other hand, the cuisine served by the chefs here, and in other aristocratic residences, was celebrated for being the finest in Europe. During the previous centuries, French cuisine had been decidedly medieval, featuring thick, spicy sauces to mask the flavour of the often tainted meat. This would only change when the Italian Catherine de' Medici arrived in Paris in 1533 to marry the future Henri II, bringing her own retinue of Italian chefs who cooked in the Tuscan fashion using fresh vegetables and meats. This imported custom had revolutionised French cuisine, so that by the Age of the Enlightenment two centuries later it reigned supreme, matched only by the subtleties and variety of Chinese cuisine. But, interestingly, meals were still taken with *service à la français*, where all the food was brought to the table simultaneously, thus creating a sumptuous display. Not until late in the nineteenth century would courses be served separately, an innovation introduced to western Europe by the Russians.[21]

Louis XV had only ascended to the throne of France by accident, at the age of thirteen, after the untimely death of no less than three more legitimate heirs. His reign got off to a rocky start under the regency of his cousin Philippe II, Duc d'Orléans, whose degeneracy resulted in him becoming the man for whom the word *roué* was coined. (*Roué* literally means 'broken on the wheel', a torture reserved for those whose behaviour was deemed so disgraceful that they were destined to eternal damnation.) Misrule would be an understatement for Philippe II's period as regent. However, he was responsible for allowing one remarkable scheme, the like of which has not been seen before or since.

This involved a Scotsman called John Law, a scoundrel who had killed a man in a duel, been imprisoned in London's notorious Newgate Prison and escaped into exile on the continent. Here he supported himself with suspicious success at the gaming tables, moving from city to city when his successes at the tables, or the boudoirs, exceeded local tolerance.

However, there was another side to Law. His exceptional mathematical skills had led him to devise an original economic scheme involving the use of paper money, an innovation at the time. In 1716 Law managed to charm Philippe II into letting him put this

---

21 The establishment of the city of Paris as the gastronomic capital of the world would come towards the end of the eighteenth century, with the French Revolution and the overthrow of the *ancien régime*. After the aristocrats had fled, their expert chefs had no one to cook for, and began flooding into Paris, opening their own restaurants, vying with each other to demonstrate their culinary expertise.

scheme into practice in France, thus alleviating the regent from the bothersome business of running the country himself.

The almost constant wars waged by the previous ruler, Louis XIV, had left France economically and financially ruined. In order to overcome this, Law was commissioned to set up a national bank, where he began printing paper money, thus considerably increasing the nation's wealth (in paper). At the same time, he also set up the Mississippi Company, intended to exploit the huge resources expected to be found in the French colony of Louisiana, which at this time extended over virtually the whole of the American Mid-West.[22] Aided by Law's propaganda, shares in the Mississippi Company quickly boomed, making many small shareholders rich overnight – this even gave birth to the term 'millionaire'. But in 1720 the bubble in both Mississippi shares and the value of paper money eventually burst, leaving many of the new millionaires penniless.

Opinion remains divided over John Law's ideas. Many reputable economists see him as the 'father of paper money' and a financial innovator ahead of his time; others, such as Adam Smith, the founder of modern economics, condemned him as a fraud. Either way, when Law's scheme resulted in a collapse of the currency, it had the unintended effect of cancelling the burden of debt that had been crippling the economy, and France emerged on its feet again. Philippe II was only too pleased to take the credit.

Law's was the first of many original ideas which emerged in Paris during this period. But, in the final year of his regency, Philippe II took an action that would in time arguably have even greater consequences than Law's paper money. With the aim of putting an end to the bitter religious factionalism that had for so many years beleaguered France, Philippe II was persuaded to issue a decree ordering an official

---

22 Law showed his gratitude to his generous patron, Philippe II, Duc d'Orléans, by naming the main trading settlement of the Mississippi Company in America La [La Nouvelle...] Nouvelle Orléans (New Orleans).

silence regarding religious conflicts. From now on, nothing could be written on such topics, either for or against. This is widely recognised as paving the way for the new freedom of thought that characterised the Enlightenment. As we shall see, it is no coincidence that in these years the young satirist Voltaire was able to achieve his first success, ridiculing certain pious behaviour without actually mentioning religion. Nor that the reformer Montesquieu was able to propose a separation of powers between the Church and the secular authorities, again without actual mention of religion.

In 1723, the young Louis XV took over France, succeeding the great 'Sun King' Louis XIV. The regency of Philippe II came to an end, just ten months before his death, aged forty-nine, in the arms of the Duchesse de Falari, his youthful mistress. Louis XV's predecessor, Louis XIV, is renowned for declaring: '*L'état, c'est moi*' (I am the state) – a definition of absolute power. In 1766 Louis XV went even further, announcing in a speech to his *parlement*: 'It is in my person alone that sovereign power resides… To me alone belongs the legislative power, without dependence and without sharing… The public order emanates entirely from me.' This was hardly auspicious, especially for the radical ideas proposed by the likes of reformist spirits such as Montesquieu and Voltaire. In order to understand the significance of such figures and their Enlightenment colleagues in such a political climate, we must now examine them in more detail.

Montesquieu was an aristocrat born in 1689 at the turreted, moated family Château de la Brède just outside Bordeaux. At the age of twenty-seven his father died and he inherited a position equivalent to a high court judge. Five years later he published *Persian Letters*, a satire in the form of an imaginary view of Parisian life as seen by two visiting Persians, which poked fun at the many absurdities of contemporary French society. This proved a success, prompting him to resign his post as a judge and embark upon a tour of Europe. During this journey he took assiduous notes, recording information regarding the governance and customs of the countries through which he passed, especially Italy and England. In this aspect, he is regarded by many as a pioneer anthropologist. Indeed, the modern British anthropologist David Pocock goes so far as to suggest that Montesquieu's observations were the first consistent attempt to survey the varieties of human society, to classify and compare them and, within society, to study the inter-functioning of institutions.

Among many other insights, Montesquieu's work is notable for introducing into the political vocabulary the word 'despot'. This is where the power of a nation is concentrated in the hands of one person – an idea that required little research for any French citizen of this era. During Montesquieu's stay in England he was able to observe first-hand the functioning of a constitutional monarchy, which had been established for William of Orange in 1688. Here the monarch was permitted to rule, but only by exercising his power according to the stipulations of the constitution and the guidance of parliament.

Montesquieu's lasting contribution included an analysis of the separation of powers. This idea had been proposed as early as the fourth century BC by Aristotle, but Montesquieu was the first to outline the practical checks and balances of how such a system should operate. He showed how the executive, legislative and judicial aspects of government should each be organised into separate bodies, thus ensuring that when one body attempted to infringe upon civil liberty it could be restrained by the other bodies.

Montesquieu divided French society into three classes: the monarchy, the aristocracy and the commons. His defence of the monarchy was explicitly reasoned, in line with the separation of powers:

> If there were no monarch, and the executive power should be committed to a certain number of persons, selected from the legislative body, there would be an end of liberty, by reason the two powers would be united; as the same persons would sometimes possess, and would be always able to possess, a share in both.

Montesquieu recognised, unlike so many before him, that there was no such thing as an ideal prescription for government. Nations were different, on account of their geography and their climate. For example, in his opinion the people of hot countries tended to be 'too hot tempered', while those who inhabited the cold north were prone to be 'icy' and 'awkward'. He proposed the differences were due to temperament, rather than race. This can be seen in his bitterly sarcastic condemnation of slavery, in which he argued that 'enslaved Africans could not possibly be human beings, because if they were, it would follow that we ourselves are not Christians'.

Montesquieu's ideas would prove fundamental to emergent modern democracy, providing inspiration for the Founding Fathers who drew up the United States Constitution. He also produced several far-reaching economic ideas that were well in advance of his age: 'The history of commerce is that of the communication of people'; 'Commerce is a cure for the most destructive prejudices; for it is almost a general rule, that wherever we find agreeable manners, there commerce flourishes'; 'The spirit of commerce is frugality, economy, moderation, labour... order and rule...The mischief is when excessive wealth destroys the spirit of commerce.' Such was the originality of his economic ideas that no less than the great twentieth-century economist Maynard Keynes would liken him to a French Adam Smith.

However, in the Paris of Montesquieu's era a different attitude prevailed, and he was forced to publish his masterpiece anonymously. Consequently, it would have little immediate effect. As with so many of the innovations and radical ideas developed during this period of Parisian supremacy, they would actually end up coming to fruition elsewhere.

At the very heart of the Enlightenment lay a project known as the *Encyclopédie*. Its full title in English hints at its huge ambition: 'Encyclopaedia, or a systematic dictionary of the Sciences, Arts and Crafts'. This was the brainchild of the philosopher and writer Denis

Diderot, along with his friend the mathematician and polymath Jean le Rond d'Alembert. They embarked upon this project in 1747, and it was intended to include a rational account of human knowledge from the earliest times right up to the latest developments.

Diderot had been born in 1713 in rural north-east France. His father was a cutler, and he was educated by the local Jesuits, who quickly recognised his exceptional intellect and encouraged him to travel to Paris to complete his education with the aim of becoming a priest. However, on arrival in Paris Diderot had other ideas and decided that he wanted to become a writer, whereupon his father disinherited him. Diderot now began to live a bohemian life, living off his wits and the occasional gift from rich lady friends. In 1747 he encountered by chance the philosopher and free spirit Jean-Jacques Rousseau while watching a game of chess at the Café de la Régence, where the finest chess players in Europe would entertain their intellectual audience. As we shall see, this meeting would mark the beginning of an intermittent but lifelong friendship, which would aid both their future work, despite their differences in temperament and beliefs. Indeed, they would become known as '*Les frères ennemis*' (The brother enemies).

In that same year Diderot wrote a book entitled *The Skeptic's Walk*, which consisted of a conversation between a deist, an atheist and a pantheist. In line with Aristotle's belief in teleology, the deist proposes that the world is constructed according to an intelligent design (by God). The atheist claims that the universe is far better explained by physics and chemistry, working according to the laws of mathematics and motion. The pantheist, on the other hand, bases his argument on the unity of the cosmos (this Greek word has connotations of both 'order' and 'the universe'). For the pantheist, the unity of mind and matter indicates that God exists in nature, the world and all creation. This work was quickly suppressed by the Roman Catholic Church, which retained far-reaching powers in France, where even the king's title included 'His Most Christian Majesty'.

Diderot's colleague Jean le Rond d'Alembert was born in 1717, the illegitimate son of an aristocratic general, whose mother abandoned him at birth on the steps of the church that gave him his name, Saint-Jean-le-Rond de Paris. Jean was consequently placed in the care of a glazier's wife, Madame Rousseau (no relation of the philosopher). D'Alembert would live in her home for almost fifty years, though from the outset she disapproved of his educated ways, telling him: 'You will never be anything but a philosopher – and what is that but an ass who plagues himself all his life, that he may be talked about after he is dead.'

Diderot and D'Alembert would play a major role in launching the *Encyclopédie* (The Encyclopaedia or Classified Dictionary of Sciences, Arts, and Trades). This echoed similar publications that had already appeared in both Britain and Italy. However, its sheer scope and depth, along with the range of intellectual contacts, meant that it would come to be regarded as the major ongoing project of the Enlightenment. According to its editors, the *Encyclopédie* was intended to do nothing less than 'change the way people think'. Knowledge was to be wrested from the hands of the Church and turned into a secular rational pursuit. The final work would end up consisting of no less than 28 volumes, including 71,818 articles and 3,129 illustrations. Indeed, this work has come to be seen by many as the first major evolution in humanity's liberal democratic ideal since the birth of this notion some one and a half millennia previously in Ancient Greece.

Despite the self-proclaimed adherence to reason of the *Encyclopédie*, over the years its running would be plagued with infighting, jealousies, disagreements and all manner of distinctly unenlightened behaviour. Its publisher came to blows with its English translator, who took each other to court; a hot-headed editor was fired for incompetence; while publication after publication was accompanied by habitual questions of plagiarism and embezzlement. Meanwhile, perhaps inevitably, the second volume was officially banned by the authorities. Over the years, several of its editors would spend time in jail, but by now it had friends in high places. Enthusiastic readers included the senior government minister Lamoignon de Malesherbes, as well as no less than Madame de Pompadour, the king's *maîtresse-en-titre* (in France, even the king's chief mistress had her own title). After officially banning the work, the authorities considered that they had fulfilled their duties, and from then on mostly turned a blind eye.

The list of contributors reads like a who's who of the finest intellectuals of eighteenth-century Paris. Montesquieu contributed to a wide-ranging article on 'taste', d'Alembert wrote on everything from abstruse mathematics to contemporary political events. At one point the leading philosopher of mind, Étienne de Condillac, put in a spell as editor. And Diderot couldn't refrain from inserting his own comments in the *Encyclopédie*:

> Aguaxima, a plant growing in Brazil and on the islands of South America. This is all that we are told about it; and I would like to know for whom such descriptions are made. It cannot be for the natives of the countries concerned, who are likely to know more about the aguaxima than is contained in this description, and who do not need to learn that the aguaxima grows in their country.

Beneath this droll observation lies a serious point on the purposes and limitations of encyclopaedic knowledge. Among the most significant (and often similarly witty) entries in the *Encyclopédie* are those by Voltaire. Though his widely attributed remark: 'I disapprove of what you say, but will defend to the death your right to say it', does not appear in this work, and may not even have been made by him, it does, however, capture precisely his attitude.

The man we know as Voltaire was born in Paris in 1694 with the given name François-Marie Arouet. His family were minor nobility, though he himself always believed that he was the illegitimate son of an aristocratic army officer called Guérin de Rochebrune. Contrary to the wishes of his nominal father, Voltaire abandoned his study of law in Caen, and made his way to Paris to become a writer. His lively mind and penchant for witty remarks gained him entry to the best salons in the city. On the other hand, a satirical verse about the regent, Philippe II, implying that he slept with his own daughters, resulted in Voltaire spending a year in solitary confinement in a windowless cell in Paris's notorious fortress prison, the Bastille.

On emerging into the daylight, Voltaire wrote to his friend Rousseau that from now on he was changing his name from François-Marie Arouet to Voltaire. Under this name he soon achieved renown as a playwright. But in 1726, after being taunted about his pseudonym by the aristocrat de Rohan-Chabret, he challenged his accuser to a duel. Consequently, he was beaten up by hired thugs and awoke to find himself once more in the Bastille. At his trial he volunteered to be exiled to Britain rather than spend more time in jail.

The two years Voltaire spent in London and travelling widely through Britain opened his eyes. He was befriended by the poets Wordsworth and Pope, met the satirist Jonathan Swift, and was baffled by the plays of Shakespeare, which violated all the rules of classical drama as practised in Paris. France's greatest playwrights, Racine and Molière, both of whom reigned supreme in seventeenth-century Paris, set a new standard. Poetic lines were declaimed, actors moved with precision about the stage; wit, elegance and rhetoric were valued above action. By such standards Shakespeare was regarded as an uncouth barbarian. Not until he was championed by the eighteenth-century composer Berlioz (who fell in love with the Irish actress Harriet Smithson while she was playing Ophelia in *Hamlet*), did Shakespeare receive his due in France. This lacuna in French judgement is indicative of the gap (or 'chasm of taste') that existed between these two cultures, both entering the modern era after their own fashion.

Voltaire was quick to discern such differences. In particular he admired the English respect for their great scientist Newton, lamenting the lack of similar adulation for the wide range of highly talented scientists in Paris. Two of these will have to suffice. The polymathic Pierre-Simon Laplace was born in 1749, and his work would appear either side of the great divide in French history: The Revolution of 1789. Laplace was both a skilled engineer, and astronomer of note, a philosopher – and, above all, a superlative mathematician. He predicted the existence of black holes, correctly described the nebular origins of our solar system, but most sweeping of all was his work on probability theory, which, according to the twentieth-century US historian of science C.C. Gillispie, he used 'as an instrument for repairing defects in our knowledge'. In line with Laplace's deep-seated belief in scientific explanation and causation, if scientists could establish all the relevant conditions pertaining to a particular moment in time, we would be able to predict everything following this event. This was the ultimate statement of scientific determinism. Not until the advent of quantum theory over a century later would this idea come under serious question.

The other supreme scientist working in Paris in this period was the aristocratic Antoine Lavoisier, widely regarded as 'the father of modern chemistry'. Along with his well-connected wife Marie-Anne Pierrette Paulze, who translated English experimental papers for him and became more a collaborator than a mere assistant in his private laboratory, they would bring about a revolution in chemistry. Most importantly, they transformed it from a qualitative science, concerned with the properties of their materials, into a quantitative science, involving precise measurements, whereby these materials could be analysed and their constituents assessed. The discoveries Lavoisier made with Anne-Marie were legion. These included the all-important role of oxygen in combustion, and the fact that sulphur is a single element, rather than a combination of different elements. Lavoisier drew up the first extensive table of the elements, which led to him predicting the existence of silicon; and he played a pivotal role in the introduction of the metric system, a triumph of universal reason over the idio-syncrasies of differing national systems of measurement.

Lavoisier and his wife in their laboratory.

Despite his great work, as an aristocrat Lavoisier would fall foul of the Revolution in 1789. On hearing that he had been guillotined, his colleague Lagrange commented: 'It took but an instant to cut off his head, yet a hundred years might not suffice to produce another like it.'

Last, but far from least among the figures who ensured that Paris led the world during this period, is the philosopher and writer Jean-Jacques Rousseau, who among all the preceding figures would probably have the most immediate effect.

Rousseau was born in the democratic city of Geneva in Switzerland in 1712, but would soon gravitate to Paris. Here he launched into a career as a writer and philosopher. His best-known works, such as the novel *Émile* and his *Confessions*, would make him famous throughout Europe, with his works avidly read by such disparate figures as the German rationalist philosopher Kant and the Scottish empirical thinker Hume. Rousseau's ideas were uncompromisingly libertarian:

> I love liberty, and I loathe constraint, dependence, and all their kindred annoyances. As long as my purse contains money it secures my independence... The money that we possess is the instrument of liberty, that which we lack and strive to obtain is the instrument of slavery. Nature and fortune had left you free... The enemy is yourself.

The controversial nature of his writings on politics and society would ensure that he was obliged to flee back home on more than one occasion. Yet he would inevitably end up back in Paris, where he had set up home with a seamstress named Thérèse Levasseur, by whom he had five children, all of whom he delivered to the local foundlings home. His excuse for this unusual arrangement was that he feared Thérèse would be unable to educate them in the manner he saw fit. As we shall see, Rousseau had his own original ideas concerning education.

After one of his flights from Paris, Rousseau received a note from Voltaire, inviting him to come and live at Ferney, his country estate, but Rousseau declined – a decision he later regretted. Voltaire himself had retired for his own safety to Ferney, on the Swiss border. Here he found himself between France and Switzerland, without coming under the control of either the one or the other.

Rousseau's political and social thinking would revolutionise philosophy, and in the process act as a catalyst that played its part in bringing about the Revolution itself. The titles of his two major works are indicative: *Discourse on Inequality* and *The Social Contract*. In the latter he would argue that kings do not rule by divine right: a long-established belief among European royalty. He believed it is the people who have legitimate political authority. After the appearance of this work in 1762, it achieved the accolade of being burned in public, prompting Rousseau to reply that such action by the authorities indicated that they 'did not have enough wit to reply to it'.

Rousseau was a free spirit who believed in spontaneous expression rather than reason, a belief to which he adhered in all its unpredictability. This rendered his personality all but intolerable. Unlike so many of the philosophers and scientists of the Enlightenment, he was far from being a rational individual, and his relations with his colleagues were frequently broken off in acrimony. Despite this, his philosophy is profound, and would influence thinkers down the years from Karl Marx to Bertrand Russell (not always positively!).

For all the faults of Rousseau's ideas, after the repressions of the past his thoughts came as a breath of fresh air. His ideas on education, for instance, have continued to resonate. He claimed that children should be left free to develop naturally, to express themselves, so that they can develop into well-balanced, free-thinking adults. Though how this could be achieved amid the corrective atmosphere of a Parisian foundlings home, rather than amid the anarchic chaos of five children running free about the house of a poor seamstress, is difficult to comprehend.

In Rousseau's ideas it is possible to see both aspects of the coming Revolution – its liberty and its repression. Meanwhile, the intellectual salons of eighteenth-century Paris were busily discussing the contents of the latest volume of the *Encyclopédie*. In a parallel, yet paradoxical development, the École militaire founded by Louis XV in 1752 had become a collection of military schools across the country. This was intended to break the aristocratic stranglehold on the army, whose purchased commissions were resulting in increasing incompetence. The new École militaire was thrown open to candidates from good families, usually of '*petite noblesse*' (petty nobility), who had fallen on hard times, subsidised by endowments gathered by a tax on playing cards. These schools began turning out the best military engineers, and France soon had an excellent network of main roads and bridges criss-crossing the country, enabling the rapid deployment of armies to oppose any threat by the several countries bordering on the 'The Hexagon', as France was often nicknamed.[23]

Yet the constant effort to maintain France as Europe's leading nation had once again required it to participate in a succession of foreign wars – against the Grand Alliance of anti-French allies (mainly England, the Dutch Republic and Austria), and then a Second Alliance, followed by a series of further wars. All this had proved a crippling effort on the nation's finances. By the 1770s taxation was ruining many *petit bourgeois* enterprises; crop failures and 'highway taxes' had reduced supplies to the cities; while both the peasants and the citizens of the slums were reduced to starvation.

The spark that lit the conflagration took place on 14th July 1789, when the angry mob stormed the detested symbol of authority, the Bastille. The French Revolution, the first comprehensive revolution in a modern European country, had begun. On that day, sitting at his escritoire in Versailles, blissfully unaware of the unfolding events, the thirty-five-year-old King Louis XVI wrote in his diary a bored: *Rien* ('Nothing').

Like Constantinople/Istanbul, Paris would quickly rise once more, in a highly transformed state, to become for a second time the leading city in Europe, and hence the world. Following the brief

---

23 This nickname for France reflects the approximate six-sided shape made by its national borders.

and bloody chaos of 'The Terror', a five-man committee known as the Directorate established the First French Republic. A measure of civil order was re-established and the Directorate despatched armies to defend the country's borders. Skilled generals who'd risen through the ranks of the École militaire led French soldiers inspired with revolutionary zeal. These proved more than a match for the might of all the European countries that now attacked France in an attempt to quash this revolution that threatened all their governments. Although the post-revolutionary French government proved almost as vicious and corrupt as its predecessors, the power balance had irrevocably shifted. The First French Republic, under the rule of the Directorate, was certainly the most progressive political rule in Europe. But it was neither stable, nor popular.

The most successful of the new breed of young revolutionary generals was a twenty-five-year old Corsican named Napoleon Bonaparte. In 1796 he crossed the Alps and in a brilliant campaign drove the powerful Austrian army back to within seventy miles of Vienna, before they sued for peace. This established the ambitious young Corsican as the most charismatic figure in the land. Fearful of losing their power, the Directorate despatched him on a campaign to faraway Egypt. Within two years he returned, and as he made his way from the south of France to Paris, he was welcomed by the cheering people who lined his route. By 1799 he had taken power.

Napoleon soon began launching French military conquests into new countries, ensuring loyalty by appointing members of his family as their new rulers. (His brother Joseph would become King of Naples, another brother, Louis, would become King of Holland.) France soon dominated the whole of Europe, with only Britain holding out thanks to its superior naval power.

Napoleon, who had been taught by Laplace, befriended many of the leading scientists in Paris. With their advice, he instigated a widespread series of educational reforms, banishing the influence of the Church, bringing universal rational education to the people.

This was so highly organised, down to the last detail, that Napoleon liked to boast he could look at the clock and know exactly what page of what book every student in France was studying at that precise moment. He also instituted a range of *grands écoles*, with highly competitive entry based on merit alone, which imparted higher education in all fields, with a special emphasis on practical studies such as civil and military engineering. At the same time, he continued to take a close personal interest in the latest discoveries, inviting leading scientists to read him their latest papers. On one famous occasion, when Laplace read out his treatise on the formation of the solar system, Napoleon asked him why there was no mention of God, the creator of this system. Laplace is said to have replied, 'Sire, I had no need of that hypothesis.'

Following Napoleon's assumption of power, Paris was once more restored to its role as the world's leading city, at the forefront of the civic, scientific and cultural revolution that was gradually coming into being around the globe.[24] Napoleon also oversaw the introduction of an entirely new legal system that become known as the Napoleonic Code. This was largely based upon Napoleon's personal understanding of the Revolution and what it meant. It was therefore informed by a large number of Enlightenment ideas, including the influence of Montesquieu and Rousseau. From now on, all citizens were equal under the law. The Napoleonic Code continues to be a basis of the legal codes of many of today's European and Latin American countries.

Although the regimes that Napoleon imposed on conquered European countries could be harsh, it is usually acknowledged that he spread liberal ideas from Paris to many other capitals. Although unconquered, Britain remained particularly fearful of the spread

---

24 In 1800 the population of Paris was probably around seven hundred thousand. Beijing had a population of over a million, and London's population was just under that figure. However, as we shall see, these larger two cities had yet to attain their peak influence.

of French revolutionary ideas, and with very good reason – harshly suppressing all signs of insurrection for years to come. As late as the 1830s, dissent such as that which characterised the Tolpuddle Martyrs, the Peterloo Massacre and the Chartists was still providing a regular supply of prisoners sentenced to 'transportation beyond the seas'; i.e. to the penal colony of Botany Bay in Australia, Britain's answer to Siberia.

Other measures introduced by Napoleon included a new more egalitarian tax system, and the establishment of the central Banque de France in order to unify and control the nation's finances. He also introduced the *legion d'honneur*, which replaced the military and civil decorations awarded by the *ancien régime*. His opponents and dissenters, of which he retained many in France, regarded him as an 'enlightened despot' at home, and a 'megalomaniac' with regard to foreign conquests.

Above all, Napoleon was a military genius of great bravery, who inspired loyalty in his men, and was on occasion not afraid to risk his own life. He was also tactically astute: 'Never interrupt your enemy when he's making a mistake.' Yet he was not above recognising the crucial part played by luck in military matters. When one of his marshals suggested a new general, Napoleon would reply: 'He may be good, but is he lucky?'

Perhaps inevitably, in the end Napoleon succumbed to his own overweening ambition. In 1804 he would declare himself emperor, undermining the entire idea of the revolutionary movement. At a ceremony in Notre Dame he was handed the imperial crown by Pope Pius VII, which he then placed upon his own head. This intentionally echoed the papal coronation of Charlemagne as the first Holy Roman Emperor a thousand years previously, yet without indicating his subservience to papal authority.

The new thirty-five-year-old emperor, Napoleon I, was determined to persist in France's campaigns of conquest, and equally determined that he alone knew the way that France should be governed. Napoleon's catastrophic overstretching of the *Grande Armée*, in the invasion of Russia in 1812, was then followed by his defeat in 1815 at the Battle of Waterloo ('a damn close run thing', according to its victor Wellington).

In just a few short years, all the influence Paris had built up as the capital of Europe and a world leader in fields from literature to military might was over. Yet, as we shall see, the ideas it produced would continue to change history.

Sequence

After Napoleon's defeat at Waterloo he fled back to France, eventually making his way to the port of Rochefort on the west coast, with the aim of escaping to America. Here he found the port blockaded by the British navy, and chose to surrender to the captain of the *Bellerophon*. Napoleon would eventually be despatched to exile on the remote south Atlantic island of St Helena, over a thousand miles off the coast of West Africa, where he would die six years later, aged just fifty-one.

Meanwhile, the leaders of the European powers had agreed to hold a peace conference at Vienna in order to decide the fate of Europe and restore legitimate governance to the countries that Napoleon had conquered. As Wellington passed through Paris on the way to this conference, he took the opportunity to sleep with two of Napoleon's former mistresses. As the modern British historian Andrew Roberts put it: 'To sleep with one of Napoleon's mistresses might be considered an accident, but to sleep with two might suggest a pattern of triumphalism.'

The Congress of Vienna, as it came to be called, marked the end of almost twenty-three years of continuous war in Europe. The aim of the Congress was to establish a balance of powers with the aim of preventing another Europe-wide conflict. The Congress was attended by representatives of countries throughout Europe, but was dominated by the delegations from the main powers: Austria, Britain, Prussia, Russia and the restored Bourbon monarchy of France. The attendance of Tsar Alexander I marked the emergence of Russia as a major European power. Another aim of the Congress was to avoid any further French-style revolutions breaking out among the downtrodden people of Europe. It is indicative that during the decades following this Congress more than 9.5 million people emigrated from Europe to the 'land of the free', as the United States became known. Almost as many emigrated across the Atlantic to Canada and Latin America. The majority of these emigrants were of Italian, German, Irish, English and Scottish ancestry.

Despite this, the Congress of Vienna would ensure that Europe remained largely peaceful throughout the rest of the nineteenth century and on to 1914. This would be the century of empire-building by the leading European powers, and even some of the lesser nations. Denmark, for instance, would accumulate an empire that included Iceland and Greenland, Caribbean islands, as well as trading ports in west Africa, India and South-East Asia. But the main empires would belong to Spain and Portugal, the Ottomans, Britain, (later) France and Russia (a country that had expanded to such an extent that it had passed beyond eastern Siberia, into Alaska, making it by far the world's largest country). Meanwhile, the sleeping giant of China continued to occupy a territory around half as large as that of Russia.

Regardless of such colonial expansion, large parts of the world remained blank on European maps. These included virtually the entire interior of Africa, the north-western quarter of North America, and much of the south of South America, all of which remained to be explored, and exploited, in the name of empire-building.

With the fall of Paris from grace, there could now be only one candidate for the world's leading city. Namely, London.

London: Heart of the British Empire

The words used by Charles Dickens to open *A Tale of Two Cities* (referring to London and Paris during the Revolution) can equally be applied to the time of London's greatness:

> It was the best of times, it was the worst of times, it was the age of wisdom, it was the age of foolishness, it was the epoch of belief, it was the epoch of incredulity, it was the season of Light, it was the season of Darkness, it was the spring of hope, it was the winter of despair, we had everything before us, we were all going direct to Heaven, we were all going direct the other way.

This is arguably true throughout the history I have so far described. Babylon, Athens, Rome, Constantinople and Paris all had their misery and their slums, as well as their transcendent achievements. Every upside has had its downside, just as Dickens describes. In Christ's words: 'The poor are always with us.' From the alleyways of Babylon, which may well have resembled the streets of Kolkata, to the thousands upon thousands of poor soldiers whom Napoleon abandoned to an icy death on his retreat from Moscow. And as we shall see, the streets of London during the century in which it led the world were to be no exception. These will appear in due course. But first the upside.

It is arguable that London would achieve more than any of the previous cities I have chosen. During the century in which London led the world, it would become the capital city of the largest stable empire the world had yet seen, one that covered almost a quarter of the land mass of the globe.[25] By 1913 Britain had a population of 43 million, while its empire contained 458 million, almost a quarter of the world's population.

How could a small island off the north coast of Europe possibly have achieved such a feat? Central to the creation and maintenance of this far-flung empire was the British Royal Navy, which had been founded in the early sixteenth century during the reign of Henry VIII. By the nineteenth century the Royal Navy was under the charge of the Board of the Admiralty in London, which ensured disciplined and efficient organisation of the fleet, in so far as this was possible during an era limited to manual messages, flag signals and lighted beacons. (In the previous century the diarist and Secretary to the Admiralty, Samuel Pepys, who had no maritime experience himself, played a significant role in reforming Admiralty practice.) And as previously indicated, the riches accumulated from the African slave trade, and the wealth of sugar from the Caribbean plantations, would also play a large part in the supremacy of Britain and other European nations. This trade too, as well as Britain's trade with India and its other overseas colonies, depended heavily upon naval supremacy.

However, the limited ability of the Admiralty in London to maintain contact with its far-flung ships on the high seas placed immense responsibility on the captains of Royal Navy vessels, who had absolute power at sea. This was bolstered by the presence on board of armed marines to protect them and their officers from unruly sailors, who were frequently flogged for indiscipline. On the other hand, the captain was expected to use his own initiative, and had to answer in person before a board of the Admiralty in case of

25 The Mongol hordes who overran much of Europe and Asia in the thirteenth and fourteenth centuries created a more extensive empire. Yet this would possess little of the administration and infrastructure usually associated with empire and would disintegrate almost as rapidly as it had been created.

defeat, loss of ship, mutiny and such. In 1757 Admiral Byng was placed in charge of a small ill-equipped fleet, whose depleted crews had been augmented by press-ganged sailors, and was ordered to relieve the British garrison besieged at Minorca. When he failed in this mission, he was ordered to appear before a court martial, where he was sentenced to death. As Voltaire ironically commented, this was '*pour encourager les autres*' – literally, to encourage the others, in other words, to make way for their promotion.

Yet the Royal Navy did far more than protect British merchant ships plying their trade in distant waters, putting down rebellions in coastal regions, or enforcing British influence (a policy that became known as gunboat diplomacy). In 1831 the survey ship HMS *Beagle* set sail from Plymouth, tasked with mapping the myriad islands, channels and inlets of the south-west coast of South America. Its commander Captain Robert Fitzroy had invited on board a young biologist called Charles Darwin, who spent much of the five-year voyage collecting biological samples. When the *Beagle* called in at the Galapagos Islands, Darwin made drawings of the finches indigenous to each of the islands, discovering that birds of the same species had developed differently modified beaks that better enabled them to live off the seeds, insects and flora of their particular island. This gave him the idea that species could change.

On his return to England, Darwin would buy a house in south London where he would spend the next two and a half decades developing this original idea into his theory of evolution by natural selection – to this day one of the most important discoveries humanity has yet made about itself and the world it inhabits.[26]

---

26 The *Beagle* was remarkable in a number of ways. It was the first ship to be fitted with a lightning conductor. And such was the accuracy of the maps made by Captain Fitzroy that many of them would remain in use well into the twentieth century. Later, Fitzroy would become an expert meteorologist, drawing up regular bulletins to describe the weather in the various coastal regions off the British Isles. He invented the word 'forecast', and one of these regions that appears in the daily Shipping Forecast is named after him.

For sixty-four years, from 1837 to 1901, Britain was ruled by Queen Victoria, a small, round lady who dressed in black for much of her life, was temperamentally averse to appearing in public, and remains renowned for her remark: 'We are not amused' (said to have been made to an equerry who deigned to recount a rude joke over dinner).

Queen Victoria was descended from Germans on both sides of her family, was educated by a German governess and ended up marrying a German prince. Many of her children and grandchildren would marry into European royalty, making half the crowned heads of Europe into close relatives. Despite such pedigree, Victoria grew up an unworldly and over-protected young girl who was isolated from the world by her mother the Duchess of Kent and her 'friend' Sir John Conroy, both of whom wished to make her utterly dependent upon their advice. Although Victoria and her mother lived in Kensington Palace, Victoria did not even have a room of her own and was forced to share her mother's bedroom each night.

In 1837, at the age of eighteen, Victoria ascended to the throne. Her position as queen meant that she could now ignore the advice of Conroy and her mother. However, her lack of worldliness meant that she was almost entirely dependent upon her prime minister. Protocol dictated that the prime minister should consult with the monarch on a regular basis, keeping her informed of all government business. Theoretically, the monarch had immense power through the 'royal prerogative', an ill-defined constitutional term that was in practice used by the prime minister, who answered to the democratic will of parliament. Even so, these strictly private consultations between the monarch and her prime minister were no mere formality. They were intended to keep the monarch informed of 'her' government's policies; the monarch also provided an element of continuity between governments as prime ministers came and went. After an election, it was the monarch who summoned the leader of the winning party and asked him to form a government. Over the years, Queen Victoria would be consulted by no less than ten British prime ministers, and her experience in such matters would prove invaluable.

Fortunately, her first prime minister was Lord Melbourne, whose solicitous manner encouraged her to regard him as a father figure. Queen Victoria was the first monarch to move into Buckingham Palace, where her mother continued to try and influence her. Lord Melbourne advised Victoria to get married, thus solving the problem of her mother's influence, and at the same time ensuring the succession. Victoria initially regarded this as a 'shocking alternative'. However, when the twenty-year-old Victoria met the German Prince Albert of Saxe-Coburg she was soon confiding in her diary 'feelings of heavenly love and happiness'.

In 1840 the twenty-year-old Queen Victoria and Prince Albert were married at Westminster Abbey, a union that would eventually produce nine children. To the consternation of many in the establishment, Queen Victoria now became partially dependent upon Albert's advice regarding matters of state. In effect, his influence was largely benign: he encouraged educational reform, and supported the international ban on slavery, among other progressive measures. Albert's main interests were scientific and technological, and he would become the driving force behind one of the most prestigious events of Victoria's reign: the Great Exhibition, which was held in London in 1851. This was intended as a showcase for British technology, and the ascendancy of the British Empire, and would contain some 13,000 exhibits from its colonies and dependencies throughout the world. Almost as an afterthought, there were fifty-four exhibits from foreign states in Europe and America. The Exhibition was housed in a vast multi-storied greenhouse-like structure, with a cast-iron skeleton covered in plate glass, occupying 26 acres of Hyde Park. This became known as the Crystal Palace. Although this was not the first exhibition of its kind – there had been a similar, smaller-scale exhibition in Paris – it came to be regarded as the supreme statement of London's leadership of the world. Despite lasting less than six months, it would attract well over six million visitors from at home and abroad.

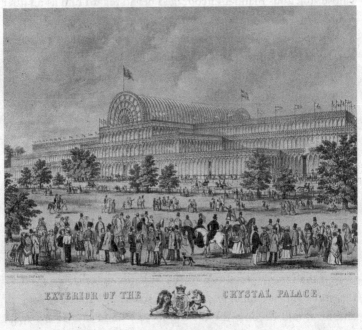

The Crystal Palace, which housed the Great Exhibition of 1851.

By 1860 the forty-one-year-old Prince Albert's health was in decline. Despite being bed-ridden he was able to use his influence to prevent Britain from going to war with the United States, which was on the brink of civil war. When Albert died in 1861, Queen Victoria was grief-stricken, and entered a state of mourning that would last through the ensuing forty years of her life. Although increasingly withdrawn, she still had to deal with a succession of formidable prime ministers. Following Lord Melbourne's advice, she learned to trust the formidably intelligent Sir Robert Peel. She would later dislike the earnest William Gladstone, and was enchanted by the flattering attentions of his great rival Benjamin Disraeli.

These prime ministers were presiding over an increasingly influential and active parliament. The MP for Hull, William Wilberforce, campaigned for decades for the abolition of the slave trade, which by 1800 accounted for no less than 80 per cent of British foreign income. In 1833, the year of Wilberforce's death, slavery was finally abolished in the British Empire. Astonishingly, slave-owners were then compensated for 'loss of property' to the tune of £20 million (anything up to £16.5 billion in present values). The 'liberated' slaves were given nothing. Some were permitted to retain small plots of land as sharecroppers. Many were forced to resort to what can only be described as serfdom.

The government in Westminster could afford such misplaced generosity towards these former slave-owners largely because the City (as the financial district became known) had by now become the largest and most influential capital market in the world. Although stock exchanges existed all over Europe, most notably in Paris, Amsterdam and Genoa, the London Stock Exchange remained unrivalled in its ability to enable entrepreneurs, merchant venturers and companies to raise capital to finance their various enterprises.

The City's reputation had been hard won. Back in 1720 the London stock market had been devastated by a financial crash, known as the South Sea Bubble. This had taken place when artificially inflated share prices in the South Sea Company, which was built upon the false promise of a monopoly on trade with South America, had collapsed. During the course of a year, £100 shares had risen to a giddying £1,000, valuing the company at £200 million, before the bubble had burst, hitting speculators large and small throughout the land.[27]

The South Sea Bubble had cast a long shadow over the London Stock Exchange, causing a bear market that would now last some forty-two years.[28] But, the following century share prices began to rise in a lengthy bull market lasting from 1797 to 1845. This was of course heavily boosted by former slave-owners investing their 'compensation'.

The end of this boom in prices was brought about by the collapse of the so-called 'Railway Mania'. Many see this as marking the end of the Industrial Revolution, which had established Britain as the global leader in commerce and London as the world's leading financial centre.

Britain had instigated the first Industrial Revolution around 1760, with the introduction of machinery into factories (especially spinning looms to manufacture cotton goods). These machines were increasingly driven by the newly discovered steam power that was developed by the Scottish inventor James Watt. Manufacturing had boomed, especially in the north of England. In 1750 Manchester had been a small market town with a population of 20,000; by 1850 it had become the nation's third-largest city, with a population of around 250,000 and factories producing cotton goods that were exported across the globe. The transportation of these goods had been transformed by the building of a network of canals linking major manufacturing centres with the ports. This had begun around 1759 and would last until 1815.

---

27 Even the finest mind of his era, Sir Isaac Newton, was taken in by the South Sea Company hype. When the 'bubble' burst he lost the colossal sum of £20,000, causing him to remark bitterly: 'I can calculate the motion of heavenly bodies but not the madness of people.'

28 A bear market is characterised by a long decline in share prices, typically when prices fall 20 per cent or more below their previous peak. A bull market, on the other hand, describes a prolonged rise in share prices.

In 1829 the civil engineer Robert Stephenson had developed steam power to drive his *Rocket*, the prototype of the steam-driven locomotive, which travelled on rail tracks. In 1830 the opening of a railway line linking the industrial hub of Manchester with the major port of Liverpool was attended by the Duke of Wellington, who had made a successful transition from the army into politics and become prime minister. During the ensuing years a railway boom had taken place, much of which was financed by money raised in the City.

Most notable of these was the Great Western Railway, which was built linking London to Bristol, and later Exeter, by the cigar-chomping Anglo-French Isambard Kingdom Brunel, widely regarded as one of the most ingenious and prolific figures in engineering history. Brunel's railway involved the digging of tunnels and cuttings through hilly countryside to ensure a level track for the locomotives, whose main drawback involved their inability to haul lines of carriages or goods wagons up steep inclines. Conditions were tough: the heavy digging work and 'excavation' involved in laying the level railway tracks was carried out by gangs of 'navvies' (navigators). These had originally been used to dig out the canals, and now turned to work on the railways. The men were paid by the day, with money docked for meals and accommodation in the temporary camps or shanty towns. To save on cash, the men were often paid in beer, and soon gained a reputation for rowdy drunken behaviour. Around a third of the navvies were Irish immigrants, and the rest were mainly former farm labourers, put out of work by the agricultural revolution, which saw the introduction of the metal plough, as well as new machinery for planting and harvesting crops more efficiently, thus rendering large numbers of farm labourers redundant.

By the 1840s the railway boom was well under way, with railway lines linking London's main terminals to all the major cities throughout the land. Other track-lines criss-crossed the country, created by companies borrowing money at low interest rates, or by launching issues of stocks and shares on the booming London Stock Market. Between 1844 and 1846 alone, 6,200 miles of railway track were laid across the country. During this period there were more navvies than there were soldiers in the British army.

Finally the day arrived when there was no need for any further railway tracks and the bubble burst. However, this was not like the South Sea Bubble, where investors were left holding debts they had incurred buying further shares, which suddenly became all but worthless. The bursting of the railway bubble left the nation with a network of railways that would be ready for use when industry once again began to expand.

The bear market on the London Stock Exchange would last from 1845 for another three years. Confidence in industrial progress and expanding markets was further damaged by the 1848 'year of revolutions'. This saw popular uprisings from Sicily to France, and the German states to Poland. These were inspired by a mix of democratic demands, nationalism and an end to the repression of civil liberties – many of the ideas proposed by the French Enlightenment. After savage repression, there were but a few significant changes. Serfdom was abolished in the Austro-Hungarian Empire, and in France the restored Bourbon monarchy was overthrown in favour of the restoration of the Republic and universal male suffrage.

Although there was widespread public sympathy in Britain with the revolutionaries, their natural supporters were deeply divided. A group called the Chartists took their name from the People's Charter. This demanded suffrage, freedom for anyone to stand as an MP, equal constituencies and the righting of other injustices. They wished to achieve their ends by legitimate political means, but when 100,000 gathered on London's Kennington Green to present their petition to parliament they were forcibly prevented from doing so.

At the same time the Irish had problems of their own. Here, in 1845, the staple crop of potatoes had been devastated by blight, which would result in what is now known as The Great Hunger.

During the ensuing seven-year period, a horrific one million people died, and hundreds of thousands emigrated to America and Britain, resulting in a 25 per cent drop in the population. Things were only slightly better in Scotland, where the landowners were clearing tenant crofters from their land in order to use this for more profitable sheep farming. The dispossessed tramped the roads to settle in the already crowded cities, with many taking steerage berths and emigrating to Canada.

Back in parliament, MPs argued and dithered. A few had sympathy for the Irish, others for the Scots, and some even recognised that the Chartists had their grievances. Prime minister Lord Russell proved totally inadequate to the situation. Even Queen Victoria took it upon herself to visit Ireland during the famine and contributed £2,000 to the relief fund.

The lack of action by the Whig leadership, Lord Russell's party, remained a disgrace from which the party would never recover. Lord Russell would be the last Whig prime minister, before the party transformed itself into the Liberals. Yet the lack of effective action at this time was more than just Lord Russell's doing; it marked a failure by parliament as whole.

The main obstacle to progress was a widespread belief throughout all parties in a policy of economic *laissez-faire*: the economy should be left to its own devices. There was no need for government to interfere in such matters, which would naturally right themselves of their own accord through the mechanism of supply and demand.

Economic understanding remained in its infancy. Adam Smith's founding work on economics, *The Wealth of Nations*, had been published just seventy years previously in 1776. Few MPs had read it, and those who had bothered had largely misunderstood Adam Smith's central notion: 'It is not from the benevolence of the butcher, the brewer, or the baker, that we expect our dinner, but from their regard to their own self-interest [...] Every individual [is] led by an invisible hand to promote an end which was no part of his intention.' However, this 'invisible hand' was neither a mystical notion nor an unalterable socio-mechanical process. It was simply a profound insight into how economics worked. Adam Smith himself never advocated a totally free market. Indeed, he was deeply suspicious of such markets, which had led from medieval guilds to contemporary cartels.

Such ideas influenced David Ricardo, who would become one of those rare MPs who knew what he was talking about and did not act solely out of self-interest. David Ricardo had been born in 1772, of middle-class Dutch-Jewish heritage. At an early age he followed his father to become a broker on the London Stock Exchange. At this time, anti-Semitism was rife and only a dozen or so Jews were tolerated in the Exchange, confined to a section of the trading floor known as 'Jews' Walk'. Despite such restriction, young Ricardo soon began exhibiting an exceptional talent for finance. By the age of twenty-five he had become a millionaire, allowing him and his family to partake of the usual social advantages of the era – a country house, and regular trips to 'take the waters' at fashionable Bath. And it was in Bath that he happened across a copy of Adam Smith's *The Wealth of Nations*. In a flash, Ricardo understood that economics was his true calling, and that he could contribute further to this subject by drawing upon his financial expertise.

Ricardo became an MP, quickly gaining the respect of his colleagues for his perceptive interventions in parliamentary debates. The outbreak of the Napoleonic Wars had left Britain in economic isolation from Europe. To prevent the flow of gold from British reserves, the government allowed the Bank of England to decouple the pound sterling from the gold standard. This allowed the Bank of England to print extra paper money. This in turn led to an inflationary rise in prices. The Bank of England flatly denied that this had anything to do with its actions. All this also led to a fall in the foreign exchange rate, where payment in gold was the norm. Not only was the Bank of England causing inflation, but it was also adding to the drain in gold reserves, which had been the original reason for the Bank's policy.

Ricardo pointed out this salient fact in a number of articles he had begun writing for leading British newspapers. As he was a poor public speaker, most of his influence on MPs, and the English establishment, came from his journalism, and later his published works.

Ricardo's analysis of society was harsh. There were three classes: the old established landowning class, the new rising capitalists and the working class. The first two were in constant conflict for supremacy, and should seek to achieve a balance, which worked for the benefit of them both. With regards to the workers, he formulated the Iron Law of Wages: any attempt to improve the lot of the workers was futile. On the other hand, they should always be paid a subsistence wage, which as we shall see was not always the case.

More influential still was Ricardo's formulation of what came to be known as the Law of Comparative Advantage. This proved to be a profound understanding of how international commerce worked, and would thus be of transformational advantage to a nation such as Britain, which relied upon overseas trade. Basically, this law explained how international trade between two nations, such as Britain and Portugal, would always be of benefit to both nations regardless of which was the stronger economy. Isolationism resulted in supplying for a home market. Free trade, on the other hand, meant an increased overall production, as both nations expanded their home market to include the export market. In the wider world this may result in certain anti-intuitive results. For instance, a country is not always best off concentrating on the production of what it does best. This may be done even better by another country. What it should concentrate upon is what it does least badly.[29]

---

29 To take an example from the modern era: Britain's forte had for many years been shipbuilding, but gradually Japan was able to produce more ships more economically. Britain was thus well advised to divert its energies from its greatest talent to activities where it had a comparative advantage over the rest of the world, such as the manufacture of supersonic airplane engines and financial services.

Ricardo's economic thinking focused Adam Smith's ideas, to the point where they could be analysed with clarity. Smith may have been the founding father, but it was Ricardo who showed how economic analysis could be conducted in a scientific manner. His ideas showed the way forward, enabling an expansion of Britain's imperial trade.

However, his friend Robert Malthus came to economic conclusions that pointed in the opposite direction. Malthus was the son of an eccentric wealthy Surrey squire, whose reading of revolutionary tracts led to him promulgating utopian ideas. He sent his son Robert to Cambridge to study maths and natural philosophy (science), where he excelled in both subjects. Upon leaving Cambridge he chose to enter the Church; however, the young Malthus was not destined to become a mild-mannered benevolent parson. His knowledge of science had led to him to precisely the opposite conclusions to his father. Far from progressing towards some utopian future, the world was in fact going to hell in a handcart.[30]

And why was this so? In his view, 'progress was killing off the human race'. In his *Essay on Population* Malthus explained how history was compelled by two irresistible forces: the need for food, and insatiable sexual desire. Applying his mathematical knowledge to this problem he predicted that the world's population was liable to increase in a geometric progression (i.e. 2, 4, 8, 16, 32...). On the other hand, food production was only increasing in an arithmetic progression (i.e. 2, 4, 6, 8, 10...). The way Malthus read the world's problems, population would always increase to the very limit of what could be sustained. At this point, 'positive checks' came into play – in the form of plagues, war, famines, natural disasters and so forth. In Malthus's view the

---

30 This particular phrase originated in London during the Great Plague of the seventeenth century, when the bodies of the dead were left outside houses to be collected by public bailiffs, who were unwilling to risk using horses and chose instead to carry off the cadavers on handcarts.

only hope of avoiding the 'population catastrophe' was by the exercise of sexual abstinence and delaying marriage. All previous attempts at amelioration of this state of affairs had only worsened the situation. In the previous century, the prime minister William Pitt the Younger had proposed poor relief, known as Poor Laws, which ensured that workers whose earnings were below subsistence level received a public dole. By the turn of the century almost one in seven of the population was receiving assistance of some kind, with the necessary £4.5 million being raised by land property taxes.

Malthus and his followers came to the conclusion that the Poor Laws did not so much relieve suffering as *increase* it. He believed such public handouts encouraged larger families among the poor. Others, who argued that larger families added to the nation's wealth, were soon cried down. Just two years after the publication of Malthus's *Essay on Population*, Pitt withdrew his support for the Poor Law.

In London, increasing population and increasing poverty seemed to go hand in hand. The first studies of the slums in London were carried out in the 1830s and 1840s by the liberal reformer Edwin Chadwick. His aim was to reform the Poor Laws and bring about sweeping changes in health and sanitation, especially in the slums of London. For centuries, London had been attracting people from all over the country, drawn by the legendary claim that its 'streets were paved with gold'.[31]

Migration into London increased dramatically in the early half of the nineteenth century – from all over Britain, Europe and the Empire. By 1800 London had become the largest city in Europe with a population of almost 1 million. Between 1800 and 1840

---

31 Long dismissed as myth, there was in fact a truth behind this legend. In Elizabethan times, several ships returned from the New World bearing cargoes of gold-bearing ore. When this was smelted, it was found to contain only iron pyrites, known as 'fool's gold'. Consequently, this cheap ore was used to provide a solid surface for the streets of London, making it look as if they contained nuggets of gold.

London doubled its population to 2 million, overtaking Beijing and making it far and away the largest city in the world.

This was the London described by the pioneer reforming journalist Henry Mayhew. With vivid accuracy he described London's streets and alleyways filled with a pell-mell of market traders and road diggers, street artists and hurdy-gurdy players, pale-faced sweatshop workers and prostitutes, watercress sellers, hucksters, tipsters and sneak-thieves. The more exotic characters included mudlarks (who searched the stinking mud of the Thames at low tide for coal, rope and wood from passing ships, along with all manner of flotsam and jetsam), as well as 'pure-finders', who scooped up dog excrement to sell to tanners. Many had no regular work, or even fixed abode, and there was inevitably massive overcrowding in poorer areas. These contained fetid 'rookeries' such as those described by Dickens in *Oliver Twist*, where the likes of Fagin ran gangs of child pickpockets.

The journalist John Hollingshead visited one of these rookeries in 1861. It is worth recording his findings in some detail:

> The small yard seemed rotting with damp and dirt. The narrow window of the lower back room was too caked with mud to be seen through, and the kitchen was one of those black holes, filled with untold filth and rubbish, which the inspector had condemned a twelvemonth before. The stench throughout the house, although the front and back doors were wide open, was almost sickening; and when a room door was opened this stench came out in gusts. In one apartment I found a family of six persons, flanked by another apartment containing five.

While families were crammed into such appalling housing, the London Stock Exchange was in the midst of yet another half-century-long bull market. Starting from the end of the three-year bear market in 1848, this bull market would continue, with only the occasional blip, through the decades until 1914. In the century between 1815 and 1914, when London was the city that led the world, the capitalisation of the London Stock Market rose from the equivalent of $250 million to $15 billion.

Once again, Dickens' words echo down the century: 'It was the best of times, it was the worst of times...' The vast discrepancy between the reality of life in many parts of London, and the City's 'capitalisation', would prove the inspiration for another economic thinker, whose critique of his subject would prove every bit as compelling as that of Ricardo and Malthus. This was the German-born Jewish philosopher Karl Marx, who settled in the immigrant district of Soho after being ejected for political agitation from his birthplace, the Rhineland city of Trier (which had become part of Prussia), as well as Belgium and France.

Indeed, throughout Marx's life in London German spies would regularly report back to their masters, informing them of what Marx was up to. This has given us a precise and intimate picture of the impecunious bohemian life Marx led. We learn that on one occasion he got drunk with some German friends, smashed a gaslight and was chased through the street by the London 'bobbies', the city's police.[32] Another report reveals that he had to remain indoors for some time because he had pawned his only trousers to provide food for his wife and children. But these were the exceptions. For most of his life, Marx spent long hours researching and writing at his desk in the Reading Room at the British Museum. Ricardo had attempted to turn economics into a science;

---

32 In 1829 Sir Robert Peel, at the time Home Secretary, had established the Metropolitan Police, the first such force in the world. This replaced the somewhat haphazard system of parish constables and watchmen, and was organised according to the principle of law enforcement with the co-operation of law-abiding citizens. Peel's policemen soon became known as 'bobbies' after the colloquial version of his first name. Peel's Metropolitan Police would become a template for police forces throughout the world.

Marx claimed not only that he had succeeded in this, but that he had also turned history into a science.

Early in 1848, 'the year of the revolutions', Marx had published his short but inspirational 'Communist Manifesto', which ends with the famous revolutionary call to arms: 'Workers of the world unite! You have nothing to lose but your chains!' In the view of the contemporary British philosopher Peter Osborne (and many others), this manifesto was the single most influential text written in the nineteenth century. But it was the opening page of the Manifesto that revealed the true direction of Marx's historical and economic analysis: 'The history of all hitherto existing society is the history of class struggles.'

Marx would spend much of the rest of his life writing his voluminous, jargon-ridden and all but unreadable masterpiece *Das Kapital* (Capital), the first volume of which would be published in 1867. This argues that the capitalist system, with the surplus value of production going to the owners of the factories, and the exploitation of the workers who actually made the products, would eventually lead to a falling of profits and the collapse of industrial capitalism. According to Marx, this process was inevitable: 'The mode of production of material life conditions the general process of social, political and intellectual life. It is not the consciousness of men that determines their existence, but their social existence that determines their consciousness.' He believed that the end result would be not only the overthrow of the capitalist system, but 'the dictatorship of the proletariat', whose consciousness would be determined by the new revolutionary order of the world. Marx (and communism) had no truck with liberal ideas such as 'the right to life, liberty and property'.

Owing to the conditions prevailing among the working class throughout Europe, it is hardly surprising that such ideas achieved a widespread following, even if they contained their own explicit denial of the liberal freedoms to which so many of these supporters aspired. Here we see the reappearance of Rousseau's message: 'Whoever refuses to obey the general will... will be forced to be free.'

Marx died in London in 1883 at the age of sixty-four, but his words of warning would live on. His work would be recognised by many non-communists as a pioneering explanation of social science. From now on, society would never again see itself in the simplistic order of previous centuries. Ideas such as 'alienation', 'social consciousness' and purely materialistic explanations of society would become commonplace. It'd be over thirty years before Marx's 'inevitable' ideas came into being in the form of the Russian Revolution. Their realisation and their practice would be quite different from the way he had foreseen. However, no matter how that revolution came about, the deep practical flaws that arose in his system can be traced back to his original theoretical ideas.

While Marx was busy scribbling in the British Museum, just a mile or two away in the borough of Marylebone an equally persistent, but in this case genuine, scientist, would be struggling with ideas about how to lay the foundations of a revolution of his own. This revolution would take almost twice as long as Marx's ideas to come to fruition, but when it did so it would arguably prove almost as transformational as the 'spectre' of world communism. The man who achieved this was Charles Babbage, who is today recognised as the 'father of the computer'.

Charles Babbage was born in London in 1791, the son of a banker. During a somewhat haphazard early education, Babbage succeeded in teaching himself advanced mathematics. By 1828 he had been appointed Lucasian Professor of Mathematics at Cambridge.[33] Babbage was essentially a polymath. He made significant advances in cryptology, founded the Royal Astronomical Society and introduced the 'Babbage Principle' in economics, which analysed how machines might best be employed in the division of labour. He also demonstrated to

---

33 This prestigious post had previously been held by Isaac Newton. In the 1930s it would be held by the pioneer quantum physicist Paul Dirac, and later in the twentieth century by the astronomer Stephen Hawking.

Brunel the advantage of a broad gauge railway, which was used on the Great Western Railway from London to Bristol.

As early as 1812, while still a student at Cambridge, Babbage found himself looking through a table of logarithms, which he recognised as being full of mistakes. The idea suddenly occurred to him that such mistakes could be avoided if all its tabular functions could be computed by machinery. Yet it was more than ten years before he set about assembling what he called a 'Difference Engine'. This was devised to solve polynomial functions (similar to algebraic equations with more than one unknown). This proved to be a complex, delicate and highly ingenious machine, involving 25,000 separate parts, weighing 15 tons and being over 8 feet tall. Despite receiving considerable government funds, Babbage never completed this project. The main reason for this was because he had conceived of an even more complex calculating machine, called an Analytic Engine, to which he now devoted his attentions.

The Analytic Engine is arguably the prototype of the modern computer. Where the Difference Engine was essentially a single-purpose machine performing mechanical arithmetic, the Analytic Engine could be made to perform all manner of different calculations and functions. This was done by inserting special printed cards of instructions. These cards were the equivalent of the modern computer program. Babbage was assisted in this task by the mathematically gifted Ada Lovelace, the abandoned daughter of the poet Lord Byron. It was she who developed an algorithm that enabled Babbage's Analytic Engine to calculate a sequence of numbers.[34]

Although Babbage never actually finished his Analytic Engine, it contains all the fundamental elements of a general-purpose computer

---

34 This is an algorithm, or sequence of instructions to be fed into the computer, to create, for instance, a Fibonacci sequence of numbers: 0, 1, 1, 2, 3, 5... The instruction (or algorithm) to continue the sequence here would be: add the two preceding numbers to form the next number. So the next number in the series after 5 is 3 + 5 = 8, then 5 + 8 = 13.

that is 'Turing Complete'.[35] Consequently, Babbage's Analytic Engine is recognised by many as the first modern computer, and Ada Lovelace as the first person to write a computer program: she went so far as to recognise that a computer 'might act upon other things than numbers'. If, for instance, it was fed with a program outlining the fundamental rules of 'pitched sounds in the science of harmony and musical composition' it could compose 'scientific pieces of music'.

By now the twentieth century was very much on the horizon. After steam-driven locomotives came steam-driven ships; and Brunel would play a leading role in this new development too. The first ship he designed was the *Great Western* in 1838. This became only the second ship to cross the Atlantic entirely under steam, and was undoubtedly the fastest, averaging a speed of just under 9 knots (around 10 mph).

Brunel's innovative mind quickly grasped the salient factors regarding the new ships. Larger ships used less fuel, propellor-driven ships were superior to paddle-steamers, and the future lay in metal ships. In 1852 he supervised the building of the *Great Eastern* in the London docks. This had an iron hull, weighed 20,000 tons, was driven by twin screws, and was six times the volume of any other ship afloat. It was intended to cover the route to Australia, and had sufficient coal holds to carry enough fuel for the return journey (coal had yet to be discovered in Australia). Brunel would live just long enough to see the *Great Eastern* launched before he died of a heart attack in 1859.

World shipping was undergoing a transformation. London, as the capital and financial heart of a vast empire, soon established itself as the busiest port in the world, as well as becoming a major shipbuilding

---

35 This term is named after the twentieth-century 'inventor' of the computer Alan Turing. Put simply, it refers to a computing machine that is capable of receiving different programs and following their instructions. For example, see the algorithm in the previous note. Another algorithm might be: take the sequence: 1, 2, 3... and square each consecutive number, thus giving: 1, 4, 9...

centre. In the very year that the *Great Eastern* was launched, the French began construction of the Suez Canal. This was intended to cut sailing time from Europe to the East by more than a half. The canal was opened with much fanfare in 1869, but faulty excavation of the waterway resulted in initial scepticism regarding the project. Even so, 80 per cent of the traffic passing through the canal was British shipping to India, the Far East and Australia. The serious implications for the dominance of British shipping were evident: France potentially threatened the British Empire 'east of Suez'.

At the time, Egypt was still officially under the control of the Ottoman Empire, to which it paid annual dues. In 1875 Isma'il Pasha, the Khedive (nominal ruler) of the country, faced severe financial difficulties, and put up his 44 per cent share of the canal for £3.6 million to French buyers, or £4 million if Britain wished to purchase them. News of this reached the British prime minister Disraeli, who immediately grasped the implications of this offer: speed was of the essence. Parliament was in recess; and without parliamentary consent the Bank of England would never loan such a colossal sum (in the region of half a billion pounds in present terms). Disraeli briefed a messenger and despatched him post haste to the home of his friend, the banker Lionel de Rothschild, to ask for a loan. When Rothschild demanded on what security this loan would be made, the messenger replied simply that the British Government was the security. Rothschild agreed at once, without requiring papers or signatures, thus making one of the greatest and most decisive gentleman's agreements in history.

Disraeli's colossal gamble paid off. The cabinet was forced to back his impulsive move, and the Bank of England reluctantly agreed to put up the money to pay off Rothschild. Although most of the other shares remained in French hands (both private and government), Britain became the largest single shareholder. The route to India was now safe, and Disraeli endeared himself to Queen Victoria by suggesting that she should now be made

'Empress of India'. This delighted the queen, who had of late become vexed at the prospect of her dwindling status among European royalty. Her oldest child Victoria, the Princess Royal, was married to Frederick, heir apparent to the German Empire, and upon his succession she would have outranked her mother.

By now Britain's need to run its empire from London, as well as the general proliferation of world trade, had set in motion a revolution in communications. In 1852 it had taken a letter twelve days to be sent from London to New York, and seventy-three to Australia. By 1858 a transatlantic telegraph cable using morse code had been laid, but this broke down after three weeks. Undaunted, engineers began laying down further cables. Over the next forty years, undersea and overland cables were laid across the globe, connecting London to San Francisco and Buenos Aires. At the same time, eastbound cables linked London overland to Vladivostok, thence to Shanghai and Nagasaki, with other cables linking the capital of the British Empire to South Africa, India, Australia and New Zealand.

Meanwhile, long-overdue improvements were being made on the home front. Through July and August 1858, central London had been afflicted by what became known as the Great Stink, when hot weather compounded the stench of human excrement and industrial waste that clogged the Thames, slopping back and forth as the tides ebbed and flowed. This miasma was (wrongly) thought to have been the cause of no less than three recent outbreaks of cholera in central London. On the recommendation of Brunel, the civil engineer John Bazalgette (also of French ancestry) was commissioned to install an extensive new sewer system under central London. This was intended to channel the waste and effluents away from the Thames to pumping stations north and south of the estuary further downstream. Bazalgette would supervise the excavation and building of over eighty miles of large brick-lined sewer tunnels, interconnected with more than a thousand miles of individual street sewers. Bazalgette proved to be a man of indefatigable energy. He personally checked every connection in this huge network; his words and comments can still be seen in the volumes of linen blueprints: 'Approved JWB', 'I do not like 6' and so forth. He purposely built the sewer tunnels double the dimensions of the original designs, remarking: 'Well, we're only going to do this once, and there's always the unforeseen.' Bazalgette's work was not only quantitative, but also of high quality. Even the balconies in his pumping stations contained some of the finest examples of coloured Victorian wrought ironwork. Such was the quality of the resultant system that it is only gradually being replaced in the present century.

Upon completion of this task, Bazalgette was commissioned as chief engineer for the Shaftesbury Avenue project, the creation of a wide street through Soho, at around the same time as Haussmann was commissioned to create the boulevards of Paris. Shaftesbury Avenue was purposely driven east from Piccadilly through the rookeries, unpoliceable thieves' dens and slums that had grown up in Soho and around the notorious Seven Dials district. Bazalgette would receive a knighthood for his troubles, marking an increasing appreciation by the Victorian establishment for engineers.

Engineers were also responsible for the next development in British shipbuilding, namely the construction of HMS *Dreadnought*. This monstrous iron battleship, so successful that it would give rise to an entire new class of 'dreadnoughts', was intended to emphasise British supremacy of the sea. The original HMS *Dreadnought* was the brainchild of First Sea Lord John Fisher, who chaired the committee that designed the ship. This would be built (from keel to launch) in just four months, at a cost of almost £1.8 million. With a displacement of 20,000 tons, it had armour up to one foot thick, and twin hulls to render it unsinkable.[36] The

---

36 This was the same principle adopted six years later by the *Titanic*, which famously sank on her maiden voyage after being struck below the waterline by an iceberg.

Dreadnought was armed with ten 12-inch guns (i.e. with a muzzle one foot in diameter) each with a range of up to 11½ miles; it also boasted twenty-seven 3-inch guns, as well as eighteen submerged torpedo tubes. Making use of the new steam turbine invented by Charles Parsons in 1884, it had four screws, which gave it a speed of 21 knots (24 mph). The ship was manned by a crew of 800 officers, engineers, seamen, gunnery crews, pantrymen, medical orderlies and so forth, all living cheek by jowl with more than eleven thousand artillery shells and twenty-nine torpedoes. Following extensive sea trials, HMS *Dreadnought* entered service in 1906.

Far from demonstrating British naval superiority, this set off an arms race in navies throughout the world, from Japan to Russia, but most especially Germany. The German Empire was now ruled by Kaiser Wilhelm II, Queen Victoria's grandson, and was beginning to flex its growing industrial might. Owing in part to its geographical location, but mostly to the recent formation of Germany in 1870 as a unified country, the German Empire was aggrieved that it had only arrived at the tail-end of the European scramble to colonise the globe. Consequently, it ended up with an overseas empire little better than that of Denmark. This mainly consisted of the grasslands of Tanganyika (modern Tanzania minus Zanzibar), a few more tracts of tropical African jungle, and south-west Africa, a largely barren territory bordering on the Kalahari Desert.

After the launch of HMS *Dreadnought*, the German navy embarked upon an extensive secret naval build-up, which involved the annual construction of two dreadnoughts and one battle-cruiser (fewer armaments, but capable of a faster 24 knots). By now the German government was also spending 60 per cent of its income on building up the German army. At the same time, German engineers were busily constructing the Berlin to Baghdad railway. This was intended to reach the Persian Gulf, and thus outflank the Anglo-French-controlled Suez Canal. Others have even gone so far as to suggest that it was part of a German plan to take over the crumbling Ottoman Empire, then widely regarded as 'the sick man of Europe'.

In 1905 the English aristocrat Sir Edward Grey had been appointed Foreign Secretary. Although he would hold this office for eleven years (a tenure unprecedented to this day), Sir Edward was an unusual choice. Having been sent down from Oxford for indolence, at twenty-three he became the youngest MP in parliament. A curious choice for Foreign Secretary, he disliked foreign travel, and preferred to spend his time fly-fishing on his country estate. Sir Edward would still be head of the Foreign Office when Britain entered the First World War in 1914. In his 1925 memoirs, he would write: 'militarism and the armaments inseparable from it made war inevitable'. By then, this had become universally accepted hindsight. However, during the years leading up to this event, Sir Edward had shown no sign of recognising this fact. Indeed, when a number of quick, vital, diplomatic decisions by Britain might just have averted the war, he put out diplomatic feelers but in effect did nothing. He is best remembered for his comment on the eve of the war he had done so little to prevent: 'The lamps are going out all over Europe. We shall not see them lit again in our time.' By now it was becoming clear that London no longer led the world.

Sequence

The First World War began in August 1914. By the end of the year, the western front was complete: a continuous double line of trenches faced each other from the North Sea to Switzerland. The western line of trenches was occupied by British and French troops (including soldiers from their empires), the eastern line by German troops. The generals of each side, most of whom had never before experienced serious warfare, would periodically launch massive offensives aimed at breaking through the enemy lines. These invariably resulted in minimal advances and vast loss of life when the advancing troops were mown down by enemy machine-gun fire. As most experts have agreed, military tactics developed before the First World War did not manage to keep up with the advances in technology and had become obsolete. Huge artillery (such as the 17-inch German 'Big Bertha', which sporadically rained shells on Paris eighty miles away), gas warfare (introduced by the Germans at the 1915 Battle of Ypres, later used by both sides), the introduction of tanks and later 'flying machines', all essentially failed to break the deadlock. Consequently, over 4 million would die on the western front alone.

At sea, Britain's surface superiority was reinforced at the Battle of Jutland, when the blockaded German fleet attempted to break out of its ports, through the North Sea, into the open Atlantic. The ships of the German fleet inflicted most damage: significantly, sinking three British battlecruisers and three armed cruisers, as against losing one battlecruiser and one pre-dreadnought battleship. Despite this the German fleet was eventually forced to return to port, where they remained blockaded for the rest of the war. However, British superiority was undermined by the German introduction of the U-boat (*Unterseebot*), which preyed on the sea routes, especially between Britain and the USA, though these submarines would eventually be neutralised by fast destroyers and depth charges.

Then, in 1917, events took place that would change the face of all subsequent history. These events were totally unexpected, although they had been predicted some fifty years previously by Karl Marx. In the end, what actually happened was somewhat different from what Marx had foreseen, but would result in the same thing: revolution.

Word quickly passed along the trenches of the western front: there had been a revolution in Russia! The tsar had been overthrown and the workers had taken over. This news was widely welcomed among the rank-and-file soldiers. It is no coincidence that 1917 saw a large-scale mutiny among French troops at Verdun, and lesser mutinies among British soldiers (for example the quickly suppressed mutiny of Scottish soldiers of the Black Watch).

Marx had predicted that the revolution would take place in an advanced industrialised society, though this description certainly did not fit Russia in 1917.

Revolutionary Moscow

It had all begun in St Petersburg in February 1917, when an explosive mix of food shortages and disillusioned peasant soldiers flooding back from the German front led to widespread civil disorders. During the course of eight days of increasing anarchy, 1,700 people were shot by government troops. On 2 March Nicholas II, Tsar of all Russia and God's representative on earth in accordance with Byzantine practice, abdicated. He retired to Tsarskoye Selo, his Versailles-like palace outside St Petersburg, along with his wife Alexandra and their five children. The tsarina was unpopular with the Russian people, in part thanks to her dependence on the notorious priest Rasputin. She was also unpopular because she was German. In fact, she was the daughter of Princess Alice of Hesse, making her Queen Victoria's grandchild. Her cousin George V was the British king at the time, and the German ruler Kaiser Wilhelm II was another cousin. This all made the First World War very much a family affair at its heart.

Following the tsar's abdication, a provisional government was installed. At this point, Germany sought to capitalise on these upheavals, in the hope that they would cause Russia to withdraw from the war. The Russian revolutionary agitator Vladimir Lenin was living in exile in Zurich. In the words of Churchill, 'The German leaders turned upon Russia the most grisly of all weapons. They transported Lenin in a sealed truck like a plague bacillus from Switzerland to Russia.' On 3 April Lenin was given an ecstatic welcome by hundreds of his supporters at the Finland Station in St Petersburg.

Amid increasing tensions and public dissent, the provisional government under Alexander Kerensky vainly attempted to restore order. When news leaked out that the Kerensky government had promised the Western allies that it would not withdraw from the war, this produced even further chaos. On the night of 24/25 October 1917, in a pre-arranged plan, Lenin and his Bolshevik Party followers seized control of the city, backed by the mutineering sailors of the Kronstadt naval base.

The following day, in line with the Marxist principles that Lenin had adopted, the new regime announced the abolition of private property and the reallocation of land to the peasants. Lenin also announced that Russia would begin negotiating a peace treaty with Germany in order to withdraw from the war. These negotiations were carried out while the German army continued its advance into Russian territory, putting extreme pressure on the Bolshevik negotiators, led by Lenin's chief henchman Leon Trotsky. The Brest–Litovsk Treaty was finally signed on 3 March 1918, with the Bolsheviks forced to cede almost a third of the old European Russian Empire, including the Ukraine, the Baltic states and territory in the Caucasus. Russia also lost a third of its working railways, three-quarters of its iron ore and much of its agricultural resources. On top of this, it was forced to surrender practically its entire currency reserves.

Five days later, on 8 March, Lenin and the Bolsheviks changed the name of their party to the Russian Communist Party. And in a move imbued with deep symbolism, they transferred the Russian capital from modern St Petersburg (Russia's 'window on Europe') to Moscow, the traditional ancient capital of Russia. Moscow, with its winding alleyways of wooden houses, was dominated by the high-walled Kremlin of painted onion-domed churches. This move of the new communist government was undertaken quickly and in strictest secrecy, with most of its participants believing that it was of a purely temporary nature.

Such a preamble is necessary to place Moscow in context, for this city would lead the world in an entirely different fashion from the previous cities in this book. Moscow's leadership of the world throughout most of its early pre-eminence would be essentially ideological, in the form of communism. This aimed at a classless society with common ownership of the means of production, and full social and economic equality for all. In time, this ideology would spread, and take root, in all four continents, proving a formative influence over a much larger population and territory than even the British Empire.

Previously pre-eminent cities, such as Athens, Rome and even London, had evolved an ethos. To be a Roman citizen, or upper-class Englishman, involved a privileged view of one's position in the world. The ideology of communism, as it was developed in its Marxist-Leninist form, declared an end to such privilege, in theory at least. And it was this element of Moscow's leadership that would spread fear, and even paranoia, among the nations of Old Europe, America, Asia, and in time Africa.

At the end of the First World War, Russia descended into civil war. Much of its territory lay in ruins, overrun by warlords of the old regime (known as 'White Russians', in contrast to the 'Red' communists), invading expeditionary forces from Britain and America, even a Czechoslovak Brigade, which took over the Trans-Siberian railway and occupied various cities in Siberia. The demented Russian general, Baron von Ungern-Sternberg, and his 'Asiatic Cavalry Division' (which included sixteen different nationalities, from Chinese and Tibetans, to Poles and Tartars), took over Mongolia. Meanwhile, a large portion of the Russian upper class fled west into Europe, south from Odessa to Istanbul, and east from Vladivostok to Shanghai. Some managed to escape with sufficient funds to continue a version of their privileged life.

Others were less fortunate: generals ended up driving taxis in Paris and Berlin, dispossessed aristocratic landowners ran brothels in Shanghai, former socialites opened restaurants in Buenos Aires.

The Red Army, under Trotsky, struggled to maintain its hold on the Russian heartland. This rapidly assembled army was largely made up of sympathetic former tsarist officers and organised battalions of peasant deserters from the Imperial army. Peasants who refused to 'volunteer' were frequently shot.

Yet at the very same time, the romance, power and hope inspired by Moscow's ideology led to communist sympathisers marching in cities from Glasgow to San Francisco. And this, despite the fact that Soviet Russia itself appeared to be on the brink of total annihilation. Meanwhile, the White Army leader General Denekin was pushing north, with Moscow itself in his sights. Only a hastily patched-up agreement between Trotsky's Red Army and the anarchist 'Black Army' (Revolutionary Insurrectionary Army of Ukraine) saved the day for Moscow.

All this news, from the front and around the world, arrived daily on Lenin's desk in the Kremlin in Moscow. Reports from Trotsky, other commanders in the field, foreign newspapers, together with Lenin's network of spies and agents, both within and outside Russia, kept Lenin abreast of the unfolding clamour of events. During all Lenin's long years of exile (three in Siberia, followed by seventeen in western European cities from London and Munich to Zurich), he had been under observation – by the local police, and tsarist agents. Consequently, one of his first acts upon seizing power was to establish the Cheka, an extensive secret police similar to the Tsarist organisation it had replaced.[37] This was more than plain paranoia on Lenin's behalf: during these years he survived

---

37 Ironically, this 'secret' police soon became known for its uniform: members invariably wore full-length black leather coats and carried orange worry beads as a standard method of recognising one another.

several assassination attempts, one where he was badly wounded after delivering a public speech.

It was Lenin's decision to rule according to so-called Marxist-Leninist principles. These differed from plain Marxist ideas, and adapted them to conditions in Russia, which was not the advanced industrialised society Marx had foreseen. Marxist-Leninist ideas required a post-revolutionary stage of socialism, with the establishment of an elite group to take charge of setting up the 'dictatorship of the proletariat'. This was handled by the Central Committee of senior party members, one of whose initial acts was the setting up of soviets (workers committees) to run the factories.

Initially, the Central Committee conducted fairly widespread discussions on matters of principle. Should the aim of the Russian Revolution be to extend the Revolution worldwide? Or should communism first be firmly established in Russia? Lenin was a masterful political manipulator, and no matter the views expressed in the Central Committee, he always seemed to get his way in the end. Lenin's tactics were carefully studied, in particular by one of the younger members of the Committee – the Georgian-born Joseph Stalin, who was not yet forty.[38]

Stalin had little time for Jews, and was quick to note the hero's reception received by Trotsky, who was Jewish, when he returned to the Central Committee after achieving victory in the civil war. By the early 1920s it was beginning to look as if Trotsky was being lined up as a successor to the ailing Lenin, who had already begun to show the strain of his constant over-working. Some were even seriously beginning to question the wisdom of his decisions. When faced with widespread urban food and supply shortages,

---

38 It is remarkable that so many of the most powerful leaders in world history were born at the outer extremities of the country they came to rule. Alexander the Great was born in Macedonia, an outlying province of the Greek world. Napoleon on the island of Corsica; Stalin in far-off Georgia; and Hitler was not even born in Germany, but just across the border at the edge of Austria.

as well as an agriculture sector ravaged by civil war, Lenin went back on his Marxist-Leninist principles. His policy of War Communism, whereby goods and agricultural products could be seized during emergencies, simply wasn't working. Eighty per cent of the population were peasants, who gave up producing more than their own needs. Meanwhile, the cities were starving, and workers were fleeing for the countryside simply to find food. To overcome these difficulties Lenin decided on the drastic step of introducing his New Economic Policy. In a party speech in 1921 he announced that Russia was reverting to 'a free market and capitalism, both subject to state control'. And in the cities, enterprises would be permitted to operate on a profit basis, in an attempt to eliminate the widespread black market that had sprung up, introducing a creeping corruption into the communism system.

Lenin faced a dilemma. The Revolution he had led was in trouble, and he appeared to have relapsed into the old bourgeois view that 'Politics is the art of the possible'. The ideals of the Revolution were being sacrificed for pragmatism.

As if this wasn't bad enough, in the eyes of many of his colleagues, Lenin continued to indulge Trotsky's increasingly peremptory behaviour, including the 'militarisation of labour', which went against the New Economic Policy. Lenin admitted that Trotsky was 'in love with organisation', while in practical politics 'he has not got a clue'. Yet still Lenin did nothing. And to top it all, he continued to support the 'internationalist' Anatoly Lunacharsky as People's Commissar for Education, with additional responsibility for the Arts. Lunacharsky had launched a campaign for the preservation of historic buildings, when zealous Bolsheviks were bent on destroying these symbols of the detested past. In the eyes of many, Lunacharsky also gave his support to a whole lot of avant-garde claptrap, with garish modernist propaganda posters plastered all over the streets, and so-called 'agit-prop' trains making whistle-stop tours spreading revolutionary ideas and poetry all over the country. A leading role in the latter was played by the formidable Futurist poet Vladimir Mayakovsky, a giant of a man with a scowling face and shaven skull, who delighted in bawling out his avant-garde poems through a megaphone, rousing the people to support the new regime. But the trouble was, the people didn't seem to understand this type of poetry. They still preferred the quaint homilies and hackneyed classics of yesteryear. The dichotomy between the 'old' and the 'new' was becoming increasingly contentious. In the ideal new society, what should be preserved and what should be transformed?

This question went to the very heart of society, and what it should be. Similar questions had been raised by the Ancient Greek philosophers, who had come to their own contradictory conclusions. But where the Revolution was concerned, there was only one philosophy that could decide the matter: Marxism. This also was utopian, yet unlike Plato it did not describe this utopia. Marx merely outlined the means to realise it: install a 'dictatorship of the proletariat', a classless society where all were free. But free to do what?

The period immediately following the Revolution saw Moscow's emergence as a leading artistic capital of Europe. Indeed, where the whole gamut of avant-garde art and modernism were concerned, it came to be seen, briefly, as a rival to Paris. The painter Marc Chagall had left Russia in 1910 at the age of twenty-three to escape the anti-Semitic pogroms taking place in the shtetl (the 'Jewish settlement' areas of western Russia). He settled in Paris, but would return just before the Revolution, his paintings imbued with a unique blend of naïf art, cubism and expressionism. He recognised that the Revolution had turned Russia 'upside down, the way I turn my pictures'. Following the Revolution, Lunacharsky (who had met Chagall in Paris) appointed him Artistic Director of the provincial town of

Vitebsk, where Chagall had grown up. Here he opened an art school 'open to all without age restrictions or admission fee'. Its approach to teaching attracted a number of established Moscow modernist artists to join its staff.

Chagall's naive character was not suited to administration though, or to dealing with the idealistic squabbles of his staff, who were largely sophisticated urbanites. He left Vitebsk for Moscow, where he began painting huge dreamlike backdrops for the theatre. These were variously described as 'Hebrew jazz in paint' and 'a storehouse of symbols and devices'. After a period of poverty, Chagall would return in Paris in 1923.

The Moscow-born painter Wassily Kandinsky was also attracted back to Russia prior to the Revolution, where he became a close friend of Lunacharsky. Abroad in Munich, his art had evolved through impressionism and expressionism to an increasing abstraction. He is generally recognised as the first abstract artist. In Moscow, together with Lunarcharsky, he set up the Museum of Painting. But Kandinsky's abstract art, far from being purely materialist, also expressed a spiritual outlook on life, and he began to question the direction the Revolution was taking. As he wrote:

> The sun melts all of Moscow down to a single spot that, like a mad tuba, starts all of the heart and all of the soul vibrating. But no, this uniformity of red is not the most beautiful hour. It is only the final chord of a symphony that takes every colour to the zenith of life that, like the fortissimo of a great orchestra, is both compelled and allowed by Moscow to ring out.

In 1922 he too would leave Russia, returning to Germany where he joined the Bauhaus, whose stated aim was: 'To attempt to unify the principles of mass production with individual artistic vision and to combine aesthetics with everyday function.' This could have been (and perhaps should have been) the ambition of Moscow's new Revolutionary art scene too. Ironically, the one to recognise this was Adolf Hitler, who in 1933 closed down the Bauhaus on the grounds of its 'communist intellectualism'.

A further twist was added to the new Russian art scene by Vladimir Tatlin, who had been born in Moscow in 1885. Tatlin's prolific activities spread over painting, sculpture, architecture and design. He is best remembered today for the so-called Tatlin Tower. This 1,300-foot spiral tower made of glass and iron was intended to surpass the Eiffel Tower in both scale complexity and utility. Its double-helix spirals contract as they rise, giving the illusion of leaning, and the entire structure is supported by a large diagonal steel girder. Its lowest level contained a large glass cube, intended to revolve once a year. This was to house the legislature of the Comintern (the Communist International organisation working for world revolution). The volume contained above this, which made one revolution a month, was a pyramid intended for the Comintern executive. Above this was a cylinder, turning one revolution a day, to house the Comintern propaganda services. And at the peak of the tower was a hemisphere, revolving hourly, to house the Comintern radio station, capable of broadcasting through a loudspeaker, as well as projecting slogans onto the clouds in the sky.

Here was a symbolic combination of architecture and sculpture, which in its way expressed the communist ideal as explicitly as the Bauhaus. It had a clarity of purpose that still seemed to elude the politicians. It was also, in the words of the twenty-first-century US architect Kim Grant, an 'ironic monument to the economic and technological limitations of early Soviet life'.

However, all that Tatlin was ever to build of his tower was a 22-foot steel model. The fate of Tatlin's actual model remains a mystery, though various copies of it have since been constructed in Paris, London and even Moscow. It is also claimed that some decades later a follower of Tatlin adapted his design to construct two pylons carrying heavy electric cables across a wide river in eastern Russia, where they are said to stand to this day, unrecognised, yet fulfilling their purpose.

This art as metaphor, metaphor as art, would extend one stage further with the painting of Kazimir Malevich, who began as a Futurist but went on to invent Suprematism. This was to be an abstract art founded upon 'the supremacy of pure artistic feeling'. Its supreme and characteristic work is a black square, followed some years later by 'white on white'.

In so many ways, the description of these artists and their works tells it all. It would be difficult to dream up such a symbolic resumé of the development and fate of post-Revolutionary Russian life. Here, indeed, was a cast of exemplary characters.

During these years any number of distinguished western foreigners visited Moscow to see first-hand what the 'great new experiment' was all about. The socialist-inclined philosopher Bertrand Russell visited Moscow in 1920, and had a half-hour meeting with Lenin, about whom he remained ambivalent. Russell couldn't help but admire Lenin, remarking of him, 'statesmen of his calibre do not appear in the world more than once in a century'. But he balked at Lenin's rigid orthodoxy, and 'the wisdom of holding a creed so firmly that for its sake men are willing to inflict widespread misery'. Lying in his hotel bed, 'in the middle of the night I would hear shots, and know that idealists were being killed in prison'.

The economist Maynard Keynes would visit Moscow in 1925, on his honeymoon with his Russian wife Lydia, a former ballerina. Keynes was appalled on several grounds: 'I am not ready for a creed which does not care how much it destroys the liberty and security of daily life.' And yet he couldn't help asking himself: 'was it just possible that Soviet communism might represent the first stirrings of a great religion', that beneath its cruelty and stupidity 'some spark of the ideal might be hid'? Such was, and would remain, Bolshevik Russia's strongest secret weapon: hope, and its apparent contrast with the class-ridden inequalities of the West, which were particularly evident at this time.

The American expressionist dancer and free spirit Isadora Duncan visited Moscow in 1921 when she was forty-six, nearing the end of her wayward career. She was so enamoured of the city that she decided to take up residence in Russia and even became a Soviet citizen. A year later she married the blond lyric poet Sergei Yesenin, who was thirty-one years her junior. The marriage would last just over a year, and would not survive her return to the West.

In 1922 Lenin's health went into serious decline, and after a series of heart attacks he died in 1924, aged just fifty-three. There followed a serious division in the Central Committee, ostensibly over whether Russia should support a worldwide revolution, or instead pursue 'socialism in one country'.

Another element of division among the members of the Central Committee had been the New Economic Policy (NEP). This had functioned so well economically that by 1928 agricultural production had returned to 1913 levels. This led to the anomalous position where the agricultural sector, which was in private hands and run in capitalist fashion, was succeeding far better than the ailing urban factories, which were all state-owned and under soviet control.

Here again Trotsky and Stalin had headed two opposing factions. Trotsky, ever the more radical, more intellectual communist, maintained that the Revolution would only succeed if the state controlled the entire economy. Stalin, on the other hand, agreed with the more moderate faction, which had supported Lenin and the need for the NEP as a temporary measure to get the country back on its feet.

The latter was supported by Stalin, while Trotsky was in favour of the 'permanent revolution' preached by Marx. Stalin became chairman of the Central Committee, and a long, bitter power struggle ensued, which ended with Trotsky being banished to remote Kazakhstan in 1927. Two years later he was expelled from the USSR altogether.

As soon as Trotsky was ousted, Stalin immediately reversed his position on the NEP. The latter was abolished, and in 1928 a new Five Year Plan put in its place. This idealist, innocent-sounding name involved a grim reality. Groups of armed party heavies were despatched to the countryside to seize stocks of hoarded grain, which was sent to feed the workers in the cities. They also enforced to the letter the requirements of the Five Year Plan. All land was seized, especially smallholdings that had been developed by peasant farmers. The dispossessed peasants were then herded onto large collective farms, where they were set to work on a communal basis and given production targets. Wholesale buyers and sellers of grain – middlemen and entrepreneurs who had profited from the NEP – were labelled 'enemies of the people', or 'kulaks'. As historian Robert Conquest wrote, even peasants with 'a couple more cows or farms with six acres more than their neighbours' were labelled kulaks. The first stage of Stalin's Five Year Plan called for the 'eradication of the kulak class'. Effectively, this meant they were shot, or shipped off to labour camps.

It quickly became clear that 'collectivisation' was not working, and famine began spreading across the Ukraine, the Volga basin and other agricultural regions. By 1932 millions were dying of starvation. When news of this eventually leaked out to the wider world, America, Britain and many other countries offered relief aid, but Stalin refused to accept such 'capitalist bribes'. Stalin's power was now such that even his closest political supporters on the Central Committee were afraid to try and dissuade him from the unfolding disaster, as millions more died while the trainloads of seized grain began pouring into Moscow and other cities.

Moscow now entered the era of mushroom government. Keep the people in the dark, like mushrooms in a shed, and every now and again throw in a bucket of shit. Reality became warped like a nightmare version of Lewis Carroll's *Alice Through the Looking Glass*, and all manner of weird and wonderful growths began to flourish in this shit-blitzed darkness beyond the laws of reality.

A strong contestant for the most surreal and exotic of all the blighted growths that emerged during this period must surely be the agronomist and biologist Trofim Lysenko, who came up with an utterly original theory that not only contradicted science but also conformed with Marxist theory.

Lysenko had been born in 1898, the son of an impeccably pro-letarian family of Ukrainian peasants. Stalin was much impressed by this pedigree, which matched his own humble upbringing. He was even more impressed by the vast agricultural improvements promised by the theory Lysenko proposed. All this from a man who had barely received an education. What could be better in a new socialist world? While Lysenko was still in his early thirties his theories were taken up by the Party. Lysenko would eventually become Director of Genetics at the Academy of Sciences, where his word became law.

So what was this revolutionary idea that promised increased crop yields, at the very time when they were most needed? Darwinism states that animals, plants and seeds have stable characteristics, encoded in their genes, which are passed on to the next generation. Lysenko would have none of this. Such ideas were reactionary, typical of farming by the capitalists. Instead, Lysenko taught that if plants and seeds could be suitably treated they could change. Environment alone, not genes, dictated how a plant developed. Exposing wheat seeds to the cold would result in cold-resistant wheat that could be grown out of season, thus doubling the crop. Plucking all the leaves off a bush would render its descendants leafless. With suitable exposure, even orange trees could be made to grow in Siberia.

Such ideas not only conformed to Marxist social theory, but they even pointed the way ahead. If people could inherit characteristics acquired during the previous generation, it was possible for a soviet government to instil good communist principles in the peasants and the urban proletariat. As a result, they would give birth to a new species of 'soviet man'. Stalin loved this idea: here at last was a science that was comprehensible, and 'politically correct'.[39]

Lysenko's ideas on plant inheritance quickly took hold as the new orthodoxy. Scientists who refused to believe such nonsense were quickly rounded up by the men in long black leather coats and incarcerated in prisons or psychiatric wards. Others were simply shot. In hindsight, it has been estimated that Lysenko's ideas set back Russian plant genetics, which had previously been on a par with the finest in the West, by as much as fifty years.

Another rarity to emerge during this period was the composer Dmitri Shostakovich. He had been born in 1906, and soon exhibited the characteristics of a child prodigy: prodigious talent, socially gauche behaviour and a retiring manner. By the age of nine he could repeat long stretches of piano music after just one hearing. At the age of thirteen he was admitted to the Conservatoire. This was 1919, making him the first Russian composer to be entirely educated under the Soviet system. His music fizzed with original ideas. To support himself during these years he played the piano in a cinema.

At the age of twenty, Shostakovich wrote his First Symphony. His biographer Laurel Fay comments on the curious mixture of

---

39 This much-misused term was originally coined by Lenin, to describe ideas that conformed to Marxist-Leninism.

'emotional restraint' and 'riveting rhythmic drive' exhibited by this work. This chimed with the feelings of many in the post-World War world, which became characterised as the Jazz Age. And Shostakovich's symphony was soon being acclaimed from America to Poland. By the early 1930s he had completed an opera, *Lady Macbeth of Mtsinsk District*, an unabashedly modernist work, with clashing chords and garish, yet deeply moving scenes. This proved an immediate success with both the public and the Party critics, who declared it 'could only have been written by a Soviet composer brought up in the best tradition of Soviet culture'. Here surely was Lysenkoism in the arts.

Around this time, Stalin decided after a hard day's work at the Kremlin he would have a night out. He enjoyed going to the opera, and went to hear Shostakovich's *Lady Macbeth*. He and his entourage were noted wincing at some of the loud climaxes, and during the poignant love scene they burst out laughing. At the end, they filed out of their box without a word, while Shostakovich took his curtain bows, his face 'white as a sheet'.

Two days later a review of Shostakovich's opera appeared in the Party newspaper *Pravda* ('Truth'). Under the title 'Muddle instead of Music', the review proceeded to lambast 'this deliberately dissonant, muddled stream of sounds... quacks, hoots, pants and gasps'. Unaccountably, Shostakovich escaped more serious punishment.

The year 1936 marked the beginning of the Great Terror, when the increasingly paranoid Stalin launched a purge of 'counter-revolutionaries', 'enemies of the people', Trotskyists and 'social deviants'. This started with generals and high-up officers in the Red Army being rounded up and flung into the cells of the notorious Lubyanka, the vast building that housed the headquarters of Stalin's notorious secret police. Having eliminated a large number of leaders of the Soviet armed forces, he then proceeded through the professions, and went on to include all ranks of society. 'Show Trials' were staged, where important figures were forced to confess to treason, acts of sabotage, even 'contacts with reactionary foreign elements'. Having made their confessions the victims were led off to be transported to Siberian labour camps, or simply shot. In this looking-glass world, many loyal comrades, who could not believe that Stalin was capable of such measures, died proclaiming 'Long Live Stalin!' before their firing squads.

Convinced that the secret police would soon be banging on his door in the middle of the night, Shostakovich, instead of going to bed, took to sitting in a chair beside his front door in a warm overcoat, his packed suitcase beside him, waiting to be shipped off to Siberia.

Fear pervaded everything – even impacting honoured 'heroes of the Soviet Union'. In a desperate effort to produce some genuinely positive news for Stalin, his underlings discovered a coal miner in the Donbass region, called Andrei Stakhanov, who was single-handedly producing prodigious amounts of coal. On 31 August 1935 he was recorded as producing 102 tons in 5 hours 43 mins. This was fourteen times his expected quota. Stalin was mightily impressed when he heard of this feat, and a campaign was launched to turn Stakhanov into a Soviet hero. This boost to public morale produced the Stakhanovite Movement. Workers who greatly exceeded their production targets were awarded medals, named 'heroes of the Soviet Union' and accorded the honour of being made 'Stakhanovites'. As part of this campaign, thousands of propaganda posters were produced glorifying Alexey Stakhanov. However, the information supplied to the campaign managers had featured a man called simply 'A. Stakhanov', and the managers had wrongly guessed that the 'A' stood for Alexey. When the mistake was discovered, everyone was terrified that Stalin would find out about it, so Andrei Stakhanov was bullied into accepting the name Alexey, and thus became famous as someone else.

Meanwhile, Stalin continued as 'the man of steel'. Party officials summoned to see him in the Kremlin were often so terrified that they would be sent to Siberia, or shot, that they shat themselves while waiting in the outer office. The secretaries quickly assembled a wardrobe of spare trousers, so that the officials could enter Stalin's presence in a suitably odourless state.

Stalin remained blissfully unaware of this, and many other such things taking place. (Though he remained very much aware of the main events: all lists of those to be sent to the camps, or shot, had first to be checked and initialled by Stalin himself. They were then sent to other leading officials to be initialled, so that if there were any 'mistakes', the blame could be apportioned where Stalin saw fit.)

Stalin now decided that Muscovites needed something to raise their spirits, something to make its population of over two million proud of their city. After four years of hectic underground work on a 'secret' project that none could escape noticing, it was announced in 1934 that Moscow was opening a new metro system that would be the envy of the world. This network would for once prove even more sensational than its preceding propaganda.

The trains and tunnels were much like those of other city metros in London, Paris or New York. But it was the underground stations themselves that were the sensation. These were described as nothing less than 'Palaces of the People' – and indeed they were. Constructed in a style known as 'Soviet Classicism', these vast underground edifices consisted of huge marble halls, complete with rows of pillared arches lit with candelabras. The world had seen nothing like it (before or since).

The Moscow Metro was of course dedicated to its creator, designer and builder, the supreme leader Comrade Joseph Stalin himself. However, supervision of this project was entrusted to the thirty-two-year-old Nikita Khrushchev, a former herdsboy from an impoverished village in Ukraine whose rough-and-ready charm appealed to Stalin. Other senior members of the Central Committee were delegated to run subsidiary departments in the construction of the mammoth project. This was to be an all-or-nothing affair. If it succeeded, 'Stalin's Metro' would become one of the wonders of the modern world. If it failed to live up to such expectations, in any way, heads would roll. This much was obvious to all concerned, from Khrushchev down to the thousands of 'volunteer' diggers. To overcome inevitable difficulties (such as deep winter freezing of the earth, and the destruction of innumerable building foundations) the tunnels were set to be dug at least thirty feet underground. Even so, progress continued to lag.

In a bold move, overseen but not signed off by Stalin, an appeal was made to the British government for the loan of a modern tunnelling shield, such as had recently been used to extend London's underground system. The shield was duly shipped to Moscow, and within months meticulously engineered copies of this machine were at work.

The opening of the Moscow Metro system in 1935 proved to be a huge success, and soon Muscovites were piling in to view the huge 'palaces' with their vast marble halls, heroic mosaics and wide arched passageways stretching far into the distance. Here was a modern subterranean equivalent of the multi-coloured onion-dome towers of the Kremlin – which were monuments of national pride, even though they were of course monuments to a forbidden religion. Yet, as with the Kremlin, the Moscow Metro also had its anomalous elements.

Alongside the public Moscow Metro system, a second secret 'Metro 2' was built. For years, this remained nothing more than a rumour. Few Muscovites, and even fewer foreigners, believed in the existence of such a folly. How could there be such a thing? Who, or what, could it be for? To this day, the existence of Metro 2 remains shrouded in secrecy. It is said to provide fast links between the Kremlin, offices of the secret services, military headquarters and other clandestine organisations. Over the years it has been developed and is now said to provide suitably luxurious emergency accommodation for high-ranking officials if ever Moscow comes under attack, as well as an escape line running twenty miles beyond the city to the VIP lounge of Vnukovo Airport.

Stalin blithely persisted with his Five Year Plan, which besides putting an end to Lenin's New Economic Policy, aimed at a drastic industrialisation of the economy, with a goal of a 250 per cent increase in industrial development. In fact, the plan achieved an increase of just 50 per cent in industrial output – something of a miracle in itself. The massacre of the kulaks, the failure of the collective farms and a famine in which millions died were deemed irrelevant, and in 1933 a new Five Year Plan came into force, with the declared aim of continuing the objectives of the 'successful' first plan. Stalin himself undertook a tour of the factories and collective farms, where he was shown production lines and fields of happy workers. Asked in a foreign interview what he thought characterised Soviet life, Stalin paused for a moment, before replying 'Unbridled joy.'

Meanwhile, pedestrians on the wide, car-free boulevards of Moscow, audiences in the cinemas, travellers on the new underground system, all made sure they wore clothes that didn't stand out, or in any way express individuality. The cowed, purposely drab Muscovites provided a curious contrast as they shuffled beneath the chandeliers and through the splendid marble halls of Moscow's new showcase. Visitors from abroad were particularly impressed by this marvel as they were led around the city, taking in this and other such sights as the arched arcades of GUM

(Main Universal Store), the multi-level department store whose windows were brimming with caviar, premium Russian vodka and other luxury items. One of a chain of similar stores in Russia's largest cities, this was proclaimed as 'democratising consumption for workers and peasants alike'. In fact, only high-ranking Party members were permitted entry. In 1932, when Stalin's long-suffering wife Nadezhda committed suicide, one shop window was used to display her body to the mourning public.

And still the foreign visitors arrived – the curious, the idealists, the ever-hopeful, come to see for themselves the 'World of the Future' in the Soviet Union. The British writer H.G. Wells, whose translated science-fiction works sold well in the Soviet Union, visited Moscow several times. In 1934 he was even allowed to interview Stalin; on emerging he declared: 'I have never met a man more fair, candid and honest.' The Nobel-Prize-winning Irish-born author and progressive playwright G.B. Shaw declared, 'I can't die without having seen the USSR.' On a visit in 1931 he was escorted around Moscow in an open chauffeur-driven limousine. After his meeting with Stalin, he said: 'I expected to see a Russian worker and I found a Georgian gentleman.' When Shaw was asked on his return to the real side of the looking glass about the famines in Russia, he replied that these could not possibly exist as in Moscow he 'ate the most slashing dinner in his life'.

Despite the purges, top-level scientists were regarded as a protected species, largely because Stalin could not understand what they did, but recognised their prestige in the outside world. Pyotr Kapitsa was an internationally recognised physicist who lived and worked in Cambridge, England, where he was regarded as the 'favourite son' of Ernest Rutherford, the father of nuclear physics. A garrulous larger-than-life character, Kapitsa wore a Russian-style heavy fur coat and delighted in telling stories in Kapitzarene, a hybrid language that appeared to be a mix of English, French, German and Russian. (It was even said that he spoke his native Russian in a similar fashion.) As a loyal Russian and a loyal communist he always returned to Russia during the summer holidays to see his parents and discuss physics with his Soviet counterparts. Then, in 1934, Stalin issued an order refusing him permission to travel back to Cambridge. Instead, he created for Kapitsa his very own Institute for Physical Problems in Moscow. When it became clear that Kapitsa would not be returning to Cambridge, Rutherford ensured that all Kapitsa's laboratory equipment was shipped to him in Moscow, where it was installed in Kapitsa's new Institute.

In 1937, the twenty-nine-year-old Lev Landau, already a world-rated physicist, was appointed head of the Institute's theoretical division. But in 1938 the reckless and exasperated Landau compared the Soviet Union to Nazi German and fascist Italy. He was immediately arrested and taken to the forbidding Lubyanka Prison, run by the NKVD. Kapitsa wrote a personal letter to Stalin explaining the importance of Landau's work, and his high regard in the West. He also rashly vouched for any future behaviour by Landau, who was then released. Years later, Landau would head the team that developed the first Soviet atomic bomb.

At the same time as Kapitsa was drawn back into the Soviet Union, many of its leading physicists were desperate to get out. One such scientist was the highly original physicist and ingenious character George Gamow, who had been a close friend of Landau at university. Between 1928 and 1931, while still in his early twenties, Gamow was chosen to represent the Soviet Union at scientific conferences in Europe, even working with Rutherford at Cambridge. Back in the Soviet Union he played a significant role in the construction of the country's first cyclotron (the early form of particle accelerator). Then, in 1931, he was abruptly refused permission to visit Europe. Undeterred, Gamow travelled with his new young wife to the Black Sea, where he launched a collapsible kayak and attempted, along with his wife, to row 150 miles across the Black Sea to Turkey. When this was thwarted by bad weather, he travelled to Murmansk on the White Sea and attempted a similar kayak trip to Arctic Norway, but was once again forced back by bad weather. Amazingly, the authorities remained unaware of both of these attempted escapes. Equally amazingly, and possibly as a result of a bureaucratic oversight, in 1933 Gamow and his wife were allowed to travel to the prestigious annual Solway Conference in Brussels – unsurprisingly they never returned to Russia. Gamow ended up in the United States, where several of his ideas were instrumental in the Manhattan Project to build the US atomic bomb, though he was not himself permitted to work on this secret project.

It proved more difficult to impose Marxist orthodoxy in advanced mathematics, which was largely beyond the understanding of the party hacks and the fearful, or compromised, mathematicians they relied upon. This meant that mathematics had a freedom that was not always apparent in the other scientific disciplines. Consequently, Moscow would in time become one of the twentieth century's most thriving mathematical centres. Pre-eminent here was Andrey Kolmogorov, rated by many (and not just in the Soviet Union) as the finest mathematician of the twentieth century.

Kolmogorov was different from the outset. His mother belonged to a family of the nobility but was unmarried when she died giving birth to Kolmogorov in 1903. His father is thought to have been a political exile, and Kolmogorov was brought up by his mother's two sisters on the estate of their wealthy grandfather. Kolmogorov's prodigious mathematical talents emerged early. By the age of five, he was writing in his notebook a regular series he had discovered: $1 = 1^2, 1 + 3 = 2^2, 1 + 3 + 5 = 3^2, 1 + 3 + 5 + 7 = 4^2...$

The young Kolmogorov advanced his study of mathematics by studying articles in the multi-volume *Brockhaus and Efron Encyclopedic Dictionary*. This was sufficiently advanced to include set theory, the latest significant advance in the foundations of mathematics. At the age of seven, Kolmogorov's aunt Vera officially adopted him and took him to Moscow to further his education. At the age of seventeen, in the midst of the civil war, he entered Moscow University, where he studied under the charismatic Nikolai Luzin. In the group that had formed around Luzin he met the highly talented topologist Pavel Alexandrov, with whom he would form a close emotional attachment that lasted the rest of his life.

In 1930 Kolmogorov travelled to Göttingen in Germany, at the time the epicentre of world mathematics. Even among such brilliant company, Kolmogorov shone. In 1933, after his return to Moscow, he wrote a ground-breaking paper that established the foundations of probability theory, one of his greatest achievements. By now, however, the authorities knew of Kolmogorov's illegal homosexual relationship with Alexandrov, and when Luzin was accused of 'mathematical mysticism' in 1936, Kolmogorov and Alexandrov were blackmailed into giving evidence against their former teacher, who was lucky to receive just a sentence of provincial exile.

In the following years, Kolmogorov developed numerous theories, many on stochastic variables (random processes linked to probability theory). When the Second World War came, Kolmogorov would develop a scheme for the stochastic distribution of barrage balloons to combat German bombers over Moscow.[40]

After the war, Kolmogorov would play a leading role in setting up Moscow schools for exceptional mathematical students, a forcing ground that would establish Moscow as the leading

---

40 Contrary to popular belief, large, high-altitude barrage balloons were not in themselves obstacles to enemy aircraft. The damage was done by the steel cables that tethered them to the ground. Invisible at night, these sliced through the wing of any aircraft that passed close to them.

mathematical centre in the years following the Second World War. Kolmogorov also continued to develop mathematical ideas in a wide range of fields, including algorithmic information, computer theory and much besides. These original ideas were published in Soviet mathematical journals, only a few of which would reach the West, where language barriers meant that the original ideas they contained were often overlooked. In this way, many of the advances that Kolmogorov made would be repeated years later in the West. In Moscow, even mathematical journals fell into the category of 'restricted information' and remained state secrets.

Stalin trusted no one, so it came as something of a surprise when in 1939 he signed a peace treaty with Hitler and Nazi Germany. This was presented to the Soviet public as a 'capitulation' by the fascists.

Despite Stalin receiving repeated warning from his spies in Germany, he continued to trust Hitler. Two years later, the long shit-blitz in the Soviet Union turned into a real blitz, as three million Nazis invaded the Soviet Union along a 1,800-mile front, catching the Red Army unprepared and even partially demobilised. Within months, the German army had swept through almost half of European Russia, with forward patrols reaching the western end of the Moscow tramline, where they were only halted by the early onset of the severe Russian winter.

In an event that chimed with the surreal atmosphere of the time, Stalin now decided to hold the traditional military parade in Red Square marking the anniversary of the October Revolution. Loud military bands led columns of marching soldiers, tanks and even horse-drawn troop-carts, as they proceeded across the red-brick-paved square past silent, watching crowds, muffled in their heavy, snow-flecked overcoats. Stalin and his dignitaries looked down from the balcony on top of the Lenin Mausoleum, inside which the former leader's mummified body had been laid out beneath a glass case. In a departure from standard practice, Stalin himself addressed the people: 'We have temporarily fallen under the yoke of German brigands.' The watching crowd was bewildered. They all knew what Stalin looked like, from the many portraits of him that adorned public buildings and the photos of him that regularly appeared in the newspapers. But they had never before listened to him speak, and were astonished to hear his thick Georgian accent, regarded by many xenophobic Muscovites as the epitome of provincial vulgarity.

In the official commentary accompanying the newsreel of the Red Square celebrations, the audiences were assured that the Red Army units taking part in the parade were promptly redeployed to the front immediately after the event.

Evolving photo of Stalin as his companions fell from power.

The annual parades held in Red Square to mark the anniversary of the October Revolution also provided another anomaly of the through-the-looking-glass variety. Each year, Stalin and his line of dignitaries on the balcony would appear in the official photographs of the Red Square celebrations. Yet as the years passed, figures began to vanish from these photographs, retrospectively replaced with air-brushed gaps where the dignitaries who had fallen from power had once stood. In a parallel move, official histories were rewritten to accommodate the fact that these people had never officially existed. Not for nothing would George Orwell begin his soviet-style dystopian novel *1984* with the memorable sentence: 'It was a bright day in April, and the clocks were striking thirteen.' Stalin's henchmen vanished into empty space, but Stalin himself remained. Just like the all-seeing, all-knowing Big Brother who dominated Orwell's dystopia.

In December 1941 Stalin and his inner circle received the British Foreign Minister Anthony Eden at a banquet in the Kremlin. With the German guns audible in the distant night, and generals hurrying in to report from the front, Eden offered Stalin British and American aid. This time Stalin decided to accept, and soon convoys were crossing the Arctic Sea to Murmansk bringing vital supplies and aid for Moscow.

The German army, like Napoleon, was unprepared for the extreme severity of the Russian winter, where temperatures plunged to -20 °C. Under such conditions, horse-drawn troop-carts easily outperformed tracked military troop carriers, whose fuel froze in their engines. Stalin transported entire factories by rail east towards the Urals, along with all manner of vital personnel (even poets); at the same time the reassembled Red Army prepared for a counter-offensive. Faced with the sheer weight of numbers, and the overstretching of its supply lines, the Nazi army was checked in its tracks.

The Red Army was headed by General Georgy Zhukov, a tough character and skilled military tactician, who had unaccountably survived Stalin's 1936 purge of the upper echelons of the Red Army. Stalin's leading ministers watched aghast as he now chose to launch another purge of the Red Army, this time for their treacherous unawareness of the Nazi surprise attack. Zhukov was relieved of his post, but was eventually allowed to 'assist' in the desperate defence of Stalingrad, the last Soviet outpost preventing the German army from pouring south to capture the vital oilfields of the Caucasus. Stalin's U-turn on Zhukov proved an astute move, and in February 1943 the Red Army line held at Stalingrad, before spilling out in a brilliant tactical move to encircle the German invaders, leading to the surrender of General von Paulus and the entire German 6th Army.

Despite Zhukov's role in the do-or-die victory at Stalingrad, it would not be until November 1944 that he was reappointed to full command of the Red Army for the long, bitter and merciless drive on Berlin. Meanwhile, Stalin made a rare trip out of Moscow, travelling south to the Black Sea resort of Yalta. Here he held a conference with the American leader Franklin D. Roosevelt and the British prime minister Winston Churchill to decide upon the shape of the post-war world. Stalin held his ground, negotiating with *realpolitik*, where his colleagues across the table attempted principles and reason. Stalin insisted upon retaining 'influence' over the territories conquered by the Red Army, at one point demanding derisively: 'How many divisions does the Pope have?'

The Soviet Union would emerge from the Second World War (still remembered in Russia as the 'Great War') as one of the two world superpowers, the other being the United States. Moscow communism led the world, or a large part of it (soon to include China). In a speech, Churchill would lament the fact that: 'From

Stettin in the Baltic to Trieste in the Adriatic, an iron curtain has descended across the Continent.'

It was now that Moscow's ideological strength emerged at its most formidable. Although the USSR controlled the eastern half of Europe, in western Europe influential intellectuals, as well as many members of the resistance movements who had fought the Nazis, favoured Marxist ideas. In France this included leading figures such as the existentialist philosophers Sartre and Camus. In Italy, the CIA was forced to prop up successive anti-communist governments. In Britain, Soviet spies held leading positions in the intelligence services and among the scientific community.

When in 1945 the new US president Harry S. Truman met Stalin at Potsdam outside Berlin, and divulged to him the secret that America was building an atomic bomb, Stalin didn't bat an eyelid: he already knew the secret, and the Soviet Union was by now pressing ahead to build its own bomb. At the same time, Stalin ensured that the German rocket scientists he had captured were set to work on a pioneer Soviet space programme (just as the Americans were doing the same with Wernher von Braun and their own captured German rocket scientists).

Stalin would finally die in his dacha just outside Moscow in March 1953 at the age of seventy-four. His death proved a traumatic event for all Soviet citizens, the large majority of whom had known no other ruler. Stalin's body was embalmed, and hundreds of thousands of Muscovites, many of them weeping uncontrollably, crammed into Red Square for his funeral. His preserved body was placed alongside that of Lenin in the Mausoleum.

Though Stalin may have died, his legacy lived on in social control, scientific advances and an international network of spies that was almost as efficient as the internal Soviet version. The world was caught by surprise when in 1957 the USSR announced the launch of the first sputnik satellite. People all around the globe raised their eyes to the night sky to witness this achievement. Another superlative propaganda coup occurred in 1961, when Soviet cosmonaut Yuri Gagarin became the first man in space. By now Moscow led the world in both scientific achievement and ideological influence. Countries from Cuba to the Congo began to embrace communism.

Only in material comforts did the materialist society lag behind the decadent capitalist West. The power of the Soviet Union can be read in the extreme paranoia that permeated the West. In America, this paranoia reached fever pitch during the 1950s, with communist 'witch-hunts' focusing on figures in Hollywood, academia and even the state department, in a farcical echo of Stalin's purges. Rock and roll was condemned as a communist plot; and in 1963 a deranged loner named Lee Harvey Oswald, who had once emigrated to Moscow, assassinated President John F. Kennedy.

But Moscow had woken a sleeping giant. Making use of its vast reserves of intellectual and actual capital, the United States soon caught up with the Soviet Union. In 1969 the US landed a man on the moon. The barely acknowledged driving force behind all this rocket science on both sides had been the development of inter-continental ballistic missiles with nuclear warheads. Soon the Soviet Union and the US were each in possession of an arsenal of weapons capable of destroying the world many times over. Yet still the US kept upping the ante in this poker game of world domination. Eventually, the arms race would bankrupt the Soviet Union.

In 1989 the Soviet Union fell apart and Moscow lost any claim to lead the world. Yet this left a curious legacy: throughout the USA there remained dozens of 'sleepers'. These were communist believers – of Russian and east European origin – who had infiltrated into the US, with the aim that they would integrate fully into American society, waiting for the moment when they could be 'awoken', to set about their allotted tasks. Some of these sleepers were uncovered, others gave themselves up to the US authorities. Yet others remained, an unknown and unknowable quantity, unsure of what to do. Were they still covert citizens of Moscow, the city that had once led the world? Or were they forced to accept that the world was now led by another city, which had long since rivalled and even overtaken Moscow?

8

New York: Beacon of Dreams

Ironically, it was Lenin who said that people 'vote with their feet'. This is precisely what the turn-of-the-twentieth-century immigrants who arrived in New York were doing after sailing across the Atlantic. These were the very people whose first sight of the New World was the Statue of Liberty, holding aloft the torch of freedom. (The statue was originally named by its French creators *La Liberté éclairant le monde:* Liberty enlightening the world.) Downtrodden workers from all over Europe had taken up the call inscribed at Liberty's feet: 'Give me your tired, your poor, your huddled masses yearning to breathe free.'[41] Here was the land where people came to begin a new life. As if this was not enough, broken chains lie at Liberty's feet – the very chains that for Marx were the only thing the workers of the world had to lose. The rallying call for communism and the rallying call for capitalism were initially all but identical.

Yet the people arriving in New York were not celebrities who had come to see for themselves what the world of the future looked like, as G.B. Shaw or H.G. Wells had done in Moscow. These were people who arrived with the intention of staying to build their own world of the future. No chauffeur-driven limousines or champagne

---

41 These words came from a poem by the resonantly named Emma Lazarus. In the Bible, Lazarus is Jesus' dead follower whom he miraculously brought back to life.

dinners for them. Instead, they were made to stand in line at Ellis Island with the bags and bundles that made up their sole worldly possessions. Here they underwent a medical and mental inspection test to ensure that they were fit to enter America, the inspectors marking with chalk the coats of those who were suspected of being sick or otherwise unfit for entry (though the immigrants soon learned to wipe off such marks). Of more than 25 million immigrants who arrived at Ellis Island between 1891 and 1936, just 4 per cent were deported on grounds of disability, disease, being unskilled, or 'likely to become a public charge'. Stowaways on the ships, or Chinese people 'regardless of status', were automatically denied entry. Yet such criteria only applied to steerage-class passengers: those who had travelled across the Atlantic first or second class were exempt from Ellis Island inspection.

The French Revolution inspired both the Statue of Liberty and the October Revolution. Yet the '*Liberté, égalité, fraternité*' (Liberty, Equality, Fraternity) of the original French Revolution would be translated very differently in Russia and America. Indeed, New York would lead the world in the very opposite direction to Moscow. The communist proletariat may have had nothing after the Civil War between the Reds and the Whites, but they had not left Mother Russia. Only the Jews, displaced by the pogroms, had been forced to do this.

The Jews arrived in New York, along with the Irish, the Italians, the Greeks, the Germans, the Slavs, the Swedes and many others. The uncle who had gone ahead, the man from the same village, the friend who had promised work in his restaurant: these were the ones you sought out as soon as you were through Ellis Island. Family clans, nationalities, races, each of them clinging together, assisting their own kind in their own specialisation: the garment industry, restaurants, the construction industry. In this way the police force of New York became predominantly Irish, inexpensive restaurants were often run by Italians, and Germans ran food stores that became known as 'delis' (after *delikatessen:* delicate food).

So the story goes: a young Jew, who had been met off the boat by his uncle, was astonished when he entered the streets of the Lower East Side to see so many shops and tailors and restaurants, all with Yiddish signs and names.

'Here we own everything! Our names are on everything!' exclaimed the young Jew.

'Look up. What do you see?' said his uncle.

'Skyscrapers.'

'No names there.'

The newcomers had a lot to learn, a long way to go. New York consisted of many elements that had arrived from somewhere else. And this was more than just immigrants.

Two archetypically American examples will suffice. Skyscrapers began 700 miles away in Chicago, where the city was expanding at truly breakneck speed, forcing up land prices on the Lake Michigan waterfront. Buildings mushroomed, making use of the new metal-frame architecture to rise into the air, and the skyscraper was born. Within years, south Manhattan Island had become even more squeezed, and New York City became the skyscraper capital of the world.

Meanwhile, a thousand miles to the south-west of New York, an entirely new kind of music had begun to emerge in New Orleans. Around the early 1900s the German oom-pa-pa music that was played on the bandstands went out of fashion, leaving trumpets, cornets, trombones, clarinets and drums available at rock-bottom prices. These were bought up by local black musicians, who began playing a loud music with subtle African rhythms and novel instrumental techniques, which became known as jazz. As this migrated up the Mississippi and on to the East Coast it developed into new styles of jazz. By the 1920s New York had evolved what became known as the 'Harlem Stride', a New York jazz of its own. (Around two decades later, New York had become the world's centre of modern jazz, with Charlie Parker's bebop all the rage among the soldiers partying before being shipped to the war in Europe.)

Like London, it had all begun with canals in the early 1800s. Or, in this case, one canal, which linked Lake Erie with the upper Hudson River. This 363-mile canal initially faced all manner of difficulties. For a start, the water level of Lake Erie was 565 feet higher than the Hudson River at Buffalo, and it was estimated that the canal would require anything up to three dozen locks. President Thomas Jefferson condemned the scheme as 'little short of madness', but the governor of New York state, DeWitt Clinton, was persuaded to go ahead with what became known as 'Clinton's Folly'. The canal would create a key transport link across the east, meaning that the grain farmers of Ohio could now ship their produce direct to the east coast. Previously, they had been forced to rely upon portage by mule train, which had led many producers to turn their grain into whiskey. With the opening of the Eerie Canal in 1825, New York had a trade link deep into the interior, connecting it to Cleveland, Detroit and eventually the Great Lakes, none of which had previously had a direct link to the sea.[42]

Next came the railways. In fact, small-scale railways had been constructed in nearby Pennsylvania and New Jersey as early as 1829, usually to facilitate mining projects. The earliest locomotives in the United States were imported from Britain, but in the 1830s home-made locomotives began appearing. One of the first of these was the *DeWitt Clinton*. Ironically, this was intended as a competitor to 'Clinton's Folly'.

Railways would play an integral part in stimulating trade in New York, with continuous railway projects extending further and

---

42 Access to the Atlantic via Lake Ontario and the St Lawrence River was still blocked by the formidable obstacle of the Niagara Falls.

further into the hinterland. A majority of these were financed with money raised by means of bonds purchased in the New York Stock Exchange on Wall Street, which had been founded in 1817. These bonds were bought by the investor (thus loaning his money to the company) and paid a fixed annual interest until the date when they could be redeemed. By this time the company was expecting to make a profit, facilitating repayment of the original loan. Such was the rapid growth of the railways that many made fortunes in this business, and by 1860 New York was connected to every leading city in the north and mid-west of the country.

This multi-owned system of linked railroads by now had reached the Corn Belt of the Mid-West (stretching from Ohio to Nebraska and the Dakota territories). Here 80 per cent of farms were now within five miles of a railway. This brought a huge increase in the transportation of grain, hogs and cattle. Much of it contributed to the miraculous growth of Chicago, but a vital factor remained New York's access to intentional trade. This too enabled many enterprising New Yorkers to accrue fortunes. Wealthy mansions began appearing in the city's suburbs that were springing up amid the woodlands and meadows of upper Manhattan, as well as in Brooklyn, where businessmen on Wall Street travelled to work by steam-boat ferries across the East River.

It is difficult to exaggerate the booming success of the New York stock market. As we have seen, between 1815 and 1915 the capitalisation of the London Market grew from $250 million to $15 billion. During the same period the US stock markets grew from a mere $50 million to an astonishing £20 billion. America was gradually growing into the world's largest economy. This was taking place in plain sight, but nobody was noticing.

In 1861 the United States plunged into the Civil War, which split the country, pitting the partially industrialised states of the Union North against the mainly agrarian Confederate South. The ostensible reason for this split was the issue of slavery, which had largely been abolished in the North: New York passed an emancipation law in 1799, but slavery would not be legally abolished in the city until 1827. In the South, cotton-harvesting by slaves remained an integral part of the life and wealth of the region. Other reasons for the civil war included the conflict between industry and farming, as well as taxation and the rights of individual states within the Union. By now New York was the most populous city in the Union, and the Empire State (as George Washington had christened it) was the most populous territory. Many Black Americans who had fled the South had joined European immigrants working on the farmlands of the prosperous agricultural region of upper New York state.

New Yorkers rallied to the flag, volunteering in astonishing numbers. New York, city and state, would contribute some 450,000 men during the four-year war. This number represented more than 20 per cent of the male population. The average age of these recruits was officially said to be twenty-five years seven months, though it was certainly much lower than this, as many of the younger volunteers lied about their age. Breaking this down into demographic groups gives an indication of the population diversity during this period. More than 50 per cent of the men enlisted (130,000) were foreign born. These included 51,000 Irish, 37,000 Germans and 20,000 from Canada. Over four thousand free Black slaves made up three full regiments of US Coloured Troops (USCT). Officers of these regiments were white. To modern eyes this suggests that although the men of the USCT were free, they remained segregated. However, it is known that a number of black soldiers fought alongside white soldiers in other regiments. The enthusiasm and bravery of the New York black troops is without doubt. They received more than their fair share of medals for bravery, and 20 per cent of their USCT ranks died in action, higher than other regiments. In fact, the overall slaughter of the Civil War was appalling: a total of 620,000 on both sides (more than the combined US losses in both World Wars, the Korean War and Vietnam). This was indeed a dress rehearsal for the world wars to come.

The geographical location of New York harbour meant that it was easily defensible from attack by warships. But it soon became known that both the North and the South were developing submarines, which posed New York with an unknown threat. Despite this, the city of New York would see no action during the Civil War. Apart, that is, from the Conscription Riots. These took place over the space of four days in July 1863. They were prompted by members of the white working class who feared that when they were conscripted freed black slaves would flood into New York to take their jobs. They also resented the fact that the rich could pay $300 to hire a man to take their place in the draft. According to contemporary US historian Eric Foner, 'These riots remain the largest civil and most racially charged urban disturbances in American history.'

President Lincoln had just delivered his celebrated Gettysburg Address, where he referred to America as 'a new nation, conceived in Liberty, and dedicated to the proposition that all men are created equal'. Following these fine words, he was forced to despatch several regiments away from the front to New York to put down the riots. During disturbances all over the city, around a hundred and twenty people were killed, and afterwards many of the black population left Manhattan to settle in Brooklyn.

New York's other direct link to the Civil War took place at Davids Island. This 78-acre island at the western reaches of Long Island Sound had been purchased some years previously by Thaddeus Davids, who ran the world's largest ink company. He had purchased the island with the intention of transferring his business there, but before he could do so the US War Department took it over. Initially, it housed a large military hospital, which ended up treating both Union and Confederate wounded. Later, it would become a Confederate prisoner-of-war camp, housing more than two and a half thousand captives.

The potent mix of class and racial divides would continue to plague New York after the Civil War. The city had taken a big financial hit during the war. Over half its exports to Europe, and especially Britain, had consisted of cotton shipments, which ceased with the outbreak of hostilities. Meanwhile, other businesses continued to flourish. In 1863, in the midst of the war, the railways began their final push westwards through the Rockies. This was financed by federal bonds sold on Wall Street, as was the Pacific Railroad, whose Irish and Chinese labourers pressed eastwards at headlong speed (the record was ten miles of track laid in a single day). On 10 May 1869 the two railways joined, with a ceremonial gold spike being driven into the track at Promontory Point, Utah. New York was now joined to the Pacific coast by a direct line, which opened up the West to all. This had been encouraged by the 1862 Homestead Act, which allowed 'any American, including freed slaves, to put in a claim for up to 160 acres of federal land'. The Native American tribes, being hunter-gatherers, had staked no claim to this territory over which they had roamed for millennia hunting herds of wild buffalo.

Then, in 1873, Wall Street suffered a collapse. This was in part caused by massive over-speculation in railway stocks, as well as by large insurance losses over property burnt in the Chicago Fire of 1871 followed by the Boston Fire of 1872. But the initial cause had taken place thousands of miles away on another continent. The collapse of the stock exchange in Vienna, capital of the Austro-Hungarian Empire, at the time Europe's largest country, had been followed by collapses on German exchanges, and then London. News now travelled fast: the telegraph had followed the railways all across America, and in 1858 the first transatlantic cable had been laid. As the New York Stock Exchange was on its way to becoming the biggest in the world, it became more and more deeply interlinked with the world, and thus more involved in its changes of fortune.

While the British Empire occupied territory all over the globe, from Australia to Africa and Canada, New York had begun to play an increasing role in financing the world's trade. From South American tin mines to South African diamond mines and the Canadian fur trade, all were quoted on the New York Stock Exchange. This was not a territorial empire like the old European empires – instead, it was a financial one. On the other hand, when the US government had bought the Territory of Alaska from Russia in 1867 for $7.2 million, this purchase was in part backed by Wall Street in the form of government bonds.

During the 'Panic of 1873', as the New York Stock Exchange crash came to be known, banks failed, insurance companies went out of business, railways went bust and construction ground to a halt. This had a rebound effect on Europe, plunging it further into depression. In a negative way, it was now clear that what happened in New York affected the entire financial world. During the ensuing depression in America, tariffs went up to protect industry and agriculture. Suddenly, protectionism was the watchword. Yet all knew that such a policy could not be sustained: America depended upon international trade. Wages sank, and in 1877 the railway workers went out on strike. But this was the low point. After three years, the economy began to haul itself out of depression. This coincided with the start of the first great wave of European immigration, and in no time New York was booming once more.

As early as 1870 work had started on a bridge to connect Manhattan to Brooklyn. This was to be the world's longest suspension bridge, with a central span of 1,600 feet, some 127 feet above high tide on the East River, enough for sailing ships to pass beneath it. The bridge's overall length would be more than six thousand feet and its steel suspension cables would be supported by two seventy-eight-foot towers. By now the stone towers had been completed, and as immigrant-filled New York underwent yet another expansion, the bridge slowly grew above the hustling market streets of the Lower East Side. And the reason for this architectural wonder? So that the horse-drawn carriages of the wealthy could drive directly from their mansions in Brooklyn to the financial district in Lower Manhattan.

Thaddeus Davids' ink company was just one of many American enterprises now beginning to outpace worldwide competitors. Singer Sewing Machines, Dupont (chemicals), Astor's American Fur Company, Wells Fargo (express mail, banking), and many such companies were now quoted on the New York Stock Exchange. A class of newly rich families began to emerge. The profligate behaviour of this novel stratum of society soon began to attract attention. Banquets were thrown featuring ice sculptures of the host's locomotives; at others, cigars were served wrapped in $100 bills.

Such behaviour came to the attention of the maverick economist Thorstein Veblen, one of the earliest and most original American practitioners in this field. Veblen had been born in 1857 of Norwegian heritage in a remote farming community of Minnesota, which only became a state a year after his birth (in fact, Sioux tribes had only recently been forcibly evicted from this territory to make way for Scandinavian immigrants). Young Veblen learned English at school but retained a drawling Norwegian accent throughout his life. According to the twentieth-century US historian George M. Fredrickson, the Norwegian society in which Veblen lived was so remote that when he left it to enter college, 'he was, in a sense, emigrating to America'. This gave objectivity to an already original but wayward mind. After graduate studies at Cornell in New

York state, Veblen remained unemployed for seven years, in part because he was 'insufficiently educated in Christianity' (he openly professed his agnosticism). He ended up obtaining a low-paid teaching post at the newly founded University of Chicago. Here, his extra-marital affairs alienated him from the staff, and his reportedly 'dreadful' lectures alienated him from the students. They were delivered in a sarcastic Norwegian drawl, and consisted of an eclectic stream of erudition, punctuated with medieval Latin quotes and Chicago slang.

But it was here that Veblen began writing his masterwork, *The Theory of the Leisure Class*, which was published in 1899. In this book Veblen described the striking behaviour of the New York rich as if they were 'the higher stages of the barbarian culture'. The new New York society was likened to the Stone Age existence of Polynesian islanders and Viking tribal behaviour in the Dark Ages. The rich had always believed that they were superior to other people, and in order to distinguish themselves from those less brilliant than themselves they had to demonstrate their superiority. And 'the only practical means of impressing one's pecuniary ability... is an unremitting demonstration of ability to pay'. Where tribal leaders in primitive society had adorned their womenfolk with rare trinkets, the modern rich felt the need to demonstrate that they were possessed of two priceless entities: namely 'conspicuous leisure' and 'conspicuous consumption'. As Veblen put it: 'In one case it is a waste of time and effort, in the other it is a waste of goods.'

Behind such vivid descriptions, Veblen was making an original and fundamental economic point. In such cases rational self-interest was not the prime motive for economic behaviour. Although it was hardly Veblen's intention, his analysis would provide guiding principles for the advertising business, which would find fertile territory in New York, taking on an entirely new lease of life. As early as 1861 there had been twenty advertising agencies in New York, centred around Madison Avenue.[43]

Making a mockery of the rich won Veblen few friends among that exclusive society. However, among the leaders of that society there now began to emerge a small group of people whose behaviour remained beyond ridicule, for the simple reason that they did not care what people thought about them. These were the so-called 'Robber Barons'. Mostly based in New York, these men accumulated untold fortunes and power that stretched throughout the land, and beyond into the wider world. Their names, along with the industries of which they gained control, still resonate to this day: Andrew Carnegie (steel), John D. Rockefeller (oil, railways), J. Pierpont Morgan (banking, railways), Cornelius Vanderbilt (shipping, railways), Daniel Guggenheim (mining).

The preponderance of 'railways' among the industries that these moguls fought to control is reflected in the sheer size of this sector. By 1880, the US rail network had 17,600 locomotives transporting 23,000 tons of freight and 22,000 passengers a year; as such, it employed more people than any other sector outside agriculture. Ten years later, with the encouragement of Wall Street, US industry began to 'rationalise'. In effect, this resulted in a flurry of takeovers and mergers as the big companies began buying up their rivals' shares. This prompted a far-sighted government to bring in the Sherman Anti-Trust Act, which was intended to put a stop to such monopolising mergers in all industries. Unfortunately, this would have the very opposite to its intended effect. With prices freed up, the larger companies began undercutting smaller competitors, then taking them over. This flurry of mergers would result in some

---

43 In a fitting parable, the original Madison Garden Square was a railway terminal, which in 1871 was turned into an open-air circus by Phineas T. Barnum. This was the man who said of himself: 'I am a showman... and all the gilding shall make nothing else of me.' He is also credited with the quip: 'There's a sucker born every minute.'

conglomerates that remained household names within recent memory. Among them, Union Carbide, Heinz, Eastman Kodak, and American Telephone and Telegraph (AT&T). Such were the economic conditions in which the Robber Barons would thrive.

The first of these was Cornelius Vanderbilt, who was born on Staten Island in 1794, the son of an illiterate sailor who ran a sailboat ferry across New York harbour. At the age of eleven young Cornelius ducked out of school to join his father's business. Five years later, his mother loaned him £100 to buy a two-masted sailing boat, capable of carrying freight and passengers. The aggressive business tactics and energetic manner of this teenage sailor soon earned him the nickname 'The Commodore'.[44] In 1817 a ferry fleet operator named Thomas Gibbons asked Vanderbilt to captain one of his ships. Vanderbilt graduated to manager, where he made up for his lack of education by learning how to run a growing, complex business. When Gibbons died and his son took over, Vanderbilt soon side-lined the son and took over the running of the business. Within years he had ships running up and down the entire coast. Then he went into railways, once again ruthlessly undercutting and picking off his competitors one by one, often going into partnership to ruin a large competitor, and then ruining his partner. When the California Gold Rush began in 1849, he made a fortune shipping prospectors to Panama, where they travelled overland to await another ship to transport them to San Francisco.[45] Vanderbilt soon bought west-coast ships to take advantage of this need. Hearing of plans to build a Panama Canal, he drew up plans of his own for a canal through Nicaragua, making use of Lake Nicaragua, but could find no backers.

---

44 This may have been ironically intended, but he liked it, and for the rest of his life Vanderbilt would enjoy hearing people referring to him by this name.
45 Before the transcontinental railway was completed in 1869, this was the only effective way to reach the West Coast from the East Coast.

When the Civil War broke out, he donated the use of his ships to the Union cause and made a further fortune on cargo charges for goods carried on these ships. But the Civil War would also bring him tragedy, when his youngest and favourite son collapsed and died on his way to the front. After a period of alcoholic depression, the seventy-two-year-old Vanderbilt snapped back into action. Faced by competitors who all sensed he was weakening with age, he ruined them all by closing his Albany Bridge, the only railway access to the port of New York, and then bought up their collapsed shares on Wall Street, gaining further railways.

Not long after this, he gave $1 million for the founding of Vanderbilt University, at the time the largest charity donation in US history. In 1877 he finally died at the age of eighty-four. Despite this being in the midst of the first Great Depression, he left a fortune arguably unequalled to this day.[46]

America remains conflicted over Vanderbilt's heritage. He is admired for having got things done, and creating vast efficient businesses in the process. But precisely how he got things done, and the broken lives he left in his wake, are another matter. The historian H. Roger Grant, of Ohio University, gives him, on balance, a positive assessment; according to Grant, 'Contemporaries, too, often hated or feared Vanderbilt or at least considered him an unmannered brute. While Vanderbilt could be a rascal, combative and cunning, he was much more a builder than a wrecker.'

In the hands of the Robber Barons money could do anything. As J.P. Morgan once said to a judge: 'I don't know as I want a lawyer to tell me what I cannot do. I hire him to tell me how to do what I want to do.' But there were positives. In 1895 Morgan bought enough gold to keep the dollar on the gold standard. This averted a US government bankruptcy, no less. Then, in 1907, there was a run on the banks, and Morgan personally stepped in to avert a Wall Street crash.

---

46 For over fifty years the 1873 depression would be known as the Great Depression – until another, even greater catastrophe would take this title.

Somewhat belatedly, the government realised that too much power was now in the hands of the Robber Barons. In response to Morgan's actions, the Federal Reserve was set up, as the national bank of the United States. This had twelve branches, one in every major city in the land; but in practice the 'New York Fed' soon emerged as the dominant force in US monetary and banking matters, with its governor fixing interest rates and the like.

By now the Sherman Anti-Trust Act was being used to break up the monopolies created by the Robber Barons. As early as 1896, the government had acted against Rockefeller and his Standard Oil Company, which controlled 95 per cent of the oil market. Rockefeller resisted with all the force he could lay his hands on, but in 1911 Standard Oil was broken up into dozens of small independent companies, each of which could compete against the others. Mobil, Exxon, Chevron and Sohio (now part of BP) were all originally part of Standard Oil.

However, financial chicanery was not limited to the rich and the super-rich. Take Charles Ponzi, who gave his name to the notorious Ponzi scheme. Ponzi was born in Italy in 1892, son of a wealthy family that had fallen on hard times. In 1903 Ponzi immigrated to the United States: 'I arrived with $2.50 in cash and $1 million in hope.' For the next sixteen years he moved about North America taking jobs in banks. At one point he arrived at the offices of one of his bank's customers to find the place deserted, whereupon he wrote himself a cheque for $423.58, forging the director's signature, which he knew from the bank. For this he got three years in jail. (To explain his new address, he wrote to his mother explaining that he was now a 'special assistant' to the prison warden.)

In 1919 he discovered a clever little scheme for making money. This scheme was based around International Reply Coupons (IRCs) – these coupons could be sent in a letter so that the receiver could exchange them for local stamps to send a reply. But IRCs were bought at the cost of international post in the country of purchase. This was often more than the stamps for the return letter would cost to European countries such as Italy. Ponzi saw his chance. Intending to capitalise on this discrepancy, he set up the Securities Exchange Company, asking people to invest in his company. This would enable him to purchase large amounts of Italian, Spanish and other European IRCs, then ship these to America and use them to purchase US stamps worth more than the IRCs had cost. He promised investors that they would double their money in ninety days.

As word of this opportunity spread, investors began pouring money into Ponzi's company. He soon began paying off his earlier investors with money from his new investors, in a form of pyramid scheme. Such was the success of Ponzi's scheme that, by March 1920, investment was flying in at the rate of $25,000 a month. By March, he had accumulated $42,000. There was a frenzy all over the East Coast, with people clamouring to invest. By June Ponzi had accumulated a staggering $2.5 million. Come July, he was receiving $1 million a week, and at the beginning of August $1 million *a day*, as people sold up everything they had, even mortgaging their houses.

Most investors did not even demand repayment, insisting instead that their profits be reinvested in Ponzi's scheme. Ponzi continued to pay those who wished to withdraw their money and take their profits, even though he had not yet worked out how to change the foreign IRCs he received into hard cash (rather than stamps).

Ponzi found himself in the money and adapted his lifestyle accordingly. He bought a mansion with a heated swimming pool, his mother came over from Italy as a first-class ship passenger, and he drove around in a Locomobile, the finest luxury automobile available. However, during July of that same year, even while Ponzi was at the height of his success, a number of perceptive journalists had begun covertly investigating the financial mechanics of Ponzi's scheme. When they made their findings public, panic set in, with a run of investors seeking to withdraw their money. Crowds gathered outside Ponzi's office. He and his staff sought to reassure the crowd by passing out coffee and doughnuts through the window, at the same time paying out $2 million in three days. In an effort to turn around his business, Ponzi hired a publicist called William McMasters, who was horrified when he discovered how it actually worked. Ponzi was simply 'robbing Peter to pay Paul'. McMasters described Ponzi as a 'financial idiot', claiming he didn't even have a grasp of basic arithmetic.

On 11 August 1920 Ponzi's scheme suddenly collapsed. On the strength of his business, Ponzi had borrowed money from five banks, which also promptly collapsed, with losses of $20 million. Ponzi pleaded guilty in court and was sentenced to five years in a federal prison. Upon his release he would try selling plots of Florida swampland on the property market, followed by another spell inside. He would end his days penniless in Argentina, where he died aged sixty-six, immortalised by the pyramid scheme that is named after him. Ponzi schemes would live on and become a regular feature of New York finance.[47]

In the midst of all this financial skulduggery, the New York Stock Exchange was in fact funding a number of schemes that would transform America, and indeed the world. Many of these would be created by the inventor and businessman Thomas Edison, at his Menlo Park laboratory in New Jersey, across the water from New York's Staten Island. Edison remains a controversial figure, with some going so far as to claim him as an inventor on a par with the likes of Archimedes and Leonardo da Vinci. Others dismiss such inflated claims, suggesting that he was mainly a businessman with a good inventive mind who was in the right place at the right time, and who knew how to exploit the talents and inventions of others working in his pioneering industrial laboratory. But there can be no disputing the aptness of the time in which he operated: this

---

47 The ones that have been detected have usually come to light after a large financial downturn, when new investors are more cautious and more old investors seek to withdraw their cash. Following the 2008 crash, 274 such schemes would come to light, the most famous of which was Bernie Madoff's $65 billion investment fund.

was the beginning of the age of electricity, the resource that would power America.

Thomas Edison was born in 1847, far from New York in Ohio. Young Thomas was largely educated at home, along with his six siblings, by his mother, who had been a schoolteacher. He had a curious mind from the outset, constructing his own little machines at home. He also suffered from scarlet fever, which rendered him hard of hearing for the rest of his life. To listen to someone playing the piano, he taught himself to clamp his teeth onto a piece of wood 'to absorb the sound waves into his skull'. He also claimed that his partial deafness helped him to concentrate and focus his mind to an exceptional degree.

Edison's first job was selling newspapers and candy on trains. Next, he obtained work as a railway telegraph operator, working night shifts so he could study and dream up imaginative electrical devices. His first patent was for an electric vote recorder; then, at the age of twenty-seven, he invented a multiplex telegraph, capable of sending two messages simultaneously. After selling the rights to this for $10,000, he established an industrial research laboratory at Menlo Park, the first of its kind. Edison began hiring talented assistants to construct and test his stream of new ideas, as well as to come up with ideas of their own. His persistence with ideas that he liked was his strength: 'I haven't failed, I've just found 10,000 ways that won't work.' Over the years this laboratory, which would eventually expand to cover two blocks, would produce various types of telegraph, a phonograph (forerunner of the record player), electric railways, and all manner of elaborate lighting devices. These were all registered as design or utility patents. He would go on to register no less than 1,093 patents. According to an 1887 press report, his lab contained:

> eight thousand kinds of chemicals, every kind of screw made, every size of needle, every kind of cord or wire, hair of humans, horses,

hogs, cows, rabbits, goats, minx, camels... silk in every texture, cocoons, various kinds of hoofs, sharks' teeth, deer horns, tortoise shell... cork, resin, varnish and oil, ostrich feathers, a peacock's tail, jet, amber, rubber, all ores...

His greatest success was with the electric light-bulb, which others had invented or produced, but he claimed to have perfected. In New York he founded the Edison Light Company, backed with money from J.P. Morgan. In 1880 Edison's electric light system, including his 'perfected incandescent light bulb', was installed on the steamship *Columbia*. His patent was challenged a year later, and his electric system was removed from the ship. Undaunted, Edison pressed ahead. On 4 September 1882 he held a grand opening ceremony at which he turned on the lighting that illuminated the entire First District of New York. This proved a spectacular success, and Edison began planning to install power generators at regular intervals all over New York, and eventually beyond.

Edison revelled in the fact that he had defeated his main rival, George Westinghouse, whose aim was to install gas lighting. Electricity was not only cheaper but cleaner. By now Edison had offices in Europe, and his Paris manager sent him a highly talented young inventor named Nicola Tesla, suggesting he be taken on as Edison's assistant. No sooner had Edison taken on Tesla than his assistant informed him that the direct current (DC) method of conveying electricity, which Edison was using, was inferior to a new method of alternating current (AC) that he had invented. Edison dismissed this idea as a 'mere complication', and Tesla left. Later, he would join Westinghouse, who eventually switched to electric power using the AC idea. Alternating current could be transmitted over long distances by cable, while direct current needed generating plants at regular intervals. Edison and Westinghouse embarked on a 'current war', each persuading different cities across America to adopt their own system.

By 1890 Edison's DC company was falling way behind Westinghouse and other AC companies. J.P. Morgan, ruthless as ever, evicted Edison from his own company, merging it with a rival AC company to form General Electric. This company soon controlled 75 per cent of the US electrical sector.

Edison moved to Florida, where he took up residence next door to Henry Ford, the automobile manufacturer. Edison ended up advising the US Navy during the First World War, as well as developing a new type of productive rubber plant that interested his friend Ford, whose new mass-produced Model T (the 'Tin Lizzie') would need a plentiful source of rubber for its tyres. And still Edison went on turning out more inventions, including rechargeable batteries, moving pictures and phenol production (used for making phonographic records and Bakelite, the early form of plastic). It was Edison's electric light-bulb and Ford's new automobile that would lead the United States into the modern age.

The United States would enter the First World War late, in 1917, but the arrival of American troops in France tipped the balance in favour of the Western Allies against Germany. At the 1919 Peace Talks held at Versailles, just outside Paris, President Woodrow Wilson was widely regarded as the prime mover among the allies. America had arrived on the world scene.

In the 1920s, while most of Europe struggled economically, the United States celebrated the Jazz Age. This era in American life was captured in all its enigmatic glory by the writer F. Scott Fitzgerald in his New York-based novel *The Great Gatsby*. The story revolves around a wealthy figure of mysterious origins (Gatsby) who throws wild parties, and pines for Daisy, the love he cannot attain. Fitzgerald, along with William Faulkner and Ernest Hemingway, brought a new American witness to bear on the modern human condition. Faulkner's faux 'clapboard' prose captured a timeless life in the American Deep South, while Hemingway's stripped-down style and wounded action figures spoke to the need for adventure in the free, modern sensibility.

However, in 1929 the boom times of the Jazz Age came to an abrupt halt with the Wall Street Crash. As with everything American from now onwards, this had to be bigger and better than everywhere else. On 'Black Monday' 24 October 1929, the Dow Jones industrial index lost 12.8 per cent. Tuesday saw a drop of 11.3 per cent. On Thursday the market went into freewheel: all wanted to sell, but no one wanted to buy. On the face of it, losses of just over 10 per cent may not sound too catastrophic. But the reality was different: such had been the previous confidence in the boom market that thousands of investors (big and small) had taken out loans (big and small) to buy shares. When these loans were suddenly called in, many went bankrupt. The hugely popular performer Eddie Cantor, who sang 'If You Knew Susie' and 'Ma! He's Making Eyes at Me' was a millionaire several times over, but suddenly found himself with just $60 in his pocket and debts of $300,000.

The Great Crash was followed by the Great Depression. This time there was no denying that New York led the world. The Great Depression sparked by the Wall Street Crash quickly spread across America, with over nine thousand banks going bust, and the song of the moment became 'Buddy, Can You Spare a Dime?' From America, the Great Depression spread all over the globe. Isolationism once again became the order of the day in the US, and world trade slowed down even further.

Despite pressure from New York and other city ports, as well as export businesses all over America, President Herbert Hoover refused to budge. He was determined to 'protect America'. Unemployment rose to 25 per cent, and tent cities of homeless people – known as 'Hoovervilles' – began springing up on the edges of cities throughout the land. New York's Riverside Park became a shanty town. Meanwhile, by 1932 world trade had slumped by a staggering 70 per cent.

The Crash caught New York in the middle of a skyscraper building boom. Since 1913 the 482-foot Woolworth Building had been the world's tallest building. Then, in 1928, plans were drawn up to build two new skyscrapers: 40 Wall Street (now the Trump Building) and the Chrysler Building. The first of these, 40 Wall Street, started construction in May 1929. It was 925 feet tall, taking over as the tallest in the world. On 23 October 1929, just a day before the Crash, the Chrysler Building reached 1,046 feet, securing the crown. Meanwhile, plans had been laid for an even higher building, to be called the Empire State Building, and construction was on a tight schedule. From now on, building was a gamble: the Depression meant that no one needed new office space, yet to have cancelled construction would have meant even greater losses. In desperation the owners of the rising Empire State Building managed to secure a loan of $27.5 million from Metropolitan Life Insurance. Two groups of 300 men worked 12-hour shifts around the clock. By the end of 1930, 3,500 men were working on the site, struggling to bring the building in on time.

On 11 April 1931, twelve days ahead of schedule and four hundred days after construction began, the Empire State building was complete. It had cost $41 million and reached a height of 1,454 feet. It would remain the world's tallest building for forty-one years. Only the construction of the twin towers of the ill-fated World Trade Center would end its reign as the tallest building in New York.

Despite the Great Depression, New York remained one of the wonders of the modern world. Yet curiously, it wasn't the skyscrapers that caught the imagination of the poets. Instead they hymned the beauty of Brooklyn Bridge, and the almost abstract geometrical patterns created by the steel hawsers that swept down from the stone towers, supporting the long deck of the bridgeway, which was now used by automobiles. When the Soviet futurist poet Vladimir Mayakovsky saw the bridge on a visit to New York in 1925, some fifty years after it had been built, he marvelled at its modernity. In his characteristic bombastic style, he stepped onto the bridge, comparing himself to a crazed believer entering a church. Four years later the young Spanish poet Federico García Lorca arrived in New York aboard the RMS *Olympic* (sister ship to the *Titanic*). Speaking of the other side of the New York experience, one insomniac night he wrote 'Sleepless City (Brooklyn Bridge Nocturne)', which expressed in surreal images his loneliness and alienation amid the modern city, comparing it to a crocodile resting beneath the stars. This aspect of New York life was perhaps best captured by Greenwich Village artist Edward Hopper's *Nighthawks*.

Edward Hopper's Nighthawks.

But the finest of all the poems concerning Brooklyn Bridge was the American poet Hart Crane's epic 'The Bridge'. In this he sought to create a myth for modern America:

> O harp and altar, of the fury fused,
> (How could mere toil align thy choiring strings!)
> Terrific threshold of the prophet's pledge,
> Prayer of pariah, and the lover's cry,—

The allusive incoherence of the poem lends it a powerful authority. Only when Crane had finished it did he discover that the room he had hired overlooking the bridge, where he wrote his epic, had previously been occupied by the chair-bound architect Washington Roebling as he had supervised the bridge's construction.

By 1933 the US had a new president, Franklin Delano Roosevelt, the scion of an old New York family. In an attempt to ameliorate the effects of the Depression, Roosevelt announced the New Deal. This put into force the counter-intuitive economics of Maynard Keynes, who advocated spending the way out of a depression, sending the unemployed back to work and creating infrastructure that would be of use when the economy recovered. Roosevelt's New Deal was responsible for creating a series of great dams, bridges and a national network of roads. These would in time supply the nation's energy and enable goods to be driven the length and breadth of the country.

A more deleterious effect during this period was an unintended consequence of the Prohibition Act, which banned the sale or use of alcohol and lasted from 1920 until 1933. When the bars were closed down, 'speakeasies' opened to dispense all manner of unlicensed hootch. These, as well as the import of illegal alcohol, mainly from Canada and Cuba, were set up by the mafia. Previously, this had been a comparatively small-scale crime syndicate mainly run by Sicilians. Now it took on the proportions of a nationwide industry; the leaders became household names. The biggest New York gang bosses were 'Lucky' Luciano and 'Bugsy' Siegel, two unsavoury sadists who conducted murder as a way of life. Despite repeated attempts, the mafia would not be dislodged from their central place in New York life, even when Prohibition ended. By then they had the money, brute power and expertise to take over entire sectors of the economy: garbage clearance, construction materials, the Manhattan waterfront, even elements of the police and the local political machine, all succumbed to mafia strong-arm tactics or blackmail. Corruption, protection rackets, prostitution and drugs would become a well-organised underbelly of New York life.

On the other side of the world, another group was spreading fear and gaining power – the National Socialist German Worker's Party (the Nazis) came to power in 1933 with Adolf Hitler at its helm. His campaign against the Jews, particularly in academia, would lead to a flow of brilliant scientists and intellectuals into America as they attempted to escape persecution and eventually genocide. The arrival of the world-renowned physicist Albert Einstein in New York in October 1933 was but the prelude to what became known as 'Hitler's Gift' to America. Six years later, Einstein would write to President Roosevelt warning him that Nazi Germany was capable of making a nuclear bomb. Roosevelt set up the top-secret Manhattan Project, which raced to become the first to assemble an atomic bomb. Many of the scientists employed on this project were Jewish émigrés from Germany. Incredibly, Einstein himself was kept in the dark about this project that he had set in motion, as military intelligence deemed him to be a 'security risk'.

At the outbreak of the Second World War in Europe, America remained theoretically isolationist. Only after the Japanese surprise attack on Pearl Harbor in December 1941 would the United States officially commit to the Allied cause, both in the

Pacific and the Atlantic (where American ships had been supplying isolated Britain for some years). America was galvanised into such action that the Depression disappeared virtually overnight: the sheer might of its industry created a war machine second to none.

Two examples will suffice. Shipping losses to German U-boats in the Atlantic were crippling. In response, the US shipyards all along the eastern seaboard, especially in New York, began a massive shipbuilding programme turning out the aptly named Liberty ships. These were standard-design merchant vessels of around 10,000 tons, with parts quickly welded together, rather than using the more reliable but complex process of riveting.

During the course of this shipbuilding drive, the New York Shipbuilding Company would become the largest and most productive the world had yet seen. Soon Liberty ships were being launched at the rate of more than one a day. And in November 1942, the Liberty ship *Robert E. Peary* was built in a record four days, fifteen hours and twenty-nine minutes. No one could compete with such production, let alone the Nazis who relied upon slave labour.

The second example comes from the 1944 winter campaign in the Ardennes, when the Nazis launched a surprise offensive aimed at piercing American lines and flooding back into Belgium and France. Among those facing the Germans was the 42nd Infantry Division, which included a large number of draftees from New York City, who had yet to see battle. The German offensive was led by the crack Waffen SS, but as the Germans were low on fuel and supplies they were ordered to scavenge these from American units they overran. One German officer later recalled that when he came across US ration dumps – with tinned Hershey bars, spam, cigarettes, and even toilet paper, all shipped directly from the United States – he realised he was on the losing side. Germany would never be able to match the sheer scale and reach of the American industrial machine.

The United States emerged from the war more powerful than ever, establishing its hegemony over what we like to call the free world (i.e. non-communist countries). The *Pax Americana* prevailed, in much the same way as the *Pax Romana* had done nearly two millennia previously. But as the United States had been born out of anti-imperialism, there could be no actual empire. Instead the term 'sphere of influence' was used.

The guiding principle of this method had been formulated in the first years of the twentieth century by the earlier Roosevelt, the Manhattan-born President Teddy Roosevelt (after whom the teddy bear is named). In seeking to dominate Latin America, without actually turning such territories into a land empire, Teddy Roosevelt spelt out his foreign policy in no uncertain terms: 'Speak softly, and carry a big stick.' Certain elements of this foreign policy endured under the later presidency of Franklin Roosevelt. The big stick had certainly worked against Nazi Germany, but how was he to deal with the ungrateful Europeans he had liberated? Despite the vast generosity of the Marshall Aid plan designed to put Europe (and European markets) back on their feet (so that they could trade with the US), the US found itself losing the propaganda war. As we have seen, the hearts and minds of many European intellectuals still preferred Marxist ideas to the so-called Coca Cola culture of America.

Surprisingly, it was the newly formed Central Intelligence Agency (CIA) that came up with the answer to this problem. If the goddam commies and intellectuals in Europe respected high culture, then that was what America would give them. The main centre of intellectual life in the United States was New York: this was where the local intellectuals wrote their magazines; this was where the artists hung out in the bars of Greenwich Village; this was where the poets scribbled their stuff about Brooklyn Bridge. Perhaps these bums and bohemians could serve some useful purpose after all.

America had already produced some fine writers, and some indisputably fine poets, but its artists had never really been taken seriously. Not compared with Pablo Picasso (who claimed he was a lifelong commie), his pal Georges Braque (a former house-painter who didn't appear to believe in anything) and Marc Chagall (who was a bona fide *Russian* commie).

The CIA began covertly funding intellectual magazines in Europe. Their editors, for the most part unaware of this arrangement, were carefully chosen from among respected independent figures, who may have been left wing but made no secret of their antipathy towards communism. And for the most part this worked. The CIA-funded *Encounter* became one of the most respected intellectual magazines, both in Britain where it was published, and throughout Europe and the USA. It would feature work by poets of the calibre of Stephen Spender and W.H. Auden, the leading British poets of their generation, as well as respected British philosophers such as Stuart Hampshire and Isaiah Berlin, and Nobel-Prize-winners like the French writer André Gide.

The painters proved a more difficult problem. According to the CIA, there weren't many good ones, and they were hardly suitable as cultural ambassadors for the United States. Jackson Pollock was a dangerous alcoholic who didn't even seem to know how to use an easel; he just laid his canvases on the floor, then splashed and dribbled paint all over them at random. Mark Rothko was a Russian immigrant, for heaven's sake, who believed his large blurred patches of colour had mystical significance. And the Dutch guy, Willem de Kooning, was obviously deranged, if his savage portraits of women were anything to go by.

With some trepidation, the CIA went ahead, presenting their chosen artists under the banner of 'American Abstract Expressionism'. Critics were hired by the CIA-funded magazines to write imaginative in-depth articles about these newly discovered artists. And it worked! The art world was taken in, and soon the New York School of Abstract Expressionism was the hottest thing on the market. Inadvertently, the CIA had picked a bunch of winners.

New York had wrested from Paris the title of leading city of the art world. Especially where modern art was concerned. And its Museum of Modern Art (MOMA) soon housed the finest collection of modern art ever assembled. Taking their cue from such developments, the rich art patrons of New York began competing for this new art in the auction rooms, bidding up prices to levels never before seen. Fashionable New York art collectors were soon paying six-figure sums for Jackson Pollocks, more even than for some of Picasso's works. New York had come of age in all fields.

The 1950s would see America embark upon a Cold War with the Soviet Union. In the 1960s the space race would end in US victory when Neil Armstrong became the first human to set foot on the moon. The 1960s would also see a cultural revolution in the US, with the Hippy generation, Vietnam War protests and a nationwide Civil Rights movement. One of the leading figures representing all aspects of this cultural upheaval would be an unlikely figure who emerged from the coffeehouses of Greenwich Village. Bob Dylan's allusive but memorable lyrics, set to the stirring music of his acoustic guitar and harmonica, would capture the feeling of this era better than any.

The Cold War would end in 1989 with the tearing down of the Berlin Wall. This presaged the break-up of the Soviet Union, leaving the United States as the undisputed leader of the world, and New York still a world leader in fields ranging from finance to art and much in between.

Sequence

The end of the Cold War gave rise to excessive expectations. The most heady of these appeared in *The End of History and the Last Man* by the Japanese-American academic Francis Fukuyama. In this, he asserted that the end of the Cold War signalled: 'not just … the passing of a particular period of post-war history, but the end of history as such: That is, the end-point of mankind's ideological evolution and the universalization of western liberal democracy as the final form of human government.'

Such wishful thinking indicated that Fukuyama had either misread history, or remained entirely ignorant of what had actually taken place in human history. Despite his book's reassurance (this was what many western people wanted to believe), Fukuyama's pronouncement appeared even more delusional than Karl Marx's 'historically inevitable' never-never-land 'the dictatorship of the proletariat'.

Take the case of the Soviet Union. At the end of the Cold War, this had disintegrated, with various Turkic republics becoming for the most part primitive dictatorships, and only the small Baltic states achieving a good measure of liberal democracy. Meanwhile, in Russia itself there had been a brief period of quasi-democratic kleptocracy under the alcoholic Boris Yeltsin, during which a mafia of oligarchs had taken over the old state industries at bargain prices. Far from evolving into a western-style liberal democracy, Russia had soon reverted to its customary autocracy. This had begun with Ivan the Terrible in the sixteenth century, and persisted under the Byzantine belief that the tsar was God's representative on earth. This belief had only been transmogrified under the personality cults of Lenin and Stalin, a tradition that, after a brief hiatus, has returned under the former secret service operative President Vladimir Putin, whose favoured henchmen continue to operate as a mafia. Not much liberal democracy here.

And what of liberal democracy in the home of the free? There is no denying that American liberal democracy survives as a powerful and functioning ethos. This, despite the country being plagued by its own mafia, big-tech monopolies that would have been the envy of many a Robber Baron, a financial system bailed out by the many for the benefit of the few, and a marginalised underclass of ethnic minorities and people of colour who make up a disproportionate section of the largest prison population in the world.

But what of the cities that led the world? Different cities have evolved in their own characteristic fashion, and it is possible to detect in the succession of these an occasionally increasing element of liberalisation. For instance, life in Ancient Rome would have been all but unbearable to the citizens of Enlightenment Paris, both for the upper classes and the downtrodden mob that brought about the Revolution.

Thus it would appear that a degree of liberalisation has often, but not invariably, accompanied the progress of civilisation. The very word civilisation derives from the Latin *civis*, the Ancient Roman word for 'a citizen', and *civitas* meaning 'a city': people who lived in a city became civilised. So civilisation is a concept rooted in urban culture. But the progressive element of civilisation has never been inevitable. The progress of the world is governed by evolution, which is blind; it is not teleological (with an end in view) as Aristotle had supposed. The fittest survive according to the prevailing conditions; and evolution is by no means biased towards the survival of humanity, which may at present be its fittest product. (In the wake of a nuclear holocaust rendering the entire surface of our planet highly radioactive, the cockroach would be fittest, and would carry the burden of progressive evolution on its small, shiny rounded shoulders.)

History has on several occasions taken a backward step. The fall of Rome and Europe's entry into the Dark Ages is perhaps the most obvious example. Similarly, it is arguable that, at least initially, Stalinist Moscow represented a retrograde step following tsarist Russia. Quite apart from such actual cases, near misses abound. Had Genghis Khan not died, and the leaders of the Mongol hordes not galloped back to Karakorum to elect a new leader, thirteenth-century pastoral Europe would have been overrun by hunter-gatherers. And what if the Nazis had succeeded in taking Britain, as they almost did? Europe would have become a fascist continent, for the foreseeable future. Or what if Stalin, in 1945, had ordered the Red Army to press on into western Europe? This would probably have led to a nuclear war.

Homo sapiens (the wise human being) has been facing this last annihilating threat since at least the 1960s. Precipitating a nuclear war, and averting one, have involved accidental near misses on several occasion, not all of them well publicised. Nuclear war would certainly spell the end of civilisation, in the sense of urban living: there would be no such thing as leading cities. As a constant threat, this remains on a par with the hoary, ever-present Four Horsemen of the Apocalypse: Famine, Pestilence, Conquest and War.[48] In true Darwinian fashion these too have evolved from their biblical stereotypes into more modern guise. Famine, recently all but eliminated from the face of the earth, shows signs of returning with the aid of ecological disaster, global warming and so forth. Pestilence, or some kind of plague, now has the potential to return as a pandemic. Conquest, accompanying the attempted formation, dissolution or collapse of empire, also remains an ever-present possibility, though it must be said that the most recent example in this sphere, namely the collapse of the Soviet Empire, was a comparatively peaceful event.[49]

---

48 These vary according to source and interpretation, but their gist remains much the same.
49 Those who regard the vicious disintegration of Yugoslavia as a direct consequence of this event would disagree.

But it is in the last of the Four Horseman, War, that we find the strongest new trend emerging. Previously piracy, revolt, war-lords and the like were minor aspects of war. Now, in the form of terrorism, this minor aspect has taken on a more formidable role. Say we assume that after the collapse of the Soviet Union a semblance of the End of History *had* begun to emerge. If so, the events of 9/11 in the United States, forever embodied in the destruction of the twin towers of the World Trade Center in New York, put an end to that delusion. More recently, the sudden rise (and collapse) of Isis in Syria has shown that war continues to thrive in its terrorist form.

But back to Professor Fukuyama and what he missed in *The End of History*. Even as attention was diverted by the end of the Cold War, the later events of 9/11, the consequent two Iraq wars and the Syrian civil war in which all the 'major powers' saw fit to par-ticipate, it soon became clear that these were not the pre-eminent events taking place in the world. Far from it. World power had begun to shift on its axis. It now extended far beyond the reaches of America, Russia or the former imperial powers of Europe. On the other side of the globe were the two most populous coun-tries on earth. India, with a population of almost 900 million was the world's largest democracy; while communist China, despite instituting its 'one child per family' policy as early as 1979, now contained a massive 1.8 billion.

Much like America's almost unnoticed rise during the nineteenth century, the emergence of India and China was barely perceived until it had become a fact.

Mumbai: A Vision of Our Future

Mumbai has everything. Indeed, the moniker that best captures the spirit of the city is the title used by the local writer Suketu Mehta for his book *Maximum City*. It is claimed that all the world's major religious beliefs – from militant Atheism to fire-worshipping Zoroastrianism – are practised here. This is the city that contains Asia's largest slum Dharavi as well as thirty of India's sixty-eight billionaires, ranking it sixth in the world of such billionaire-resident cities.[50] Mumbai also contains the world's most expensive home, Antilia, a twenty-seven-storey high-rise valued at £2.2 billion. Bursting at the seams with over 10 million inhabitants, its population increases by 500 people per day, seven days a week, year in year out.

Mumbai is both the ancient and the modern name for the city that used to be known as Bombay, from the fifteenth-century Portuguese *bom bahia*, meaning 'good bay'.[51] The name Mumbai comes from the ancient temple of Mumbadevi, which stood by the long-gone Bora Bundi creek, where the local Koli fishermen used to haul in their boats. This temple burnt down some time in the mid-eighteenth century, and the present Mumbadevi temple stands a mile or so to the north, beyond the Zaveri Bazaar, with its maze of alleys and jewellery shops, where 65 per cent of India's ex-

---

50 After New York, Moscow, London, Hong Kong and Beijing.
51 To avoid confusion, I have chosen to use the name Mumbai throughout, even when it is historically anachronistic.

tensive gold trade is carried out. The present, somewhat run-down Mumbadevi temple houses a statue of a wide-eyed Mumbadevi clad in multi-coloured robes, a silver crown atop her head and an ornate nose-jewel with pearls falling down over her face. In many statues Mumbadevi is depicted with an orange face and no mouth – an incongruous detail, as she is often claimed to be an incarnation of the fearsome mother-goddess Kali, devourer of evil, who is usually depicted as a blue-skinned, multi-armed goddess with her red tongue stuck out. (The Rolling Stones logo of a stuck-out tongue was apparently suggested by Mick Jagger after he had seen a statue of Kali.)

Mumbai is best known around the world as the city of Bollywood (Bombay-Hollywood), the Hindi film industry, whose extensive film studios are situated in the northern suburbs. In fact, Bollywood's output far exceeds that of Hollywood – both in size, productivity and the sheer exuberant extravaganza of its over-the-top performances. Films are typically three to four hours long (with gasping interval), replete with much stylised song and choreographed dance routines, often featuring more than a hundred extras. Nowadays, films are liable to include location shots in such exotic far-off spots as London, Paris, New York, Brazil and Switzerland (to name but a few). However, these exotic locales are invariably populated with Hindi-speaking extras, bullock carts, beggars and sacred cows, while the main narrative takes little account of its foreign surroundings.

The most popular films are what is known as *masala*, meaning 'mixed spices' (as in the most popular Indian dish in Britain, Chicken Tikka Masala[52]). These involve a mind-spinning *mélange*

---

52 There is no such dish in authentic Indian cuisine. This was in fact concocted by Indian restaurants in Britain to cater for local tastes. This has been such a success that recent polls have found it to be Britain's favourite national dish. In much the same way, chop suey was originally concocted by Chinese chefs in San Francisco to suit local tastes.

of genres: action, comedy, drama, as well as ingredients of melodrama and romance. Action is based on the Hong Kong variety, rather than Hollywood, and thus includes all kinds of Indian-version Kung Fu, replete with acrobatics and stunts. Plots, too, include a regular menu of ingredients such as crossed lovers, outraged traditional parents, long-lost relatives, love triangles and the benevolent courtesan. All this has to be achieved with the star-crossed couple displaying no hint of sexuality and absolutely no kissing.

Such films are wildly popular throughout India, as well as all over the Indian diaspora (especially in the UK and Canada). A sixth of the globe's population are said to obtain their wider worldview from Bollywood, much as America's view of the world remains coloured by Hollywood.

Bollywood makes up to one thousand six hundred films a year; the entire US makes less than half this amount. According to the latest figures there are almost ten thousand cinema screens in India, which are attended by 2.2 billion people. In Mumbai alone the number of screens fluctuates at around one thousand three hundred. A well-known Bollywood actor expects to make around £6 million per film, and to feature in around four to five films annually. On top of this come lucrative commercial endorsements.

All these Bollywood numbers are even more astonishing when one takes into account the fact that there are some twenty-three culturally recognised languages in India, and hundreds more locally spoken languages and dialects. Mumbai has around nine main spoken languages, and many dozens of other minority languages and dialects. The city's official language is Marathi, with Hindi and English also widely spoken. The language in the majority of Bollywood films is colloquial Hindustani, recognisable to both Hindi and Urdu speakers. This is often interposed with a language known as Hinglish, a blend of Hindi and English that is becoming increasingly popular, especially in the advertising industry, which aims at reaching out to as many people as possible. Examples of Hinglish in high-profile adverts abound. Domino's Pizza ran on the slogan 'Hungry kya?' (Are you hungry?). Pepsi Cola's most successful advert in all its history proclaimed: 'Yeh hi hai right one, baby' (You got the right one, baby). Coca Cola replied with 'Vaah! Life ho to aisi' (Wow! Life should be like this).

But back to Bollywood, whose stars are regarded with something approaching religious awe. These are the gods of the silver screen, and their lives provide a continuous soap opera for the popular press and social media: their marriages, their affairs, their misdemeanours... When Sonam Kapoor, of the Bollywood Kapoor dynasty, claimed that 'good karma' was the reason she was born into privilege and riches, the press were quick to denounce her statement as 'casteist'.

Which brings us to the vexed question of caste. The societies of all the previous cities in this book have invariably, to a more or less degree, been stratified by class. Such divisions were practically institutionalised in nineteenth-century London. Meanwhile, in the 'land of the free', New York had a mobile but similarly delineated class system. Even in 'classless' Moscow the Party evolved its own social gradations: ironically, in the 'dictatorship of the proletariat' it was the proletariat who were on the receiving end of the dictatorship. Yet all these are as nothing compared to the Indian caste system, which remains categorically in a class of its own, so to speak. The class divisions of London, New York and Moscow were socially sanctioned; the caste system in Mumbai is reinforced by the rigidity of religious sanction.

Put with brutal simplicity, the caste system stems from the Hindu belief in the endless cycle of reincarnation. According to the karma achieved by individuals during their lives, they return in a higher (or lower) caste. The highest caste are the Brahmins (whose very name derives from Brahma, the God of Creation). Beneath these are the Kshatriyas (according to ancient tradition, these were warriors and rulers), the Vaishyas (likewise said to be farmers and merchants) and the Shudras (labourers), each of which have several sub-castes. Condemned to the bottom of the heap are the Dalits, the 'untouchables', who traditionally have been assigned the roles of street-sweepers or latrine cleaners.

Before we condemn out of hand such a hierarchy, it should be noted that this bears a striking resemblance to the ideal society as conceived by Plato, whose work remains so admired in the West. (After all, many still regard western philosophy as nothing more than 'footnotes to Plato'.) Also, it is worth noting that British colonialists encouraged the caste system as part of their 'divide and rule' policy, which enabled 165,000 British administrators and military personnel to rule over 330 million Indians.

However, it comes as something of a surprise that many of those who strove to free India from the yoke of British colonial rule did not seek to free their country from the constraints of the caste system. Like so much else that is forward-looking in India, the Indian independence movement was founded in Mumbai, during the Congress Party meeting in August 1942. It was on this occasion that Mahatma Gandhi delivered his famous 'Quit India' speech before a massive crowd gathered at the Gowalia Tank Maidan in central Mumbai. In this speech, Gandhi called for an extension of his passive non-violent resistance to British rule, involving 'do or die'.

Gandhi's campaign of passive resistance had given birth to a new and powerful form of political resistance. This would involve crowds of his followers taking part in novel forms of protest, such as lying down on railway lines to prevent the passage of trains, or accompanying Gandhi on his march to the sea to gather free salt in protest against the British monopoly tax on this vital commodity. Gandhi's exemplary campaign would eventually rouse the whole of India against the British, and be instrumental in the subcontinent achieving independence.

However, despite such widespread and popular success, the leaders of this movement stopped short of liberating India from the shackles of the caste system. The South Africa-born Gandhi may have shed the conventional three-piece suit he had worn as a lawyer in London in favour of a native dhoti, but he refused to disown the notion of caste. Gandhi's vision of India involved a return to the ancient ways of tradition. Similarly, his political colleague Pandit Nehru put aside the conventional garb he had worn during his English public school education in favour of a white outfit echoing his Brahmin status, along with the white cap of the Congress Party, and refused to publicly condemn the caste system.[53] This, despite the fact that Nehru's vision for India was more progressive, even egalitarian than Gandhi's, in many of its intentions. Only the 'father of the Indian constitution', the lawyer and polymath Babasaheb Ambedkar, adamantly rejected all notion of caste (while at the same time adhering to western dress). As India's first Minister of Justice he would campaign tirelessly against social discrimination, especially with regard to his own 'untouchable' caste, the Dalits.

The Indian Constitution specifically forbids discrimination on grounds of caste or race, and mandates education for all castes. The notion of caste is recognised and legislated against, rather than simply banned – which would probably have been impossible, on religious and social grounds. Following independence in 1948, however, caste would continue to permeate all aspects of Indian life – from marriage to notions of 'purity' and even diet.

---

53 Nehru's actual first name was Jawaharlal, but he was popularly known as 'Pandit', reflecting his membership of the Kashmiri Pandit Brahmin caste. Similarly, Gandhi's first name was in fact Mohandas, but he was popularly known as 'Mahatma', which means 'saintly', on account of his ascetic lifestyle.

(Brahmins are meant to be vegetarian, refraining from 'unclean' meat, which is the diet of the lower-caste warriors. Dalits were particularly shunned, as they ate beef, product of the sacred cow.)

In modern India the caste system remains closely associated with Hinduism, and still remains a decisive element of social life, especially in the villages and rural areas. Yet an indication of how far urban life has progressed can be seen in the fact that the Dalit Kocheril Narayanan would become president of India in 1997. Another indication can be seen in the fact mentioned above that the Mumbai popular press could accuse Bollywood royalty, in the form of Sonam Kapoor, of 'casteism'. As Suketu Mehta put it: 'In fifty years, independent India has done what 5,000 years of history could not do: it gave the people who are in the majority a voice in the running of the country.' India remains the world's largest democracy: all castes are permitted to vote. This includes women, who in the 2019 election even became the majority of voters.

Of the eight Indian Nobel-Prize-winners since independence, only its three prize-winners for peace have been resident in India. Great scientists such as the physicist Subrahmanyan Chandrasekhar, as well as the economists Amartya Sen and the Mumbai-born Abhijit Banerjee, have only managed to fulfil their potential in exile, free from the constrictions of caste. Although this is less prevalent in other fields, a similar pattern can be seen in the lives of writers from Nirad C. Chaudhuri to the Mumbai-born Salman Rushdie. And as the Indian literary critic Amit Saha has pointed-ed out: 'Indian-English writers like Anita Desai, Bharati Mukherjee, Shashi Tharoor, Amitav Ghosh, Vikram Seth, Sunetra Gupta, Rohinton Mistry, Jhumpa Lahiri, and Hari Kunzru have all made their names while residing abroad.' Yet the heartening fact here is that these figures belong largely to previous generations. The younger generation of talented and ambitious Indians may feel the need to travel abroad to widen their horizons, but fewer are choosing to live in exile. And even those who do, tend to make regular return visits to re-establish contact with their roots.

Following independence India quickly established itself as a major player on the international scene, with Nehru leading the Non-Aligned Nations of the Third World. In the original meaning of this last term, the Third World consisted of the many (often newly independent) countries that wished to steer an independent course between the First World (the US and its Western allies) and the Second World (the Soviet Union, communist China and their more or less socialist-inclined allies). As early as 1953, Nehru outlined the Five Pillars of the Non-Aligned Movement. These included mutual respect, non-aggression, non-interference, equality and peaceful co-existence. Though it is worth noting that Nehru's speech was originally intended as a guide to relations between India and China.

Relations between the world's two most populous nations have long been prickly, to say the least. The inexact frontier they share in the high Himalayas has seen frequent incidents, one of which escalated into outright war in 1962, though it was evident that both sides sought to contain this war within the immediate region.

The twin presence of Mumbai and Beijing in this book is intended to reflect their differing status in leading the world. Beijing would appear to heavily outrank Mumbai, and the notion of any competition between them would seem to be simply 'no contest'. The miracle of Beijing's recent economic transformation has but a pale echo in the billionaires, skyscrapers and vast slums of Mumbai.

Yet, beyond this competitive aspect, there remains a categorical difference between these two cities, one that is indicative of the different ways in which they both lead the world. Beijing's growth has been strictly calibrated by Chinese Communist Party control. Mumbai's growth, on the other hand, has been part of the raucous free-for-all of capitalism, with its analogous whirligig of Bollywood extravaganza along with all the innumerable slum dogs who do not win the lottery and become fairy-tale millionaires. Surely even in this aspect, communist Beijing has certainly won, and capitalist Mumbai can only be judged a poor second?

So it would appear, at least for the moment. But as we shall see, the cracks are already beginning to appear in the strictly maintained facade of Beijing's command economy (and command society). The cracks in Mumbai are gaping holes that the city has learned to live with (while striving to fill these vast fissures of social injustice). And here lies the point. Mumbai is living with its failures; something that Beijing cannot bring itself to admit. Both are in need of long-overdue reforms. But Mumbai will persevere, no matter how much, or how little, these reforms are enacted. In a fundamental sense, Beijing refuses to admit such freedoms, which it knows would destroy its entire credo (and almost certainly a lot more besides).

This fragility, and Mumbai's 'freedoms', are the reason why it is a leading city in today's world. Mumbai can be seen as an exaggerated example of all the ambitions and ills of the 'Free World'. Its attempts to solve its multiple ills are the paradigm the world must follow if it is to succeed while retaining notions of freedom and democracy. Seen from this perspective, it is Beijing that appears fragile, and Mumbai that carries humanity's hopes.[54]

---

54 Rapid economic development throughout India means that it now has a middle class larger than the entire population of the United States. On the other hand, China's larger population and faster economic development ensures that it has an even more populous middle class. In both countries, this class is driven by entrepreneurial and social aspirations. The Indian middle class expects freedom of speech and other democratic freedoms as their right. By contrast, the emergent middle class in China is denied such political freedoms. As this class increases, the demand for such liberty will inevitably grow. As the Indian middle class increases, the country as a whole will benefit. For the communist rulers of China, the emergence of an increasingly demanding middle class is a political time bomb.

India's new status as an independent country would have a transformative effect on Mumbai, the country's major port on the western seaboard. Indeed, it was this very location that had been responsible for Mumbai's first leap to prominence well over a century earlier, another occasion when international affairs had moved in its favour. This time it was the American Civil War that benefited Mumbai. With the Unionist North blockading the cotton ports of the Confederate South, as well as preventing cotton reaching the ports of the north-eastern seaboard by rail, the mills of Britain's thriving cotton industry were suddenly bereft of raw material. This gap was filled by the shipping to Britain of Indian cotton, exported through the port of Mumbai. In 1869, four years after the end of the American Civil War, Mumbai would further benefit from the opening of the Suez Canal, which reduced sailing time to Europe by almost two-thirds. Six years later, Mumbai would establish itself as the financial centre of India, when twenty-five local equities brokers came together to form the Native Shares and Stock Brokers Association. This was the first stock exchange in all of Asia.

In fact, such trading had begun as early as the 1850s, when five Indian brokers took to gathering beneath a banyan tree in front of the town hall (on the present site of the Horniman Circle). Nowadays, the BSE (formerly the Bombay Stock Exchange) is among the dozen largest in the world. The total market capitalisation of the companies trading on the exchange in 2019 was just over $2 trillion.[55]

Naturally, such a market soon began attracting the usual crop of financial innovators, some of whose inventiveness would lead to them spending time 'at His Majesty's pleasure' (i.e. in jail). However, the coming of age of a world financial centre is frequently

---

55 By comparison, New York was $23 trillion, Tokyo $5.7 trillion and London $4.5 trillion.

marked by its first great scandal, and here the BSE would prove no exception. In 1992 the BSE would play host to what is now known somewhat unimaginatively as the '1992 Securities Scam'. This was orchestrated by the stockbroker Harshad Mehta, already known for his fabulous wealth, having been christened by the popular press 'The Amitabh Bacchan of the Stock Market'.[56]

From an early age, Mehta seems to have wanted to be a millionaire, regardless of whether this was achieved by legal or more imaginative means. Financial chicanery often involves all manner of impenetrable jargon, technical juggling of non-existent items and so forth, and Mehta's scams would prove no exception. On the other hand, the techniques he used were refreshingly simple.

Previously, Indian banks were not permitted to deal in the equities (shares) market, but were required to hold their assets in stable fixed income bonds, which could only be purchased through bona fide brokers. The low interest rates of these bonds provided a low income. Despite this, the banks were expected to post healthy profits. Mehta offered his services as a broker, assuring the banks that he had a solution to their problem. The banks could transfer large sums into his personal account, with the stated expectation that he would use these to purchase for them fixed income bonds. Some time later, Mehta would return the borrowed sum, along with a generous surplus that had allegedly been accumulated from fixed income bonds. The banks were happy, no questions asked. And Mehta was even more happy.

The sums loaned by the banks were invariably bank-sized, in other words vast. Mehta would use these sums to purchase shares in some of India's most respected companies, such as ACC (the

---

56 Amitabh Bacchan is a Bollywood god: a 'one-man industry', 'star of the millennium', leading actor, director, producer, famous throughout the worldwide Indian diaspora, and host of the real life Indian *Who Wants to Be a Millionaire?* (as distinct from the purely imaginary show that featured in the eight-Oscar-winning *Slumdog Millionaire*).

Indian concrete conglomerate) or Videocon (the world's third-largest tube manufacturer, with worldwide assets). A clue to the figures involved can be seen in what happened to ACC shares during 1991. When Mehta began surreptitiously purchasing these shares, word soon got out; brokers suspected that Mehta knew something about future developments in the concrete market of which they were not aware, and piled into ACC shares. Consequently, during a three-month period, ACC shares rose from 200 rupees per share to an eye-watering 9,000 rupees, making Mehta a huge profit. A small percentage of Mehta's profit would be sufficient to satisfy the bank from whom he had borrowed the money (larger sums would have raised unwanted suspicions among the regulators), and the rest he kept for himself.

Come 1992, and Mehta was operating another version of this scam, involving himself as a broker in loans between two banks. These banks were often not aware of the other bank they were dealing with, while Mehta held the money. As security for his short-term borrowing, Mehta would sometimes use Bank Receipts (BRs), which he had bullied some small banks into issuing to him. These were of course worthless, but they gave him credibility. Thus they enabled Mehta to borrow from one of the larger banks and hold this money during the fifteen-day period before he was required to pass it on as a loan to the other bank.

As part of the freeing up of the markets, which was taking place all over the world during this period, Indian banks were now permitted to invest in the equities market. During the fifteen-day period in which Mehta held the money he'd been loaned to pass on to another bank, he would play the markets. To maintain an appearance of legality, he would claim to be acting on behalf of the bank from which he had borrowed. But it was now that Mehta started becoming excessively greedy. As a security for his loans from the banks, he began widescale use of his BRs, which only he knew were worthless. Soon the market was flooded with these BRs, which were soon being used as currency for interbank business.

By now Mehta's lifestyle had become legendary. He owned a fleet of luxury cars, had collected a veritable Aladdin's cave of expensive jewellery, and lived in a 15,000-square-foot penthouse (the size of more than five tennis courts). Unfortunately for Mehta, the skilled financial journalist Sucheta Dalal grew suspicious of this excessive lifestyle and began investigating how it was financed. She got wind of his schemes and started writing an article for *The Times of India* exposing what he was up to.

On 23 April 1992 Dalal's article was published, causing a flurry of alarm on the BSE. Banks holding BRs began demanding their money back, and the market for BRs collapsed. Even so, it was 9 November before Mehta was arrested on a charge of gaining possession of some 28 million shares (worth $35 million) using forged share transfer forms. But this was not all. The true extent of Mehta's activities became clearer when the banks found themselves left holding a total of $560 million of worthless BRs.

Along with his initial charge, Mehta was banned from the BSE and any activities connected with it. Ever resourceful, Mehta took up journalism while awaiting his trial. He began writing a highly successful weekly column in the popular *Navdesh Samachar*, passing on a stream of market tips. Mehta's column attracted a large following in Mumbai, where his expertise was widely appreciated by those who had not fallen foul of his scams. Consequently, the tips in his weekly newspaper columns were largely self-fulfilling because so many readers were following his advice. 'Friends' who held stocks for Mehta under their own name benefited accordingly from advance tips before his column went to press.

The wheels of Indian justice are notoriously slow (to the immense benefit of the participating lawyers), and it was 1999 before Mehta was finally sentenced to five years' rigorous imprisonment, along with a fine of just $350. In 2001 he would die of a heart attack in prison at the age of forty-seven. Mumbai's BSE could now rank itself on a par with great stock markets throughout the globe; it too had produced its own major financial scandal, to rank alongside the likes of Ponzi and Enron.

The newspaper that exposed this scandal, *The Times of India*, is a Mumbai institution. Founded in 1838, it is now the largest English-speaking daily newspaper in the world, and it regularly ranks among the world's top half-dozen newspapers in any language.

The paper began during the colonial era and, despite being run by a British editorial staff, it established its independence from the colonial government from the outset. Its great long-term editor was Sir Stanley Reed, who ran it for seventeen years until 1924. Reed corresponded with Mahatma Gandhi when he was organising his campaign for civil disobedience and refused to be put off from publishing Gandhi's opinions. The paper would remain similarly independent when an Indian staff took over after India achieved nationhood in 1948. Its most famous example of this would come twenty-seven years later when the country was ruled by its first woman prime minister, Indira Gandhi.[57]

On 25 June 1975 Prime Minister Gandhi declared a state of emergency, imprisoning many of her opponents, ruling by decree and curbing press freedom. In response, the following day *The Times of India* published in its obituary column an entry that read:

D.E.M. O'Cracy, beloved husband of T. Ruth, father of L.I. Bertie, brother of Faith, Hope and Justice expired on 25 June.

---

57 Indira Gandhi was Pandit Nehru's daughter, and no relation to Mahatma Gandhi, whom she knew during her childhood. Indira Nehru received the name Gandhi from her husband Feroze Gandhi, who was a freedom fighter and journalist.

Nowadays *The Times of India* does its best to expose the city's ills: crime, corruption, housing. The sheer scale of this unending task is indicated by writer Suketu Mehta:

> The city is full of people claiming what's not theirs. Tenants claim ownership by virtue of having squatted on the property. Mill workers demand mills to be kept open at a loss to provide them with employment. Slum dwellers demand water and power connections for illegal constructions on public land.

Government employees are little better, frequently demanding *baksheesh* ('bribes') from petitioners to look into their cases, claiming overtime for hours not worked, etcetera, etcetera. And why? Frequently wages are inadequate. Such demands are not limited to the lowest-paid workers: 'Commuters demand subsidies for train fares, which are already the lowest in the world. Moviegoers demand that the government freeze ticket prices.' Economic reality in Mumbai is something of a never-never land, for the government 'has long believed in the unreality of supply and demand; what you pay for an item, for a food or for a service, has no relation to what it costs the producer'.

It is hardly surprising that crime flourishes in such conditions, and that even the behaviour of the police force itself is often barely distinguishable from that of the criminals they are meant to pursue. On the other hand, there are heroes. One of these is senior police officer Ajay Lal.[58] With his cropped hair and athletic build, Lal has the appearance of an intelligent boxer. He is well-dressed, well-spoken and sophisticated, with the charisma of a Bollywood

---

58 Ajay Lal is a pseudonym. This is the name of a character who appeared in the movie *The Attacks of 26/1*, playing the part of a well-known Mumbai police commissioner. The reasons for my use of this pseudonym will become apparent, as Lal unbuttons himself when describing his deeds and intentions.

star. During his rise to the top, Lal won medals for bravery and a deserved reputation for motivating his force with fiery speeches.

This was the man who arrested the godfather of the Mumbai underworld, Dawood Ibrahim, an unsavoury character whose multifarious criminal activities at home and abroad enabled him to become one of the richest men in the world, with a fortune estimated at over £5 billion. The machinations of Ibrahim's lawyers enabled him to flee the country, where he received the accolade of reaching No. 3 on the FBI's 'Most Wanted' list. He is thought to own a dozen or so residences in countries as far afield as Pakistan, the UAE, Bangkok and even Luxembourg.

Ibrahim's activities are known to have extended far beyond organised crime, and he is thought to have been behind several acts of terrorism (hence the FBI's interest). The most notorious of these incidents was the 1993 bombings in Mumbai, during which no less than 257 people lost their lives and 1,400 were injured.

Commissioner Lal openly admits that when interrogating Ibrahim's henchman he has not been afraid to use waterboarding and electric torture. Though he claims that his most effective method is to give a suspect 'one kilo of *jalebi*s' (a popular Indian sweet). 'If you have a kilo of sweets, you must have water,' Lal explains. 'A man will do anything for water after so many sweets.'

Lal reserves his deepest contempt for his corrupt colleagues and announces that he has big plans to mark his retirement. He says he will go to Police HQ with a megaphone, and here he will unzip his trousers and wave his penis at the building, while at the same time yelling through his megaphone abuse at all his colleagues, revealing everything. He promises to shout, '"Fuck you, fuck you, fuck you, gentlemen." Then I will pee in their direction and turn around and leave the force.'

Another contentious aspect of Mumbai life (and indeed that of all India) is the gold market. Mumbai's colourful Zaveri Gold

Bazaar, with its maze of twisting lanes, 11,000 shops and many thousands of craft jewellery makers, may account for well over half the nation's gold trading, but it remains the tip of the iceberg where gold in India is concerned. Indians have traditionally favoured storing their savings in the form of gold, which is usually held as a hedge against inflation, to disguise accumulations of income from the tax authorities, or as a reliable means of transporting an internationally recognised form of wealth. Over the centuries this covert hoard has increased many times over.

In 2019 the Indian federal government held 557.7 metric tonnes of gold, making it the tenth-largest official holder of gold in the world.[59] The gold held in private hands in India is certainly far in excess of that held by the government. Indeed, historical investigators have come up with an estimate that over the centuries Indians have built up a collective fortune of some 20,000 tonnes of gold. This does not take into account corporate business holdings, many of which follow the predilection of private citizens for this commodity for similar covert reasons. Then there is the gold wealth held in temples and other religious institutions that favour gold as a mode of decoration. These range from the stupendous six-storey golden facade of the Sree Padmanabhaswamy Temple in Thiruvananthapuram to the Sikh Golden Temple at Amritsar. Such buildings may be among the wonders of India, but they are far from being unique in their wealth of gold. Add all this together, and one begins to get an idea of the true enormity of India's gold holdings.

In the light of all this gold, India might in fact be one of the wealthiest nations on earth, though, measured by normal, more open criteria, such as the IMF rankings, it is a lowly 116th, with a GDP per capita of just $9,027. Gold hidden away under the bed

59 By contrast the USA holds 8,133.5 tonnes, and China 1,797.5 tonnes.

or buried in the garden may be a tangible asset, but it earns no interest. Indeed, it plays no real part in the economy at all. For years, economists have puzzled in vain on how to release all this wealth into the market, making it productive in the real economy. If this could only be managed, in an economically prudent fashion, India might even be able make a great leap forward enabling it catch up with its Asian rival China.[60]

Another difficulty facing the economy of a city such as Mumbai is the flourishing black market. With a pool of cheap labour in slums such as Dharavi, 'off books' employment and transactions of all kinds have become a widespread way of avoiding tax. The black economy has been estimated to account for around 30 per cent of the actual economy of the city. Indeed, release of the official figures has led to the official economy being widely regarded as an Indian rope trick.

In 2016 the Indian government took drastic action to overcome this problem. The Mumbai-born populist prime minister Narendra Modi announced his plan to de-monetise the high-denomination 500- and 1,000-rupee notes. At the same time, the Reserve Bank of India announced that such notes could only be cashed in for lower-denomination notes over a period of fifty days, ending on 30 December 2016. This was intended to bring to light (or de-monetise) any income that could not be accounted for, as it was known that many black marketeers stashed away their profits in secret hoards of high-denomination notes.

---

60 Towards the end of the last century, the Black Sea coastal region of Turkey faced a similar problem, with its economy moribund and its citizens choosing to hold their savings in gold rather than the collapsing Turkish lira. Then, in 1989, the Berlin Wall fell and Russians were soon free to travel abroad. One side-effect of this was an influx of blonde Russian prostitutes crossing the Black Sea to Turkey on the newly opened ferry route. Consequently, many men in northern Turkey began cashing in their gold in order to pay these prostitutes, and this sudden release of liquidity soon brought about a revival of the entire economy of the region.

Further measures were announced in November of that year. The cashing in of these high-denomination notes was limited to 4,000 rupees per person, reducing to 2,000 rupees per person by the end of the month. Limits were also placed on withdrawals from ATM machines.

The results of this campaign were highly revealing. Income tax returns for 2016/17 rose by 25 per cent. And in line with the government's intentions, the shortage of ready cash resulted in a large increase in digital payments (which are registered and can be traced). An unexpected side-effect was a decrease in funding for terrorist organisations, and a consequent decrease in bomb incidents. On the other hand, there was such chaos at the ATM machines that several people lost their lives in the scramble to get their hands on their money before the machines ran out of cash. The Mumbai stock market may have immediately crashed, but it soon began climbing again when it became clear that the prospect of de-monetisation had resulted in a retail spending boom. Such heavy-handed innovative economic measures were not well received by many local professional economists, with Vivek Kaul claiming that 'demonetisation had been a failure of epic proportions'. Similarly, several of Mumbai's billionaires and millionaires lost a fortune in the stock market crash. Many of these high-net-worth investors panicked at the prospect of a huge devaluation of the Indian currency. They quickly liquidated their holdings at a loss and transferred their savings to foreign markets. Yet after the initial dip, the Indian rupee soon regained its value.

Regardless of such drastic measures, the central feature of Mumbai life remains the polarisation of the filthy rich and the dirt poor. This is epitomised by the contrast between the Antilia building and the Dharavi slums, which are separated by less than five miles.

The Antilia building, home of Mukesh Ambani and his family.

The Antilia building is almost 600 feet tall, and from its upper storey the rising smoke of the Dharavi slum is just visible through the trembling heat haze. The average annual temperature in Mumbai is well over 30 °C, which is stifling at the best of times, even more so during the humidity of the summer monsoon season. Naturally, the Antilia building has air conditioning throughout its 400,000 square feet of floor space, which is spread over twenty-seven storeys. These include several projecting decks with extensive gardens, including lawns, pools and statues of Hindu deities.

The building is occupied by Mukesh Ambani and his family, along with 300 staff. Mukesh Ambani, who is now in his sixties, is the tenth-richest man in the world, according to the 2021 Forbes list. He made his £60-billion fortune as the largest shareholder of Reliance Industries, the most valuable company in India by market value (i.e. what it would cost to buy the company, in this case well north of £120 billion). The company was co-founded in 1973 by Mukesh's father Dhirubhai, who expanded the business beyond its initial polyester manufacturing interests into a wide variety of commercial enterprises. Mukesh joined the firm at the age of twenty-three after leaving Stanford University, and he played an active role in moving Reliance into retail, telecommunications and petrochemicals. In 2002 Reliance would discover what was at the time the largest supply of natural gas in the world. This was in the Krishna Godavari Dhirubhai 6 field in the Bay of Bengal off southeast India.

In 2008 Mukesh Ambani founded the Indian Premier League cricket team Mumbai Indians, which played its home games at the Wankhede Stadium, a venue that was then capable of holding 45,000 delirious spectators. The Mumbai Indians team included the Mumbai-born Sachin Tendulkar, another of India's 'gods', who ranks alongside Bollywood's greatest in legendary and monetary status. Known as the 'master blaster' for his explosive batting skills, he would play for India for twenty-four years before his retirement in 2013. He captained India in test cricket, and in 2011 he was a member of the Indian OTD (one-day cricket) team that won the World Cup. Many commentators rate him as the greatest batsman of all time.

More recently, in 2018 Mukesh Ambani celebrated the wedding of his twenty-seven-year-old daughter Isha to her childhood friend, property tycoon Anand Piramal, scion of another of Mumbai's richest families, whose fortune was accrued largely through financial services. As befitted the union of two such prestigious dynasties, the marriage was suitably over the top, with celebrations in the fabulous lakeside city of Udaipur lasting four days and costing some $100 million. Guests were entertained by the likes of Beyoncé, and the father of the bride donated sufficient food to provide 5,100 local people with three free meals a day for the four days of the wedding celebrations.[61]

Dharavi 'village'.

---

61 To put this into perspective, the marriage of Prince Charles and Lady Diana Spencer in London in 1981 is estimated to have cost $110 million.

The other side of the social equation provides some similarly extravagant figures. The slum of Dharavi, quaintly marked on some maps as 'Dharavi village', is thought to house anything up to a million people in an area of less than one square mile (almost three-quarters the size of New York's Central Park, or almost twice the size of London's Hyde Park). Dharavi is the most densely populated spot on Earth; but it is not the only slum district in Mumbai, and it is estimated that some six million (roughly 60 per cent of the city's population) live in slum conditions. In Dharavi these range from ramshackle, home-made, three-storey hovels overlooking a fetid creek of floating refuse, acres of corrugated iron-roofed shacks whose brick walls form warrens of alleyways, to a hillside of colourfully painted primitive block-built dwellings. Incongruous amid a jumble of corrugated iron rooftops rise the pale walls, striped minarets and green dome of the Moinia Masjid mosque. Muslim districts sit uneasily alongside those of Hindus and other religions, strife often being incited by outside interests for political gain.

The United Nations, World Health Organization and other international and Indian aid agencies work in co-operation with the Municipal Corporation of Greater Mumbai to alleviate some of the worst pockets of abject poverty. Such commodities as potable water and liquid gas cylinders will soon be available throughout the 'village'. Driving down one of the main roads that pass through this district may present an overwhelming experience of smoke, filth and poverty in the raw, but inside the huts that line the maze of alleyways prejudicial stereotypes are frequently overturned. Huts are swept clean, cheap trinkets hang from the walls and objects of devotion lend a homely aspect. Colourful frayed curtains cover the windows, with little beds of flowers.

In some districts of Dharavi there are row upon row of bulbous brown clay pots in yards outside potteries. Other districts have cramped sweatshops where women in coloured saris labour over sewing machines. The inhabitants may be marginalised, ignored or exploited, but in many aspects Dharvi is a hive of small-scale entrepreneurship – evidenced in the home-made buildings, and basic ingenuity of everyday living. Today, there are also schools in Dharavi, which has a literacy rate of 69 per cent, with a handful of students even making it to university.

Yet there is no denying the harsh criminal reality, such as that exposed in the fictional *Slumdog Millionaire*.[62] The film shows the sheer vulnerability of the slum-dwellers, especially the children who pick their way through the city's rubbish tips, some recruited into begging gangs by local Fagins similar to those who haunted the slums of nineteenth-century London.

And here, if anything, is a ray of hope. London has come a long way since Dickensian times. And Mumbai too is already progressing along its own path. The streets of 1960s Kolkata that I described at the opening of this book were home to the homeless, with death by starvation and disease an ever-present possibility. Despite the rise in population, the death rate in India is now one-third of what it was then. And Mumbai, with its Antilia building and its Dharavi 'village', is recognisable as a leader of similar cities across the globe. From Rio de Janeiro to Cape Town, from Mexico

---

62 This multi-Oscar-winning movie will be many people's only experience of Mumbai, and especially Dharavi, which forms a backdrop to much of the action. *Slumdog Millionaire* is often derided as a 'British-made' film. In fact, it is based on the book *Q &A* by the Indian novelist Vikas Swarap and co-directed by Indian Loveleen Tandan (alas not included in the Oscar credits). Most advisers and technicians were locally hired, as indeed were many of the extras, some of whom actually came from Dharavi. All the main actors were of course Indian. The conscious 'Bollywood' element added a slight sentimentality (but nothing compared with Dickens' descriptions of nineteenth-century London). Salman Rushdie, who lives in exile but grew up in Mumbai, slated the film. Local and national film critics included it in their top-ten lists – some feat for a 'serious' drama in competition with Bollywood entertainment hits. As a 'sleeper' it has gone on to attract worldwide attention and acclaim.

City to Manila, eyes are watching Mumbai. What happens here will echo throughout the so-called Free World.

It is in this sense that Mumbai leads the world. It has, and manages to live with, some of the most appalling urban problems. In the 1960s Kolkata was an unrecognised 'failed city' before its time. In the 2020s Mumbai is the unrecognised 'city of the future' before its time. The problems it faces are the world's problems, now and to come, writ large. It is the future playing out before our eyes. And perhaps most interestingly of all, it is attempting to do this in an arguably liberal democratic manner. Corruption may be an infection, just as abject poverty in juxtaposition with extreme wealth may be a bleeding sore, but the body politic of democracy remains alive. Somehow, miraculously. This is the political system to which the so-called 'free West' adheres, and in which it invests its future. Should this fail here, the implications would be worldwide for whatever other system might rule the world.

The main alternative is a state-control system, as in Beijing. This is undeniably some years ahead in the race at this point. But will its system of authoritarian government prove more resilient, and ultimately more beneficial, than that of Mumbai? Government of the people by the people, or government of the people by the government?

Beijing: The Alternative Future

Beijing has no Dharavi, and no Antilia building, but then neither could it be described as part of the Free World. On the other hand, it has one of the most imaginative skyscraper landscapes of any city in the world. This ranges from the celebrated Bird's Nest Stadium, home to the 2008 Beijing Olympics, based on an idea by artist Ai Weiwei, to the unique 630-foot Pangu Plaza building, whose top floors expand and curve into a flowing flare resembling a dragon's head (others claim it is meant to resemble the flame of the Olympic torch).

Yet the most accomplished of all these many architectural feats is surely the Wangjing SOHO development, designed by the late Iraqi-British architect Zaha Hadid. This consists of three towers – 387 foot, 417 foot, and 656 foot high – each moulded in Hadid's trademark sensual curves. Together, they form a sculptural juxtaposition unique even in this modern age of fantasy architecture. Only a city open to the most daring and ambitious of new ideas could have permitted such a design. Yet, paradoxically, when a local internet technology company called Zuhai Shengun criticised the building for having bad *feng shui*, it was fined 200,000 yuan ($30,000) for defamation.[63]

---

63 *Feng shui* literally means 'wind-water' and harks back to a belief that is older than China itself. This is rooted in metaphysical ideas regarding how constructions – such as tombs, homesteads or even furniture – should be aligned in an auspicious manner, often with regard to the position of stars in the heavens or nearby waters.

Beijing may not have a giant Dharavi slum, but it does have its own smaller shanty towns, most of which have sprung up among the suburbs at the edges of the city. An exception is Huashiyung, a makeshift village that lies literally in the shadow of the pristine glass skyscrapers of Chaoyang, Beijing's central business district. The narrow winding alleyways lined with haphazard brick-built and tiled-roof dwellings would be immediately recognisable to any inhabitant of Dharavi.

Huashiyung is largely populated by the migrant workers who stream into Beijing from poor villages in distant provinces, drawn by tales of the riches to be found in the new China. Many men find work on construction sites in the city; women often use contact networks to find employment as maids or cleaners. Others are not so lucky. On the walls of the alleyways are posters advertising for blood donors; a pint of blood can earn enough to rent a tiny space in shared accommodation.

In the evenings the air of the alleyways is thick with smoke, mingled with the smell of food from the cooking fires. And during the daytime there is the eye-watering miasma of Beijing's notorious air pollution. Tangled electricity cables loop over the rooftops, and sewage flows down the centre of many alleyways. Such shanty towns are often short-lived, bulldozed away to make room for new high-rise buildings. But as quickly as they disappear, other new settlements sprout up. In 2015 the metropolitan area of Beijing had a population of 18.2 million. By 2020 this had grown to 20.4 million, making it twice the size of Mumbai. And it continues to increase at something over 2 per cent, year on year – that's 1,200 new inhabitants arriving every day (well over twice as many as arrive in Mumbai).

Beijing has engineered the greatest economic transformation in history, while at the same time being ruled by the Chinese Communist Party (CCP). Anomalously, the city has embraced free-market capitalism, while at the same time remaining at its heart an autocratic command economy.

This creative leap forward is all the more remarkable when one considers that less than half a century ago, this very same CCP, under the leadership of Chairman Mao Zedong, all but destroyed the social fabric of the city, and indeed the entire country, during the Cultural Revolution. This violent period would last in various forms from 1966 until after Mao's death in 1976.

In pursuance of the Cultural Revolution, Chinese youth and young urban workers were encouraged to weed out and destroy all remnants of traditional and bourgeois culture. During this period previously respected figures – including an entire strata of society, such as professors, administrators and other 'enemies of the people' – were despatched to far-flung peasant villages. Here they were set to work at menial and demeaning tasks as part of their 're-education' in 'correct thought'. The purest form of this Maoism, as it came to be known, was found in Chairman Mao's Little Red Book. This publication, which was freely distributed throughout China, and indeed in translations all over the world, contained the thoughts of Chairman Mao. These were expressed in 267 aphorisms concerning class struggle, correct thinking, revolutionary behaviour and the aims of the revolution. They are recognisably derived from the writings of Karl Marx, but with a modern, characteristically Chinese twist. Like Marx, Mao believed in the 'scientific' nature of communist thought, as well as the inevitability of its outcome:

> The socialist system will eventually replace the capitalist system; this is an objective law independent of man's will. However much the reactionaries try to hold back the wheel of history, eventually revolution will take place and will inevitably triumph.

Other aphorisms stress the 'realism' required for this approach:

> A revolution is not a dinner party, or writing an essay, or painting
> a picture, or doing embroidery. It cannot be so refined, so leisurely
> and gentle, so temperate, kind, courteous, restrained and magnan-
> imous. A revolution is an insurrection, an act of violence by which
> one class overthrows another.

All that matters is the Revolution:

> Don't make a fuss about a world war. At most, people die... half
> wiped out – this happened quite a few times in Chinese history.

The aim of the Revolution is not any materialist goal:

> People say that poverty is bad, but in fact poverty is good. The
> poorer people are, the more revolutionary they are. It is dreadful
> to imagine a time when everyone will be rich... From a surplus of
> calories people will have two heads and four legs.

The aim of the Revolution is nothing less than perpetual revolution:

> Everything under heaven is in utter chaos; the situation is excellent.

The publication of Chairman Mao's *Little Red Book* was the culmi-
nation of a personality cult that put even Stalin's efforts to shame.
All schools, army barracks, offices, factories, government buildings
and main squares throughout the land were adorned with their
large portrait of Chairman Mao. Here was George Orwell's fictional Big Brother come to reality with a vengeance.

Chairman Mao's thoughts are now considered a thing of the
past. His beliefs have, of course, been modified by the modern

CCP. Yet Chairman Mao's large portrait still looks down over Tiananmen Square, and it is necessary to remember these are the foundations upon which the Party's present ideas are based.

Throughout almost all of China's history it has been an autocracy. For millennia, it was ruled by dynastic emperors 'holders of the Mandate of Heaven... God's representative on earth'.[64] As with the Roman emperors, and the tsars of Russia, the ruler's word was law. It was also sacred: to contradict the ruler was blasphemy. In China this absolutist power was centralised in Peking, the city now known as Beijing. Such God-reinforced rule was deemed necessary in order to hold such a vast, multifarious country together. From the outset, the people who lived within its boundaries were subject to 'sinicization': the process by which 'non-Chinese' were absorbed into Chinese culture, beliefs, social structure and even writing. Any reversal of this trend, any resurgence of a national identity other than that of the one overarching whole, the Chinese identity, was (and still is) regarded as a betrayal of the Chinese identity. Any such deviance strikes at the very heart of Chinese self-conception.

In this, as in many other aspects, China was always a monoculture. Its laws, its ethos, its deepest beliefs, are integral to the very notion of what it means to be Chinese. Such notions have barely changed over the millennia. They have survived famine, disaster and revolution. They even survived the frenzy of national self-destruction during the Cultural Revolution. This monolithic aspect remains as true of China today as it was some two thousand two hundred years ago during the founding Qin (or Ch'in) Dynasty, after which China takes its name.

For almost all of China's history, Beijing has been its capital city. Unlike most of the earlier leading cities in this book, it had no close

---

64 A Chinese philosophical concept said to date back as far as the Zhou Dynasty of emperors (1046–256 BC). The 'Mandate of Heaven' meant the backing of the gods, with the emperor as 'son of Heaven'.

link to the sea. (Only Babylon, Paris and Moscow were similarly isolated.) This had the effect of limiting Beijing's contacts with the outside world. Often for centuries on end, Peking would remain in splendid isolation, visited only by merchant travellers along the Silk Road. Consequently, the emperors of Beijing developed a belief in the innate superiority of Chinese culture. Beijing came to see itself as the centre of the world. The emperor had no foreign policy as such. Relations with neighbouring territories were handled by the Ministry of Rituals, whose task it was to determine the gradation of tributary homage due to the emperor. When Europeans began to arrive in east Asia, profound misunderstandings were inevitable.

Take two historical examples. Both of these examples involved the British, who harboured similar delusions of superiority themselves. In 1793, the first British envoy to Beijing, George Macartney, travelled to the city with the aim of establishing diplomatic relations. The boat on which Macartney travelled inland to the capital was required to display a flag; unknown to Macartney, this flag proclaimed to the watching Chinese people: 'The English ambassador bringing tribute to the Emperor of China.' Macartney bore a letter from George III proposing free trade and the setting up of reciprocal embassies in Beijing and London. He also brought along various products of the Industrial Revolution – globes, intricate clocks, and (irony upon irony) much fine porcelain china.[65] These gifts were intended to show how China could benefit from trade with such an advanced country.

The Emperor Qianlong accepted Macartney's gifts, pointedly referring to them as tribute. He then dismissed the letter from the British king, George III, explaining that no ambassadors

---

65 Not for nothing is this known as 'china'. The process for making porcelain had been discovered in China as early as the Shang Dynasty around 1,500 BC. Europeans had only discovered how to make porcelain early in the eighteenth century.

could possibly be permitted to reside in Beijing. As the politician and diplomat Henry Kissinger describes it: 'The Emperor saw no need for trade beyond what was already occurring in limited, tightly regulated amounts, because Britain had no goods China desired.'

Two decades later, the British despatched another envoy, William Amherst. By now the British had conquered Napoleon and saw themselves as ruling the waves throughout the world. On his way to China, Amherst called in at St Helena where Napoleon was in exile. Napoleon was in the bath when Amherst arrived, but still delivered him a warning: 'China is a sleeping giant. Let her sleep. For when she wakes, she will shake the world.' Undaunted, Amherst pressed on and met the Emperor Yongyan. When Amherst omitted to kowtow before the emperor, his mission was abruptly dismissed.[66] Whereupon the emperor sent a letter to the British Prince Regent saying it was all very well that 'thy kingdom far away across the oceans proffers its loyalty and yearns for civilisation', but he considered it 'a waste of travelling energy' to send any further missions if their barbarian envoys could not even learn the proper protocol, 'which was the true way to turn toward civilization'.

It is no accident that Kissinger refers to both these missions in his book *World Order*. It was as US secretary of state that Kissinger travelled to Beijing with President Nixon in 1972 on their historic visit, which after decades of isolation, opened up China once more to the world. Following this visit, the People's Republic of China would be admitted to the United Nations in place of the Republic of China. This latter was the remnant Chinese democratic government on the island of Taiwan, all that remained of the Kuomintang government and the forces that had opposed Mao

---

66 This obligatory act of obeisance before the emperor required one to prostrate oneself so that one's forehead touched the ground.

and the Red Army. (The Taiwan government occupied territory that was viewed as an integral part of greater China, and as such could never be recognised by any ruling government on the mainland, whether communist or otherwise.)

The entry of the People's Republic of China into the United Nations was a step of huge symbolic significance. China was now irrevocably part of the wider world. Yet this was more than just a symbolic step. Upon entry to the United Nations, China would take a place as a permanent member of the ruling Security Council – alongside the US, the USSR, the UK and France. From its status as an outsider in world affairs, China now leapfrogged into a central role in world governance during the last quarter of the twentieth century.

Yet ironically, even Kissinger himself would continue to have misgivings about China's suitability for such a role. Mindful of China's long self-centred history, yet referring to the present, Kissinger now warned that: 'China has no precedent for the role it is asked to play in the twenty-first-century order, as one state among others… Chinese thinking is shaped in part by Communism but embraces a traditionally Chinese way of thought to an increasing extent.' Despite such a caveat, he remained guardedly optimistic: 'the Chinese were intensely and proudly parochial in their perception of the world outside their immediate sphere. Contemporary Chinese leaders are influenced by their knowledge of China's history but they are not captured by it.'

Although the nation's leaders may not be 'captured' by such historic beliefs, the evidence suggests that these still underpin much of Beijing's foreign policy, to say nothing of their present governance. Take what is probably the most important event in the Beijing calendar: the National People's Congress, which takes place in the Great Hall of the People every spring. This is the closest Beijing comes to a democratic institution. It is attended by almost three thousand members and is incontestably the largest parliamentary body in the world. Delegates from all over China, some wearing their colourful ethnic costumes, gather in the Great Hall of the People.

The Great Hall of the People.

The architecture of this building speaks volumes. Its imposing facade is 1,200 feet long and occupies the entire western edge of the vast central Tiananmen Square. At the centre of this structure, ten pillars dominate the wide stone stairs leading up to its entrance. Inside, the State Banqueting Hall can accommodate up to seven thousand guests. This was where Nixon and Kissinger attended a state banquet on their historic 1972 visit. But the largest room in the building is altogether something else. This has the same name as the building itself, being called the Great Hall of the People, and it is here that the delegates gather for the annual National People's Congress. The room resembles a huge cinema, with row upon row of seats, as well as a tiered balcony and gallery. In all, this can accommodate some ten thousand people. Instead of a cinema screen, the raised dais at the front of the auditorium has room for 500 leading Party members, seated in long rows behind the Party leader as he addresses the assembled Party delegates, outlining government aims, progress on present policies, and new initiatives to be taken by the government.

According to China's constitution, this 'assembly of the people' has the power to oversee all aspects of national government. It is at the same time the government legislature, the supreme court, as well as the arbiter of financial policy and controller of all aspects of the nation's military. In fact, this is one huge charade. The only purpose of the assembly is to publicly rubber-stamp any proposal put to it by the supreme leadership.

At the National People's Congress in 2017, China's present leader Xi Jinping presented to the world his personal philosophy. This would later be published as 'Xi Jinping Thought on Socialism with Chinese Characteristics for a New Era'. According to Bethany Allen-Ebrahimian, writing in the magazine *Foreign Policy*, Xi's work is a 'mix of stilted Communist Party argot, pleasant-sounding generalizations, and "Father Knows Best"-style advice to the world'. She writes that others see this work as 'a continuation of Marxist-Leninism, the thought of Chairman Mao Zedong and Deng Xiaoping Theory, in keeping with Marxism adapted to Chinese conditions'.

It is difficult not to see Xi's 'Thought on Socialism' as a continuation of Mao's *Little Red Book*. In fact it goes even further, fostering a personality cult that looks set to supersede that of Chairman Mao. The first volume of 'Thought on Socialism' even ends with a political biography of Xi. Following the Congress, Xi Jinping's 'Thought on Socialism' was incorporated into the constitution of the Chinese Communist Party, no less.

Xi's 'Thought on Socialism' would later be extended to include 'Xi Jinping Thought on Diplomacy', which was characterised as follows: 'the fundamental guideline for China's diplomatic work is an epoch-making milestone in the diplomatic theory of New China'. Such empty phraseology prefaces a far more ominous agenda. In this work, China is seen as an exception to the rest of the world, and the present is seen as 'an era that sees China moving closer to centre stage and making greater contributions to mankind'. Xi makes three main points:

1. From now on China wants international relations to take on a more 'Chinese characteristic'.
2. China must achieve more of a leadership role. This involves diminishing the present hegemony of the United States.
3. China should 'safeguard' its sovereignty, security and development interests.

The attitude prevalent in this last document would be readily recognised by the emperors Qianlong and Yungyan. Though unlike the emperors, Xi Jinping's 'Thought on Diplomacy' seems to be laying the groundwork for external expansion. This work, too, has been incorporated into the constitution of the Chinese Communist Party.

Some commentators have sought to allay alarm over Xi's stated policies by claiming that they are principally intended for home consumption, with the aim of further boosting his personality cult. However, this is difficult to reconcile with the fact that Xi's 'Thought on Diplomacy' would soon be translated into twenty-six languages and published in over a hundred and sixty countries worldwide.

What came after Xi's addition of his 'Thought on Socialism' and his 'Thought on Diplomacy' to the constitution of the CCP should come as little surprise. Megalomania feeds on itself. At the following year's annual National People's Congress, Xi Jinping put forward the proposition that he should remain leader for life. This was passed by 2,964 votes, with just 3 abstentions.

In support of these developments, Beijing argues that authoritarianism has been a permanent fixture of its long history, and as such it is necessary to secure national unity over such a vast and disparate territory. This unity is said to be under present threat from a number of sources. First, there are the 12-million-strong Uighur people, whose belief in the Muslim religion is deemed incompatible with communism, while at the same time their adherence to their Turkic ethnicity of dress and culture goes against the time-honoured process of 'sinicization'. Likewise, the central government perceives a similar threat from 5.8 million Mongolians. Ironically, perhaps the greatest threat comes from the thoroughly 'sinicized' 7 million Chinese inhabitants of Hong Kong, who demand democracy and a return to the limited freedoms that they enjoyed under the previous British colonial administration.

Even so, it is worth putting all this into context. Just as the West has its unshakable belief in liberal democracy, so Beijing has long held its similar belief that the Chinese way is the right way. Looking back over recent history, it is easy to see why the western world has little faith in autocracy – or, not to mince words, outright dictatorship. The fall of Hitler and Nazi Germany would eventually be followed by the disintegration of the Soviet Union, giving rise to Fukuyama's claim that we had come to the end of such history. From now on, he believed, history would be replaced by the inevitable spread of liberal democracy and free-market capitalism. If only...

However, if we look at the recent history of democracy, we can see that this does not always provide the kind of lasting stability so necessary for a country like China. In 1920, following the Treaty of Versailles after the First World War, all the states in Europe were ruled by a democratically elected government. Just two decades later, in 1940, only four democracies remained intact (Britain, Ireland, Switzerland and Sweden).

Yet it was Beijing's daring liberalisation policy following Mao's death in 1976 that would result in arguably the greatest socio-economic transformation in history. This was initiated under the rule of Deng Xiaoping, who held the reins of power in Beijing from 1978 to 1992. This fourteen-year period would see the gradual loosening of government control over both the economy and the people of China. Officially it was named 'Socialism with Chinese Characteristics', and it would result in an increasingly mixed economy called 'market socialism'.

According to all previous orthodox economic theory, such a contradiction in terms could not possibly work, let alone flourish. Admittedly, it had been a success on a small scale in post-war Sweden, which had a population the size of London spread over a territory almost twice the size of Britain, as well as its own liberal democratic tradition. But on a huge scale such as in China, which had its own very different authoritarian tradition, it was unthinkable. Much like Darwinian evolution, the market had to find its own way: it could not be 'guided to freedom'.

The man who oversaw this economic miracle that would modernise China and lift hundreds of millions out of poverty deserves recognition far beyond that which he has received. Indeed, from the hindsight of the future, Deng Xiaoping may well appear among the most significant figures of the twentieth century – his effect as great as that cast by the long shadow of Marx, the apocalyptic horrors inflicted by the likes of Hitler, Stalin and Chairman Mao, or even the legacies of Roosevelt, Gandhi and Mandela. So who was this remarkable figure? And how did he manage to do what he did?

Deng Xiaoping.

Despite Deng's worn, battle-hardened features, he came from a family of educated landowners. He was born in 1904 in the inland province of Sichuan in south-west China. After a local education, the sixteen-year-old Deng was sent along with 200 others to France on a work-study programme. He studied in Paris and worked as a fitter in a metal factory in the south-west suburbs. At the age of twenty he joined the Chinese Communist Party in exile, then travelled to Moscow. On his return to China in 1927, he joined the Soviet-backed army in north-west China. Indicatively, the modern Chinese-Australian historian Mobo Gao argues that Deng Xiaoping and many like him in the Chinese Communist Party were not really Marxists, but basically revolutionary nationalists who wanted to see China standing on equal terms with the great global powers.

In 1929 Deng led a failed uprising against the central republican government of the Kuomintang. Later, he would take part in the famous Long March, led by Mao Zedong, during which the remnants of the Red Army retreated thousands of miles on foot through the Chinese hinterland, avoiding the Kuomintang forces. He would also be at Mao's side in 1952 when he took power in Beijing.

Over the ensuing decades Deng began a perilous rise through the ranks of the CCP, falling from favour more than once over factionist squabbles. During the Cultural Revolution he and his family were targeted by Red Guards, who threw his oldest son from a fourth-floor window. Deng was banished to a provincial tractor factory, where he resumed his old trade as a fitter. Four years later he would return to Beijing. After the death of Mao, he eventually emerged as supreme leader and began his programme of reforms.

These consisted of the 'Four Modernisations', which related to a reform of the Military, Agriculture, Industry and Science/Technology. Out of the ruins of the Cultural Revolution, Deng was determined to build China into a global power, and he was willing to be pragmatic about the means he chose to achieve this. As he said: 'No matter if a cat is white or black, so long as it can catch mice it is a good cat.' In a direct contradiction of Mao's claim that 'poverty is good' and that it makes for good revolutionaries, Deng stated unequivocally in 'Thought on Socialism': 'Poverty is not socialism. To be rich is glorious.' In fact, Deng consciously modelled his reforms on Lenin's New Economic Policy, which had sought to alleviate famine in Russia after the Civil War. Understandably, Deng met with strong opposition from Party loyalists. Likewise, he was equally strongly opposed by Reformists, who wanted to move all the way to western freedoms.

Deng's control and his reforms required a precarious balancing act, which was not always successful. Consequently, many of his policies would receive sharp criticism. In an attempt to limit China's booming population, in 1979 Deng initiated the One Child Policy, which limited the size of China's families. This would have a number of grim side-effects, such as forced abortions. Also, as families traditionally favoured male offspring, many new-born daughters 'vanished'. The effects of this policy remain to this day, years after it was abandoned in 2015. Today, China has 0.05 per cent more males than females. This may sound negligible, but in a total population of 1.394 billion it amounts to 70 million excess males.

Beijing's policy of rapid growth would lead to widespread corruption, and Deng sought to control this too. In 1983 he launched a 'Hard-Strike Anti-Crime and Corruption Campaign'. In line with command economy principles Beijing set quotas for this plan, which involved some five thousand executions by the end of the year. In all, it is estimated that as many as four times this amount may have been killed by zealous Party officials, many of whom were simply settling old scores.

Despite such measures, and the introduction of a new economic freedom, many began pressing for more social freedom – most notably, freedom of expression and open democracy. This would come to a head in 1989, the year that saw the collapse of the Soviet Union and the fall of several communist regimes. Three years previously, Deng had pushed for political reform, but this had been resisted. In April 1989, thousands of students began camping out in Tiananmen Square in central Beijing. The Party saw this as a threat to its authority, and after some argument Deng was persuaded to send in the army. One student famously stood in front of the line of advancing tanks, forcing them a halt. But the heroics of 'tank man' only postponed the inevitable. The ensuing crackdown would see the deaths of anything up to a hundred thousand students.

Later that year, Deng would retire from his top posts, though he did not entirely relinquish power. In 1992 he undertook a widely reported Southern Tour through the provinces, travelling much of his journey along the river systems on a naval destroyer. The leader speaking to his people, carried into their midst on an armed and armoured gunboat. Some sources claim that Deng's Southern Tour actually helped prevent a civil war, yet at the same time reinforced the popularity of the reformists. After this, he stepped down. Deng would finally die in Beijing at the age of ninety-two.

In the opinion of John Pomfret, the *Washington Post*'s China expert, Deng turned China from a totalitarian backwater into the power it has become today and accomplished something that had eluded Chinese leaders for almost two centuries: the transformation of the world's oldest civilisation into a modern nation.

The economic figures that chart this transformation are nothing less than miraculous. In 1978, when Deng took power, China's GDP was the equivalent of $149.5 billion. By the time he left office in 1992 this had risen to $426.9 billion (statistics from World Bank GDP figures in current US dollars). But in many ways, Deng had simply laid the groundwork for what was to come. From then on China's GDP would shoot up, reaching $5.1 trillion in 2009. A year later, China would overtake Japan as the world's third-largest economy, and in 2018 it would overtake the Eurozone and become the world's second-largest. By 2019 China's GDP had risen to $14.3 trillion (in the same year, the US GDP was $21.4 trillion), During the course of this economic miracle, 800 million people were lifted out of poverty.

China's GDP figures were largely export driven, with comparatively small import figures. In line with the declared aims of Xi's 'Diplomatic Thought', the surpluses were used to invest in such ambitious foreign projects as the Belt and Road Initiative, intended to forge shorter rail and seaway routes between China and Europe. This has involved massive infrastructure projects such as the building of new super-ports in Pakistan (Gwadar) and Sri Lanka (Hambantota). Less trumpeted have been widespread investments all over Africa. Many of these projects left the host nations indebted to China, only able to repay their debts by granting China strategic territory on long leases.

Beijing's increasing economic success has created an entirely new class of Chinese citizens. These constitute a young cash-rich, tech-savvy, ideologically indifferent, growing middle class. Their economic power within the shell of Beijing's world economic power will continue to grow, and with it their expectations. Initially satisfied with materialistic rewards, these expectations are liable to become increasingly libertarian. So far, such expectations have been successfully reined in by the older generation that controls the levers of power. Such power, along with the government's control of the internet and other media, has played a large part in this precarious balancing act. But for how much longer?

Xi Jinping initially consolidated his power by building on the foundations laid by Deng Xiaoping. But Xi's lust for power now seems to have extended beyond such limits. As Xi continues to indulge his megalomania, one of his contemporaries continues to raise a dissenting voice on the world stage.

Like Xi Jinping, the artist Ai Weiwei is a native of Beijing. They were born within four years of each other, but the round, scruffy artist and the plump, smooth statesman are very much opposite sides of the same coin. Ai Weiwei is the son of a famous poet, and spent much of his twenties on the United States avant-garde art scene. On his return to China, he curated an art show called 'Fuck Off'. By deliberately provoking the authorities he raised the question: why should he conform to a culture that is alien to his nature, that limits his freedom and attempts to distort his humanity to fit its own ideas?

Ai Weiwei has produced all manner of disparate art, and more recently has been known for his documentary films. He has been continually harassed, imprisoned and finally exiled for his troubles. Yet even in a different continent he remains a thorn in the side of the authorities. His very existence, to say nothing of his creations, raise fundamental questions. These can be blatant and obvious, but are frequently subtle and oblique.

Take the hundred million handmade and hand-painted porcelain sunflower seeds that he spread over the floor of the Engine Room at the Tate Modern in London. These have been compared to the two-thousand-year-old Terracotta Army of Qin Shi Huang, the first emperor of China, and to the millions of forgotten Chinese who were displaced or lost their lives in China's many self-inflicted tragedies, such as the Cultural Revolution (during which 20 million are thought to have died), a population of individuals reduced to nothing but identical sunflower seeds spat on the floor for generation after generation.

In another of his art works, Ai Weiwei dips old Chinese pots into garish modern paint, while in the background are three consecutive photos of him holding a million-dollar Han dynasty vase, letting it fall from his hands, and watching it smash on the floor at his feet. This work is literally iconoclastic (from the Greek 'image' and 'breaker'). Similarly, the old pots dipped into brightly colour-ed modern paint suggest desecration, the ancient being overlaid with modern monochrome, old culture being obliterated. Ai Wei-wei's beguiling art examines China's very definition of itself and its history in its art. He may have learned his provocative avant-garde art in the US, but he has transformed this process into a uniquely Chinese form of expression.

So what can a mere artist achieve in the face of such over-whelming power? History has many quirks. In 1940 the composer Béla Bartók fled his native Hungary when it was taken over by the fascists. Streets and squares through-out the land were named after Hitler and Mussolini. Bartók swore that he would never return to his native country as long as there was a single street named after Hitler or Mussolini, at a time when fascist power extended over the length and breadth of mainland Europe, from Norway to Greece, from Poland to Portugal. Bartók died in New York in 1945. Forty-three years later his body was carried in state back to his native land, where not a single street remained named after Hitler or Mussolini. There are now streets named after Bartók in cities and towns throughout Hungary, as well as statues of him in major cities across Europe and North America. As the Ancients put it: '*Ars longa vita brevis*' (Art is long, life is short).

Beijing's future power lies in its relationship with the outside world, in particular with Washington. The dealings between the present world superpower and its prospective successor are com-plex and symbiotic. The historian Niall Ferguson has compared this to a marriage, referring to this partnership as 'Chimerica'. At present, the balance of trade between the US and China is heavily tilted in China's favour. In an attempt to ameliorate this, China has used its trade surplus to buy up billions of dollars-worth of US Treasury Bonds. But this has also had the effect of keeping China's currency artificially cheap compared to the US dollar. In this Chimerica marriage, neither side can afford a divorce. If China stopped purchasing US dollars, the dollar could easily collapse. But if this happened, China would see the value of its $800 billion-worth of US bonds drastically reduced, to say nothing of its large trade-accumulated dollar reserves. China needs Americans to spend large amounts on its cheap imports, just to keep its economy expanding. These may help Americans sustain an unwarranted high standard of living, but if Americans stopped buying cheap Chinese imports, the Chinese economy would collapse. Of course, China could always retaliate by dumping vast amounts of dollars on the market. This may reduce the price of the dollar, but it would also devastate the US economy.

So does this mean that China is in the driving seat, its economy set to continue growing until it overtakes the United States and becomes the world's next superpower? As we saw at the start of this book, China's relentless drive to keep up its GDP has involved such ploys as the building of ghost cities. How long can it keep up such policies?

Compared to previous leading cities in world history, Beijing's options are limited. London led the world through its banking and its colonial empire. New York's ascendancy came as a result of its financial and industrial might. Moscow's leading role was due to ideological appeal on the one hand, and sheer military might when this failed. Compared to these cities, Beijing's strengths are limited. Ideologically, its communism has little appeal in the modern world. Its commercial ascendancy might result in foreign indebtedness, but this is far from colonisation. And militarily it remains no match for the United States. On the other hand, there appears to be little that will stop it increasing its economic ascendancy.

How this can dislodge America's continuing quasi-hegemony remains to be seen.

All this assumes that China remains stable, able to settle (or simply contain) the perceived problems posed by its Uighur and Mongolian minorities, and Hong Kong's agitation for democracy. Is Xi possessed of the ability to maintain power while at the same time continuing to satisfy its increasingly affluent citizens' thirst for liberalisation? In short, can Xi hold course against the siren song embodied by Ai Weiwei and his beguiling art? Can power as old as China itself prevail against an artistic tradition whose roots reach deep into the very definition of what China is?

Similar questions have been asked of every city that has led the world. The answers provided by that city to such a predicament have decided upon its contribution to history, both in the grander sense, as well as in minor matters. As we have seen, 'greatness', in whatever form that is translated, is only one ingredient of many in such leadership. There are often minor, even serendipitous, factors that determine a leading city's legacy. For instance, Roman numerals still appear on things ranging from public buildings to movie credits. Eclipses of the sun still occur with the clockwork regularity predicted by the Babylonians.

But these are matters of the past. It is in the coming rivalries that our future will be decided. Emblematic of these is the contrast, and contest, between Mumbai and Beijing. On the one side we have democracy as conceived by Athens, liberty as conceived by revolutionary Paris, and the heritage of these ideas in cities throughout the so-called 'free world'. On the other lies the rigid social stratification of ancient Babylon, imperial Rome and 'revolutionary' Moscow. Is individual freedom integral to our future? Or is our future destined to arrive in the form of a centrally controlled power that sees itself as its own *raison d'être*, rather than that of the individuals whose collective destiny it seeks to guide?

Again and again the cities that have led the world – in power, organisation, ideas or inventiveness, or a blend of these qualities – have all answered these questions after their own fashion. We are now entering a period when such issues are once again central to whichever city will lead the world into the coming age. This will be a capital in an age of contested hegemony, with growing frictions between contenders such as the United States, China and possibly even a revived Russia. This contest will also take place on a planet increasingly ravaged by climate change. Even if this 'increasing' is somehow miraculously halted by combined international agreement, the ravages are unlikely to be reversed. Then there is the Covid-19 pandemic, whose marks will remain with us for many years to come.

On top of this there will inevitably be the 'unknown unknown' that appears out of left field. This may be something that promises a positive effect, one that is already being hatched in the next leading city of the future. For whatever happens, we can be sure that this city will also herald an age of unrivalled human self-transformation and ingenuity, with each new decade giving birth to concepts that were inconceivable to previous generations. The next city to lead the world will be the one that provides some solutions to our besetting problems, as well as leading the world into an undreamt-of future. Precisely how it provides these solutions – politically, socially, scientifically – will determine the future of the human (or partly artificial) race.

Acknowledgements

First of all I would like to thank my long-term agent Julian Alexander, who came up with the idea for this book, and has been a great encouragement during my time writing it. I would also like to thank my editors at Hodder, Kirty Topiwala and Anna Baty, who played such a leading role in the editorial process, excising my errors, making suggestions, and generally making a great improvement to the finished text. Thanks also to Nick Fawcett, Richard Rosenfeld, Matthew Everett, Lesley Hodgson, and Sarah Christie.

Alas, this book was begun during the Covid period. The first lockdown I spent in Vienna with my family. Thank you to Matthias and Oona for having me, for their advice, and for providing piles of books for research. Also, thanks to my grandsons Tristan and Julian, who managed to tolerate the company of their aged, shrinking Opa. Also to Hanna for some great Italian cooking, and Erno who was always such cheery company.

When I got back to London, I was able (occasionally) to book a seat at the British Library. But more importantly, I would like to thank the London Library, which was able to provide so many books.

During the entire period of writing this book I also had constant useful advice from my partner Amanda, without which I would have made many blunders.

Notes

Prologue: What Survives

pxi 'to house nine out of ten of Latin America's tallest buildings…', according to Andrew Beatty of *Business News*, in his article 'Construction Boom in Panama Built on Drug Money', consulted 20 April 2021.

pxiv 'I'll go to another city…', et seq., translated by author from the original Greek. For the original, see C.P. Cavafy, 'Η πόλη' ('The City'), *The Collected Poems* (London, 2007), p. 28.

pxix '*Carthago delenda*…', F.E. Adcock, 'Delenda Est Carthago', in *The Cambridge Historical Journal* 8(3) (1946): 117–28.

pxix 'One boy in each school class…', David Platt, cited by Maggie Fox in article 'Gene Study Shows the Phoenicians Still With Us', *Science News*, 30 October 2008.

pxx 'the whole scientific world…', W.J. Colville, *Ancient Myths and Modern Revelations* (London, 1910), Ch. VII, p. 10.

pxxi 'The past is a foreign country…', L.P. Hartley, *The Go-Between* (London, 1953), opening line.

Chapter 1: Babylon

p1 'In this palace…', Josephus, *Contra Appion* (Against Appion), Book 1, Ch. 19.

p2 recently published a book…', Stephanie Daley, *The Hanging Garden of Babylon* (Oxford, 2013).

p3 'The house, the foundation...', Schøyen collection, MS 2063.

p6 For details of saros etc. see *The Book of Numbers* by John Conway and Richard Guy (New York, 1996), esp. Ch. 1: 'How to Read Babylonian Cuneiform'.

p6 'all Western efforts...', for much of this material see Asger Aaboe, 'The Culture of Babylonia: Babylonian Mathematics, Astrology, and Astronomy', in *The Assyrian and Babylonian Empires and other States of the Near East, from the Eighth to the Sixth Centuries B.C.*, ed. John Boardman, I.E.S. Edwards, N.G.L. Hammond, E. Sollberger and C.B.F. Walker (Cambridge, 1991).

p7 'could abdicate briefly...', et seq., see *Haaretz* (Israeli newspaper), 21 August 2107: 'How Ancient Babylonians Could Have Predicted the 2017 Eclipse', by Ruth Schuster.

p9 'driven from men...', King James Version, Daniel 4:33.

p9 'By the rivers of Babylon...', opening of Psalm 137, verses 1–5, KJV.

p10 'free to develop...', see Jonathan Tenney, *Life on the Bottom of Babylonian Society* (Leiden, 2011), p. 88.

p10 'water sprinklers', et seq., see article 'Slaves or Not, Babylonians Were Like Us', by Linda B. Glaser on Phys.org website, 6/1/2012.

p10 'If a man destroy the eye...', et seq., 'The Code of Hammurabi', Internet Sacred Text Archive (Evinity Publishing, 2011). Retrieved 7 May 2020.

p14 'Therefore the desert creatures...', Jeremiah 50:39

Chapter 2: Athens

p25 'There is only one...', et seq., Diogenes Laertius, *Lives of Eminent Philosophers*, trans. James Miller and Pamela Mensch (London, 2008), entry on Socrates.

p25 'How can one live...', see opening of Plato, *The Symposium*, trans. W. Hamilton (London, 1951).

p26 'corrupting the young' and ensuing details, see Plato, *Apology of Socrates*, trans. B. Jowett (London, 2021 edn).

p27 'God forever geometrises...', Plutarch attributed the belief to Plato, writing that 'Plato said god geometrizes continually' (*Convivialium disputationum*, *liber* 8,2).

Chapter 3: Rome

p40 'making public calamities...', see Plutarch, *Life of Crassus*, 33.2–3, in *Plutarch: Lives of the Noble Grecians and Romans*, trans. Arthur Hugh Clough (London, 2011).

p42 'the gloomiest of men...', Pliny the Elder, *Natural History*, remark cited by many, including Tacitus.

Chapter 4: Constantinople/Istanbul

p59 'like melons along a canal...', Niccoló Barbaro, *Diary of the Siege of Constantinople*, trans. J.R. Jones (New York, 1970).

p59 'If you embrace Islam, we will leave you alone, if you agree to pay...', Mehmet II, citing Sahih Bukhari 53: 392.

p65 'Mathematics is the language in which God has written the universe...', Galilei Galileo, *Opere Il Saggiatore* (Roma, 1623), p. 171.

p68 'It is a tale / Told by an idiot...', Shakespeare, *Macbeth*, Act 5, scene 5.

Chapter 5: Paris

p69 'utmost power and cunning...', René Descartes, *Meditations on the First Philosophy*, trans. John Cottingham (Cambridge, 2013), p. 17.

p74 Louis XV's speech before the *parlement* of Paris, 1766, cited François Furet, *Revolutionary France, 1770–1880* (Oxford, 2004).

p75 'goes so far as to suggest...' see D.F. Pocock, *Social Anthropology* (London, 1961), p. 9.

p76 'enslaved Africans could not possibly...', *The Complete Works of M. de Montesquieu* (London, 1777), 4 vols: Vol. 1. *The Spirit of the Laws*.

p76 'If there were no monarch...', et seq., Baron de Montesquieu, Charles-Louis de Secondat, *On the Spirit of the Laws*, Book XI (Paris, 1748).

p78 'You will never be...', cited in *The National Cyclopaedia of Useful Knowledge*, Vol. I (London, 1847), p. 417.

p79 'Aguaxima, a plant...', see entry for 'Auguaxima' in *the Encyclopédie*, Readex Microprint Corporation (New York, 1969), 5 vols. The full text and images reduced to four double-spread pages of the original appeared on one folio-sized page of this printing.

p81 'as an instrument for repairing defects...', entry on Pierre-Simon Laplace in C.C. Gillispie, *Dictionary of Scientific Biography*, 16 vols (New York, 1970–80).

p82 'It took but an instant to cut off his head...', Joseph Louis Lagrange, see William Hughes, *Annual Editions: Western Civilization* (Connecticut, 1997), p. 64.

p83 'I love liberty, and I loathe...', et seq., see Jean-Jacques Rousseau, *Confessions*, Books 1 and 5 (first published in English in 1790, widely available from Gutenberg, Penguin, Oxford etc.).

p84 'they: "did not have enough wit..."', Ian Davidson, *Voltaire in Exile* (London, 2004), pp. 186–7.

p88 'an "enlightened despot" at home...', see Wikipedia entry for Napoleon Bonaparte, consulted 1 June 2021.

p88 'Never interrupt your enemy...', Thomas Carlyle, *The French Revolution*, 3 vols (London, 1836).

p88 'He may be good...', ibid.

p89 'a damn close run thing…', this quotation is widely cited in collections of quotes by Wellington. Though considered by some to be apocryphal, it certainly captures the spirit of the battle and accords with Wellington's character.

p89 'To sleep with one of Napoleon's mistresses…', Andrew Roberts, *Napoleon and Wellington* (London, 2001).

Chapter 6: London

p91 'It was the best of times…', Charles Dickens, *A Tale of Two Cities* (London, 1859).

p93 '*pour encourager les autres…*', Voltaire, *Candide* (1759).

p95 'Victoria initially regarded this as a "shocking alternative"…', *The Girlhood of Queen Victoria: A Selection from Her Majesty's Diaries between the Years 1832 and 1840*, Part I (British History Monarchs and Royalty Book 1), by Queen Victoria (January 2016).

p101 'It is not from the…', see Adam Smith, *Works and Correspondence* (Glasgow, 1976 edn), Vol. 2a, pp. 26–7.

p104 'progress was killing off the human race…', Robert Malthus, *An Essay on the Principle of Population* (London, 1798).

p106 'The small yard seemed rotting with damp…', John Hollingshead, *Ragged London in 1861* (London, 1861).

p108 'Whoever refuses to obey the general will…', Rousseau, *Du contrat social; ou, Principes du droit politique* (Netherlands, 1762), Book 1, Chs 6–9.

p111 'might act upon…', Rowan Hooper, 'Ada Lovelace: My Brain is More than Merely Mortal', *New Scientist*. Retrieved 16 October 2012.

p114 'Well, we're only going to do this once…', Stephen Halliday, *The Great Stink of London: Sir Joseph Bazalgette and the Cleansing of the Victorian Metropolis* (London, 2013).

p116 'militarism and the armaments inseparable from it...', Viscount Grey of Fallodon, *Twenty-Five Years 1892–1916* (London, 1925).

p116 'The lamps are going out all over Europe...', ibid., p. 20.

Chapter 7: Moscow

p119 'The German leaders...', cited in many sources, including Robert Fulford, *National Post*, 9 December 2016.

p124 'a free market and...', *Lenin's Collected Works*, 2nd English edition, Progress Publishers (Moscow, 1973), first printed 1965, Vol. 33, pp. 186–96.

p124 'Politics is the art of the possible...', interview (11 August 1867) with Friedrich Meyer von Waldeck of the *St. Petersburgische Zeitung*.

p124 'Trotsky was "in love with organisation"...', Geoffrey Swain, *Trotsky* (London, 2006), p. 211.

p125 'Upside down...', Marc Chagall, *My Life*, (Phoenix, 1960).

p126 'Hebrew jazz...', et seq., cited Brian Moynahan, *Comrades 1917: Russia in Revolution*, (Boston, 1992), p. 334.

p126 'The sun melts...', Hajo Duchting, *Kandinsky*, Taschen (Berlin, 2007), p. 7.

p127 'Kim Grant, an "ironic monument to the economic"...', Dr Charles Cramer and Cr Kim Grant, 'Tatlin's Tower', SmartHistory website, consulted 1 June 2021: https://smarthistory.org/tatlin-tower/.

p128 'statesmen of his calibre...', et seq., Bertrand Russell, 'The Practice and Theory of Bolshevism' (London 1920), reprinted in excerpt, 'Lenin, Trotsky and Gorky'.

p128 'I am not ready for a creed...', et seq., J.M. Keynes, *Essays in Persuasion* (London, 2009 edn), from *A Short View of Russia* (1929), p. 161f.

p130 'a couple more cows or farms with six acres more than their neighbours...', Robert Conquest, *Reflections on a Ravaged Century* (New York, 2001), p. 94.

p133 'could only have been...', Dmitri Shostakovich,. *Shostakovich: About Himself and His Times*, compiled by L. Grigoryev and Y. Platek, trans. Angus and Neilian Roxburgh (Moscow, 1981), Progress Publishers.

p137 'Unbridled joy...', this anecdote appears in various forms in most biographies of Stalin. I have taken it from Solomon Volkov, *Testimony: The Memoirs of Shostakovich* (London, 2004 edn). p.68.

p138 'I have never met a man more fair...', H.G. Wells, *New Statesman* supplement, 27 October 1934.

p138 'I can't die without...', 'Bernard Shaw: I can't die without having seen the USSR', *Russia Beyond*, 26 July 2016, consulted 1 June 2021: https://www.rbth.com/arts/literature/2016/07/26/bernard-shaw-i-cant-die-without-having-seen-the-ussr_615147.

p138 'I expected to see a Russian worker and I found...', et seq., cited in *Russia Beyond* (*Rossiyskaya Gazeta*) 26 July 2016, website consulted 23.4.21.

p143 'We have temporarily fallen under the yoke...', Stalin, 'Speech at the Red Army Parade on the Red Square, Moscow', www.marxists.org. Retrieved 2 June 2021.

p145 'How many divisions...', cited in *Time* magazine, New York City, Monday 27 December 1943.

pp145–6 'From Stettin in the Baltic to Trieste in the Adriatic...', Winston Churchill's Iron Curtain Speech, 5 March 1946; for text see National WWII Museum, New Orleans, website, posted March 2021, consulted 1 June 2021.

Chapter 8: New York

p149 'vote with their feet...', see, for instance, T.H. Wintringham 'The Road to Caporetto', *Left Review* 2(2): 63–5 (November, 1935).

p155 'These riots remain...', Eric Foner, 'Reconstruction: America's Unfinished Revolution, 1863–1877', *The New American Nation* (New York, 1988, updated 2014 edn), pp. 32–3.

p158 'he was, in a sense...', et seq., George M. Fredrickson, 'Thorstein Veblen: The Last Viking', *American Quarterly* 11(3) (autumn 1959): 403–15.

p159 'the higher stages...', et seq., ibid.

p162 'Contemporaries, too, often hated...', H. Roger Grant, 'Review', *Journal of American History* 98(2) (2011): 544.

p162 'I don't know...', J.P. Morgan quotes (n.d.), Quotes.net. Retrieved 12 March 2021, from https://www.quotes.net/quote/49089.

p163 'I arrived with $2.50...', 'In Ponzi We Trust', Smithsonian, December 1998. Retrieved 26 April 2021.

p166 'to absorb...', see 'Thomas Eddison's Greatest Invention', *atlantic.com*. Retrieved 26 April 2021.

p166 'I haven't failed...', as quoted in J.L. Elkhorne, 'Edison: The Fabulous Drone, in XLVI(3) (March 1967): 52.

p166 'eight thousand...', Seth Shulman (1999), *Owning the Future*, Houghton Mifflin Company (Boston, 1999), pp. 158–60.

p172 'O harp and altar...', Hart Crane, 'Brooklyn Bridge' (London, 1992), verse 8.

p175 'Speak softly...', Suzy Platt, *Respectfully Quoted: A Dictionary of Quotations*, Barnes & Noble (New York, 1993), p. 123.

p178 'not just...', Francis Fukuyama (1989), 'The End of History?', *The National Interest* 16: 3–18.

Chapter 9 Mumbai

p185 'When Sonam Kapoor, of the Bollywood Kapoor…', see front page of *The New India Express*, 22 June 2020: headline: 'Sonam Kapoor attributes her "privilege" to "karma", netizens give lesson on "casteism"'.

p186 'footnotes to…', Alfred North Whitehead, *Process and Reality*, Free Press (New York, 1979), p. 39.

p188 'Indian-English writers like Anita Desai…', Amit Saha, 'Exile Literature and the Diasporic Indian Writer', *Rupkatha Journal of Interdisciplinary Studies in Humanities* 1(2) (2009), pp. 186-196.

p195 'D.E.M…', *Times of India*, 26 January 1975, obituaries column.

p196 'The city is full…', et seq., Mehta, op. cit., p. 149.

p196 'One of these is senior police officer Ajay Lal…', Suketu Mehta, *Maximum City*, (London, 2004), pp. 145–6.

p196 'If you have a kilo…', et seq., op. cit., 'Number Two After Scotland Yard', pp. 144ff.

p200 'demonetisation had been…', Vivek Kaul blog *Econ Central*, speech delivered mid-November 2020.

Chapter 10: Beijing

p209 'The socialist system…', et seq. quotations from Chairman Mao Tse-Tung, *The Little Red Book* (London, 2018 edn).

p211 'holders of the Mandate…', see Kallie Szczepanski, 'What is the Mandate of Heaven in China?', *About Education*. Retrieved 26 April 2021.

p212 'proposing free trade…', see J. L. Cranmer-Byng, 'Lord Macartney's Embassy to Peking in 1793', *Journal of Oriental Studies* 4(1–2) (1957–58): 117–87.

p213 'The Emperor saw no need…', et seq., see Henry Kissinger, *World Order* (London, 2014), p. 217–18.

p213 'which was the true...', see E. Backhouse and J.O.P. Bland, *Annals and Memoirs of the Court of Peking* (Boston: 1914), pp. 322–31.

p214 'China has no precedent for the role...', et seq., Kissinger, ibid., p. 226.

p216 'a mix of stilted...', Bethany Allen-Ebrahimian, 'We Read Xi Jinping's Book So You Don't Have To', *Foreign Policy* (5 February 2015).

p217 'the fundamental guideline...', et seq., Bill Bishop, 'Xi's thought on diplomacy is "epoch-making"': www.axios.com. Axios. Retrieved 26 April 2021.

p220 'Mobo Gao argues...', Mobo Gao, 'The Battle for China's Past: Mao and the Cultural Revolution (London, 2008). Cited in Wikipedia article on Deng Xiaoping, consulted 26 April 2021.

p221 'No matter if a cat is white...', see Mark Buckle, 'White Cat, Black Cat', *China Daily*, 2 August 2018.

p223 'Deng turned China...', John Pomfret, 'In its own neighborhood, China emerges as a leader', *Washington Post*, 18 October 2001.

Recommended Further Reading

Chapter 1: Babylon

J. Boardman, I.E.S. Edwards, N.G.L. Hammond, E. Sollberger and C.B.F. Walker (eds.), *The Assyrian and Babylonian Empires and other States of the Near East, from the Eighth to the Sixth Centuries B.C.* (Cambridge, 1991).

Stephanie Daley, *The Hanging Garden of Babylon* (Oxford, 2013).

Mario Liverani, *Imagining Babylon: The Modern Story of an Ancient City*, trans. Ailsa Campbell (Boston, 2016).

Joan Oates, *Babylon* (London, 1986).

'The Code of Hammurabi', Internet Sacred Text Archive (Evinity Publishing, 2011).

Chapter 2: Athens

T.D.J. Chappell (ed.), *The Plato Reader* (Edinburgh, 1996).

Herodotus, *The Histories* (Penguin, 2003). The 'father of history'. Not always reliable, but filled with revealing and interesting tales of the ancient world.

Simon Hornblower, *The Greek World 479–323 BC* (Abingdon, 2011).

Konrad Kinzi, *A Companion to the Classical Greek World* (Blackwell, 2006).

Thomas Martin, *Ancient Greece: From Prehistoric to Hellenic Times* (Yale, 2013).

Bertrand Russell, *History of Western Philosophy* (Routledge, 2004). Contains a good general introduction to Ancient Greece and its philosophers.

Chapter 3: Rome

Edward Gibbon, *The Decline of the Roman Empire* (London, 2010).

Ross R. Holloway, *The Archaeology of Early Rome and Latium* (London, 1996).

Nathan S. Rosenstein and Robert Morstein-Marx (eds), *A Companion to the Roman Republic* (Oxford, 2006).

Walter Scheidel, Richard P. Saller and Ian Morris, *The Cambridge Economic History of the Greco-Roman World* (Cambridge, 2007).

Tacitus, *The Annals of Imperial Rome*, trans. Michael Grant (London, 1956).

Chapter 4: Constantinople/Istanbul

Warwick Ball, *Rome in the East: Transformation of an Empire* (London and New York, 2016).

Niccoló Barbaro, *Diary of the Siege of Constantinople*, trans. J.R. Jones (New York, 1970).

Caroline Finkel, *Osman's Dream: The Story of the Ottoman Empire 1300–1923* (London, 2005).

Philip Mansel, *Constantinople: City of the World's Desire, 1453–1924* (New York, 1998).

John Julius Norwich, *A Short History of Byzantium* (London, 1998).

Warren Treadgold, *A History of Byzantine State and Society* (California, 1997).

Chapter 5: Paris

Daniel Brewer, *The Enlightenment Past: Reconstructing Eighteenth-Century French Thought* (London, 2008).

Denis Diderot, *The Encyclopédie of Diderot and D'Alembert: Selected Articles* (Michigan, 1996).

Peter Gay (ed.), *The Enlightenment: A Comprehensive Anthology* (London, 1973).

Patrice Higonnet, *Paris: Capital of the World* (Harvard, 2009).

Alistair Horne, *Seven Ages of Paris* (Maryland, 2003).

Jean-Jacques Rousseau, *Confessions* (Oxford, 2008).

Chapter 6: London

Charles Dickens, *Selected Journalism 1850–1870* (London, 1997).

Isambard Brunel, *The Life of Isambard Kingdom Brunel, Civil Engineer* (London, 1970). Written by Brunel's son.

Henry Mayhew, *London Labour and the London Poor* (London, 2015).

P.J.G. Ransom, *The Victorian Railway and How It Evolved* (London, 1989).

Lytton Strachey, *Eminent Victorians* (Oxford, 2009).

Kate Williams, *Becoming Queen Victoria: The Unexpected Rise of Britain's Greatest Monarch* (London, 2016).

A.N. Wilson, *The Victorians* (London, 2003).

Chapter 7: Moscow

Simon Sebag Montefiore, *Stalin: The Court of the Red Tsar* (London, 2003).

Natalia Murray, John Miller, et al., *Revolution: Russian Art 1917–1932* (London, 2017).

Boris Pasternak, *Doctor Zhivago* (London, 2015).

John Reed, *Ten Days that Shook the World* (London, 2007).

Karl Schlogel, *Moscow, 1937* (London, 2014).

Robert Service, *The Russian Revolution, 1900–1927* (Studies in European History) (London, 2009).

Chapter 8: New York

Jack Beatty, *Age of Betrayal: The Triumph of Money in America, 1865–1900* (New York, 2008).

F. Scott Fitzgerald, *The Great Gatsby* (London, 2013).

Kenneth T. Jackson (ed.), *The Encyclopedia of New York City* (New Haven, 1995).

Zachary Kent, *The Story of the New York Stock Exchange* (New York, 1990).

John Dos Passos, *Manhattan Transfer* (London, 2000).

Jules Stewart, *Gotham Rising* (London, 2016).

Chapter 9: Mumbai

Mihir Bose, *Bollywood: A History* (New Delhi, 2008).

M.D. David, *Bombay, the City of Dreams: A History of the First City in India* (Mumbai, 1995).

Guku Ezekiel, *Sachin: The Story of the World's Greatest Batsman* (London, 2003).

Sunil Kilnani, *The Idea of India* (London, 2012).

Baljinder K. Mahal, *The Queen's Hinglish: How to Speak Pukka* (London, 2006).

Suketa Mehta, *Maximum City: Bombay Lost and Found* (London, 2005).

Chapter 10: Beijing

Gordon Kerr, *A Short History of China: From Ancient Dynasties to Economic Powerhouse* (London, 2013).

Colin Mackerras and Amanda Yorke, *The Cambridge Handbook of Contemporary China* (Cambridge, 1991).

John Naisbitt, *Megatrends: Ten New Directions Transforming Our Lives* (London, 1982).

Alexander Pantsov and Steven I. Levine, *Deng Xiaoping: A Revolutionary Life* (Oxford, 2015).

Mao Tse-Tung, *Quotations From Chairman Mao Tse-Tung* [aka Little Red Book] (London, 2018).

Ai Weiwei, *Spatial Matters: Art Architecture and Activism*, ed. Anthony Pins (London, 2014).

General /Further Reading

Edward Glaeser, *Triumph of the City* (London, 2012).

Leo Hollis, *Cities Are Good For You: The Genius of the Metropolis* (London, 2013).

Laurie Winkless, *Science and the City: The Mechanics Behind the Metropolis* (London, 2016).

Peter Yapp, *The Travellers' Dictionary of Quotation: Who Said What, About Where?* (London, 1983).

Picture Acknowledgements

Index